THE CRESCENT OBSCURED

This popular engraving, first issued just before the Civil War, shows two American heroes and two Muslim enemies. Stephen Decatur learned, after the fierce naval battle of August 3, 1804, that his brother James had been killed by a Turkish officer who had surrendered. Decatur tracked down his brother's killer, shown here with Decatur's pistol aimed at his throat. Decatur himself was almost killed by the Tripolitan sailor shown raising his sword. But American sailor Daniel Fraser, also known as Reuben James, put himself between the Turkish sword and his captain. This engraving calls the Tripolitan enemy an "Algerine," thus confusing America's Muslim enemies of 1804 with those of 1793.

THE CRESCENT OBSCURED

The United States and
the Muslim World
1776–1815

ROBERT J. ALLISON

The University of Chicago Press
Chicago and London

The University of Chicago Press, Chicago 60637
The University of Chicago Press, Ltd., London
Copyright © 1995 by Robert J. Allison
All rights reserved. Originally published 1995
University of Chicago Press edition 2000
Printed in the United States of America

05 04 03 02 01 00   6 5 4 3 2 1

Frontispiece: "Decatur's Conflict with the Algerine at Tripoli" (engraving, 1874). Courtesy United States Naval Historical Center.

Library of Congress Cataloging-in-Publication Data

Allison, Robert J.
    The crescent obscured : the United States and the Muslim world, 1776–1815 / Robert J. Allison.
        p. cm.
    Originally published: New York : Oxford University Press, 1995.
    Includes bibliographical references (p.) and index.
    ISBN 0-226-01490-8 (paper : alk. paper)
    1. Africa, North—Relations—United States. 2. United States—Relations—Africa, North.
3. Islam—Public opinions. 4. Africa, North—Foreign public opinion, American. 5. Public
opinion—United States. I. Title.

DT197.5.U6 A45 2000
303.48´273061—dc21
                                                                            00-025311
                                                                            CIP

For Phyllis

Contents

Acknowledgments

Many people have helped bring this project to a close. First, Sheldon Meyer of Oxford University Press has been a source of encouragement since an early stage. Helen Greenberg has done a marvelous job editing, and I thank her for her patience.

Virtually all the faculty and students in Harvard's History of American Civilization Program have contributed to this project. Stephan Thernstrom deserves special thanks for his kindness and generosity; Werner Sollors has been a steadfast counsellor since I enrolled in his Harvard Extension School classes; Drew McCoy, now at Clark University, set for his students an example we have yet to equal; Alan Heimert read an early draft of this manuscript and offered encouragement and criticism; and Warner Berthoff's good humor and good sense have been inspirational.

Bernard Bailyn advised me on this project from the beginning. From a second-hand copy of *Ideological Origins of the American Revolution* I learned that ideas matter, that what people think makes a difference, and I decided to finish college. On the day I bought that book, I became a student of history; ten years later I thank Professor Bailyn for helping me become a historian. I cannot thank him enough for his patience and kindness. His questions and comments have not only improved this work, but have made me a more thoughtful writer and teacher. His influence is on every page and will be on each page I write.

Fellow-students at Harvard, now scholars and teachers in their own right, have helped this project immeasurably. I thank especially Pleun Bouricius, Richard Bennett, Cynthia Blair, Steve Holmes, Dan

B. Miller, Daniel Terris, Andrew Walsh, Robert Johnstone, Jeffrey Pasley, Gretchen Konig, Benjamin Schmidt, Martha Burns, Mark Peterson, Yin Xiao-Huang, Rosemary Crockett, Heather Richardson, and Ted Widmer for each one's individual contribution. Two others deserve special thanks: Fred Dalzell often had more enthusiasm for this project than I did, and Thomas J. Brown shared his insight into the problems of writing.

Ruth DiPietro, Christine McFadden, Susan Hund, Marcia Dambry, Laura Johnson, and Sharon Lenzie have helped to make my years at Harvard and Suffolk enjoyable, and their professional skill have also helped make them productive for me and rewarding for my students. Christopher Marrion and Elizabeth Mullin of Harvard's financial aid office helped me finish graduate school, and I owe a special thanks to the Herbert Lehman fund at Harvard for a year of research. My students at Harvard, Suffolk, and in the Harvard Extension School have contributed to this work in ways they can hardly imagine.

I thank the person who assigned Louis P. Masur to the office next to mine; having Lou Masur next door, literally and figuratively, has been one the great boons of life. Wilfred Rollman I thank for sharing his knowledge of North Africa, and his enthusiasm for the intersection of American and Muslim history. Dennis Skiotis offered ideas in his inimitable way. Thomas G. Slaughter gave a kind yet critical reading of an earlier version, and this one is much improved thanks to his comments. Fred Anderson's critique also improved the finished product.

A number of libraries offered their resources to make this project possible. The Henry E. Huntington Library is a joy to work in, and I was fortunate to be a Robert Middlekauff fellow. I thank Mary Wright and Susan Naulty, as well as the scholars who were assembled during my brief but important stay: Martin Ridge, Paul M. Zall, Claudia Bushman, William Pencak, Brooks Simpson, and of course Howard Shorr. I also thank the American Antiquarian Society, the Boston Public Library, the Boston Athenaeum, in particular

Catharina Slautterback of the Print Room, the Essex Institute in Salem, the New York Public Library, and the staffs of Harvard's library system, particularly Houghton Library, the Harvard Theatre Collection, and the Government Documents room.

My wife's parents, Philip and Evelyn Gaudiano, have been extremely generous, perhaps in hope I would not lecture them on American history. Michael Gaudiano owns the only garage I know of that has a picture of James Madison in it. He and his son Michael have kept our car on the road, and on more than one occasion have made me realize that no one has ever said, "Thank God my wife's uncle is a historian." I also thank Joseph and Margaret Gaudiano, and their children, Alison, Philip, and Joseph, who might also have thoughts on historians as uncles. I thank them for trying so hard to be quiet as I studied; I treasure the times they failed.

My mother is responsible for my own encounter with the Muslim world and showed great prescience in taking me through Mashad and Shiraz at an impressionable age. My father read and commented thoroughly on an earlier version of this book, and this one would have greatly improved had I followed all his suggestions. Matthew Galbraith and Susan Galbraith have been unfailing sources of encouragement and put me up during research trips to New York. Frank and Susan Johnson made sure Shea Stadium was on my research itinerary. Jean Davies made it possible for me to finish college; more than that, she made me think I could do it without her.

Friends, too, have contributed. I give special thanks to Karen Leighton, Maureen Connolly and her son Michael, Mary Frances Daviess, and Keith and Margaret Bergman. Doug Shidell might wish I had said more about bicycles, though he has yet to mention Jefferson in his books.

Finally, when I come to thank Phyllis, I realize how ineffective a writer I am. Her contributions far exceed what I know how to say. She continues to bring great moments of joy which shine in memory, despite my own professional distractions which make those moments too short. Professor Bailyn and the other colleagues mentioned above have struggled to make me a better historian; to her has fallen the harder task of making me a better person. She also has struggled to keep this book in its proper perspective. John Robert, who arrived during the early stages of research, and Philip, who joined us during the writing, have helped her to succeed. To her the book is dedicated; to all of them my life is.

Introduction

In 1978 I was vacationing in Iran when a revolution broke out. The Iranian revolution caught many Americans by surprise, but as an admirer of Thomas Paine, I saw it coming. Iran's leaders enjoyed the benefits of rapid modernization and the trappings of Western luxury, while most of the Iranian people lived in poverty. The abyss separated rich and poor as it does in most of the world, but it also separated the more urbane and cosmopolitan Iranians from those who had only their religious faith to sustain their desperate lives.

But though Paine and other writers on revolution had prepared me for the tumult, I did not expect the religious turn Iran's revolution took. Most revolutionaries of the past two centuries have pursued progress and liberty, but the Iranian people rejected both of these tenets of Western faith. Indeed, the Iranian revolution was less a repudiation of Muhammad Reza Pahlevi and his corrupt, despotic dynasty than it was a rejection of the Western social order he had embraced. The Iranian people did not rebel against their own failed rulers but against ours. The full fury of the Iranian revolution eventually turned on the United States, and in 1979 Iranians captured the American embassy in Teheran, taking fifty-two Americans hostage. Iran had exploded after years of oppression and glaring inequality; now the United States exploded over this attack on its embassy. In American cities Iranian students were beaten by angry mobs, songs like "Bomb Iran" played on the radio, the nightly news reminded us of how many days the fifty-two Americans had been deprived of freedom, and President Jimmy Carter, who tried to negotiate an end to the crisis, was perceived as weak and voted out of office.

Bewildered by these events in America caused by a revolution few

Americans understood, I went back to study our own, more explicable Revolution and the early national period of American history. But even here, the specter of the Iranian revolution against progress and liberty would not go away. Like some *Arabian Nights* genie changing the familiar into the strange, images of the Muslim world appeared everywhere I turned in the early history of the American republic. Virtually every American knows that the United States fought a war with the "Barbary pirates" in the early 1800s, a war memorialized in the Marine Corps hymn. That had been the extent of my own knowledge of this American encounter with the Muslim world.

But this war was not an isolated phenomenon, not a chance encounter. The American encounter with the Muslim world actually began before there was a United States and almost before Europeans became aware that America existed. When the Christian kingdoms of Castille and Aragon conquered the Muslim kingdom of Granada in 1492, their most Christian majesties Isabella and Ferdinand had extra capital to pay for Columbus's voyage to the Orient. But however important this voyage would be to our history, Ferdinand and Isabella hoped that by securing a new route to the Indies, they would find a new source of revenue to pay for their continuing holy war against the Muslims they had driven into Morocco and Algiers. Sixteenth-century Europeans would remain more interested in driving the Turks from the Mediterranean and Eastern Europe than they would be in colonizing the Americas. John Smith, before he turned his attention to America, fought the Turks in Eastern Europe and was captured by the bashaw of Nalbrits. No Turkish Pocahontas came forward to offer her life in exchange for Captain Smith's, so he killed the bashaw and escaped. This may have been the first "American" encounter with a Muslim tyrant, but it would not be the last. In 1625 Morocco captured an American ship, and twenty years later a ship built in Cambridge, Massachusetts, with a crew from that colony, defeated an Algerian ship at sea, in an action James Fenimore Cooper would later call the first American naval battle. In 1673, when Britain and Algiers were at war, the Algerians captured a ship from New York. Churches in that city raised money to redeem their sailors. At the close of the seventeenth century, Joshua Gee, a sailor from Massachusetts, was held captive in Sallee, Morocco. When he got home to Boston, he was a celebrity: He wrote the story of his captivity and redemption, and Cotton Mather celebrated his deliverance with a sermon.

These episodes are important, and must be considered as part of a larger struggle that did not end when the Ottoman Turks were driven from the gates of Vienna or their navy beaten at Lepanto. This was more than a struggle for trade routes or territory. Americans at the time saw these episodes as part of the contest between Christians and Muslims, between Europeans and Turks or Moors, and ultimately, between what came to be called civilization and what the newly civilized world would define as barbarism. The Americans inherited this understanding of the Muslim world and pursued this enemy more relentlessly than the Europeans had done.

By the end of the eighteenth century, the Barbary states of North Africa (Algiers, Morocco, Tunis, and Tripoli) threatened only weaker nations, such as Denmark, Sweden, the states of Italy, and the United States. Their naval strength had not kept pace with that of the British or French. No longer a threat to England or France, instead the Barbary states became their tools. It was a common eighteenth-century maxim in England, France, and Holland that if there were no Algiers, it would be worthwhile for England, France, or Holland to build one. The British, Dutch, and French could pay Algiers to attack their competitors, making the Mediterranean dangerous for the Danes, Swedes, Spanish, Portuguese, and Italians. The British were quick to inform Algiers when the United States became independent, and in 1785 Algiers captured two American ships and eleven more in 1793. These captures created problems for America's political leaders—John Adams, John Jay, Benjamin Franklin, and Thomas Jefferson—and equally vexing troubles for American citizens. Jefferson, who was minister to France in 1785, immediately proposed war, which he said would prove to both the states of Africa and Europe that the United States was a new kind of nation, which would not play the games of European power politics. John Adams, whose presidential administration would adopt the rhetorical position "Millions for defence, not one cent for tribute," thought the United States, like the Europeans, should pay tribute to Algiers. Peace would be less expensive than war, Adams believed, and tribute to the Algerians and Tripolitans was the price of doing business in the Mediterranean.

Adams won the argument. Once relations with Algiers, Tunis, and Tripoli were smoothed by treaty, President Adams sent consuls to the Barbary states. These consuls had dual roles as diplomats and independent businessmen, who would supplement their meager salaries through their own commercial enterprise. They bickered with one another and could not see that their own commercial interests were different from their country's interest. Instead of preserving American peace in the Mediterranean, this policy brought on the war with Tripoli.

The war with Tripoli carried great ideological importance for the Americans, who imagined themselves doing what the nations of Europe had been unable or unwilling to do: beating the forces of Islamic despotism and piracy. This war proved to Americans their real status as a nation and affirmed that theirs was to be a different kind of nation—different both from the nations of Europe, which were content to pay tribute to the Barbary states, and from the Muslim states, ravaged by their rulers and torn apart by their impoverished and savage people. For the Americans, the war had a significance far beyond military objectives. Pope Pius VII said the Americans had done more in a few years than the rest of Christendom had done in centuries: They had humbled the Muslim states of North Africa. The war against Tripoli was meant to do this, but it was also meant as a lesson to Europe. The Americans had proved that they would behave better than the Europeans, that they would not stoop to the demands of Tripoli or use the Barbary states to drive their own competitors from the sea. The war inspired the American people with a renewed sense of their mission and destiny.

This is the story. But just as Scherezade would tell many small tales in the course of telling one large one, this large story has many smaller narratives within it. Scherezade used her minor stories to bring out the points of her larger one, and so the minor facets of this history all contribute to the whole. All the minor parts of the story of American relations with the Muslim world bear on the larger themes, the themes of liberty, power, and human progress. A flood of books on the Muslim world poured from American presses in the 1790s: captivity narratives; histories, including two biographies of Muhammad; novels and poems; and the first American edition of the *Arabian Nights.* This literature conveyed a consistent picture of the Muslim world, an inverted image of the world the Americans were trying to create anew. The ability to create the world anew gave the Americans endless chances to improve people's lives but just as many chances to ruin them. In the literature on the Muslim world, Americans saw what could happen to people who made the wrong choices. Muhammad had offered people a chance to change, and change they did, adopting a new religion, building new states and empires, reorganizing family life. But each change had been a tragic mistake. The once prosperous people of Egypt, Turkey, Mauritania, and Syria were impoverished by bad governments, and their fertile lands turned to deserts. In Algiers, Tunis, and Tripoli, honest commerce was perverted into piracy by avaricious deys and pachas. Everywhere, women were debased in harems and seraglios, the victims of unrestrained sexual power. The Muslim world was a lesson for Americans in what not to do, in how not to construct a state, encourage commerce, or form families. Power had to be controlled, liberty had to be secured, for men and women to prosper and for societies to progress.

But though the American people had avoided some evils, they had not avoided them all. How could the United States condemn Algiers for enslaving Americans when Americans themselves enslaved Africans? If slavery was wrong for Americans, was it not also wrong for Africans? Slavery in the United States made the congratulations Americans bestowed on themselves for avoiding political, religious, or sexual tyranny sound hollow, hypocritical, and shameful. Perhaps the war against Tripoli did prove that the Americans had created a different kind of nation. But Americans came home from "slavery" in Algiers, Morocco, and Tripoli to a nation in which slavery was much more deeply rooted than in any Muslim society. By avoiding the mistakes of Muslims, who submitted without question to their rulers and religion, Americans for an instant thought they had avoided the fate of every empire that had risen only to fall. But slavery in America constantly reminded them of their failure. The degree to which their countrymen submitted to it as a necessary evil, or endorsed it as a positive good, was the degree to which all Americans would be condemned by their just God, the God of the Christians and the Muslims, who judged all men.

This book begins in a time of fear, in the years after the American Revolution, before the Constitution was established, before the United States had a government, an army, or a navy. It concludes in a time of triumph, after the United States had defeated not only Tripoli but England, the world's greatest military force. The Americans had overcome the fears of the 1780s and 1790s, the fears that they might fall into the traps of anarchy or despotism. The successful creation and maintenance of constitutional government, and the military victories over Tripoli and England, ushered in a period of confidence and national assurance. But the Americans were left with the unresolved dilemma of slavery, a constant reproach to their own sense of moral superiority. Slavery's legacy still haunts us, proving a more dangerous and resilient phantom than any genie, sultan, or ayatollah.

THE CRESCENT OBSCURED

CHAPTER ONE

American Policy Toward the Muslim World

Patrick Henry was worried. Three mysterious strangers, two men and a woman, had arrived in Virginia in that November of 1785, and Governor Henry suspected they were up to some bad tricks. One of his predecessors, Thomas Jefferson, had left office under a cloud four years earlier, having failed to defend the state from a British invasion. Britain no longer threatened Virginia's peace and security, having recognized American independence, but Henry feared these three strangers were the advance scouts of a more dangerous enemy. He believed they were spies sent to Virginia by the Dey of Algiers.

Henry's fear of Algerian spies was not farfetched. Algiers had declared war on the United States in July 1785, encouraged to do so by the British, who wanted to scare American commerce out of the Mediterranean. British papers reported that Algiers had already captured "an infinite number" of American vessels, including one carrying Benjamin Franklin home from France. Franklin, it was reported, bore his "slavery to admiration."[1] A New York paper reported that an English ship was mistaken for an American, and the Algerians stopped it five times between London and Lisbon. Virginia legislator John Bannister wrote to Thomas Jefferson, now U.S. minister to France, in December 1785 that "The Inhabitants of these States are greatly alarmed at the hostility of the Algerines," and this fear had stopped Americans from trading with Spain and other Mediterranean countries. This was "of the utmost consequence to our grain trade." Under these threats, America's carrying trade would fall into the hands of the British, "whose interest it is to depress us by becoming our Carriers."[2] From Philadelphia, Samuel House wrote that business lagged, that no American ship could pick up freight in Europe. This fear that American ships would be taken by Barbary cruisers meant indeed that either British ships would capture all the carrying trade or Americans would have to pay exorbitant insurance premiums.[3] Frenchman James le Maire warned Henry that if the Algerians themselves did not molest Virginia's coast, then "some ill-designed Brittons, Irish, Jersey, or Guernsey men, under the cloak of a Barbarian, with an Algerine Commission" might do so. Le Maire suggested that he be sent to France to buy a frigate and commissioned by Virginia to protect the commonwealth from the impending Algerian attack.[4]

Jefferson found this fear frustrating. Algiers had not captured any American ships, and he believed the British were using fear of Algiers to ruin American trade. Morocco, it was true, had captured the American merchant ship *Betsey* in October 1784. But Morocco had done this for a particular purpose: Emperor Mawlay Muhammad (reigned 1757–1790) had recognized American independence in 1778, but the Americans had so far failed to send a negotiator. To get the Americans' attention, he ordered an American ship captured and promised to hold it hostage until the United States sent a diplomatic agent.[5]

Jefferson's friend John Page asked, when he heard of the *Betsey*'s capture, if it was true that "the Emperor of Morocco had made advances to Congress" that had been ignored, in consequence of which the emperor had sent his cruisers after American ships. Page hoped that this, like the Algerian captures, was "a british Tale" but still thought "a little Flattery, a few Presents, and the Prospect of our Trade with them" would secure American trade in the Mediterranean. Richard Henry Lee hoped American negotiators could accommodate the Barbary states and open the Mediterranean to trade, and he criticized the "avaricious, monopolizing Spirit of Commerce and Commercial Men," such as the British, who had closed the Mediterranean to Americans, preventing contact "between the human species in different parts of the world."[6]

After the *Betsey's* capture, John Adams went to France's foreign minister, the Comte Vergennes, for advice. Vergennes advised Adams that Emperor Mawlay Muhammad, whom he called the greediest and "most interested man in the world," was piqued at the American failure to send him presents. Vergennes told the Americans of this but refused to offer any more advice. He suggested they consult the Marquis de Castries, France's minister of marine, for more information. When John Adams asked if France had renewed its 1684 treaty with Algiers, Vergennes smiled, amused that Adams knew this, but he would not answer Adams's question. It was not in France's interest to help the Americans to the Mediterranean trade, and Vergennes, Adams, and Jefferson all knew this. Vergennes told Adams to direct his questions to Castries, who Adams knew would reveal even less than Vergennes.[7]

It was in England's interest to hurt American commerce, but it was not in France's interest to help the United States. It was, however, in Spain's interest to do the Americans and the Moroccans a favor. Spain had become convinced that the United States was likely to endure, and Spanish Foreign Minister Floridablanca thought the United States could be a valuable ally against the British in North America. Spain was preparing an expedition against Algiers, and Floridablanca wanted Morocco as an ally in North Africa. So Spain interceded in Morocco, and in March 1785 Mawlay Muhammad returned the *Betsey*, and the U.S. promised to send a negotiator.[8] Congress appropriated $80,000 for negotiations with the four Barbary states (Morocco, Algiers, Tunis, and Tripoli). American Foreign Minister John Jay told the commissioners that they would "find it expedient to purchase the Influence of those...able to impede or forward your views," particularly in "Courts where Favoritism as well as Corruption prevails."[9]

While the American diplomats struggled to secure European support and North African treaties, Governor Henry and his council worried about what to do with the three North African strangers in Virginia. Henry ordered them locked up in Norfolk, then sent them to Williamsburg, and finally had them brought to Richmond. Henry sent Richmond doctor William Foushee to interrogate the strangers as best he could and to search their luggage. Foushee found a little cash, no weapons, and some documents in Hebrew, along with their English traveling papers. Though this did not look like the stuff with which to launch an invasion, Foushee was not satisfied with the strangers' story. They said the Hebrew documents were to admit them to a temple; since Foushee could not read Hebrew, he could not vouch for that. Their story, that they were travelers from England, did not correspond with the English documents they carried, which suggested the three were from Morocco. The strangers explained to Foushee that since they could not read English, they could not vouch for what papers in that language said. Foushee's interrogation of the three was less satisfactory. He was not satisfied with either their looks or their story, but he could prove nothing. Foushee sent them to Norfolk, and Henry gave orders to send them back to their native land, wherever that was. The three were disappointed not to be going to Philadelphia, where they thought they might have had a friendlier reception.[10]

With these three strangers being shipped out of the commonwealth, the Virginia legislature passed a law to prevent such dangerous aliens from ever again molesting the people or disturbing Virginia's safety. The legislature gave the governor power to deport aliens from countries at war with the United States. This Virginia act anticipated the Enemy Aliens Act of 1798, which gave the president of the United States power to deport aliens from countries at war with the United States. Virginia would declare the 1798 federal Enemy Aliens Act an unconstitutional abuse of power. In 1786, the Virginia legislature tried to control suspicious-looking characters, but it also restricted the power of the state. The legislature gave the governor power to ship out undesirables, but it also passed the statute for religious freedom, preventing any future legislature from entertaining, in the words of the bill's sponsor James Madison, "the ambitious hope of making laws for the human mind." Not merely tolerating different religious faiths, the Virginia act, according to its author Thomas Jefferson, guaranteed religious freedom to "the Jew and the Gentile, the Christian and the Mahometan, the Hindoo, and infidel of every denomination." The Virginians shipped the mysterious travelers out of the country, while protecting their right to worship in a temple or mosque.[11]

Jefferson would later regard this statute granting religious freedom as one of his greatest achievements. But freeing the American mind proved easier than freeing the seas for American ships. Jefferson and Adams waited throughout the summer of 1785 for Congress to send a negotiator. Jefferson's friends in America assured him that he was not the only one wondering what Congress intended to do. Francis Hopkinson wrote from Philadelphia that "we know little more of Congress here than you do in France—perhaps not so much." Congress was "seldom or ever mentioned in the papers and are less talked of than if they were in the West Indies." Eliza House Trist wrote that "Every now and then we hear of an Honble Gentleman geting a wife or else we shou'd not know there existed such a body as Congress."[12]

Congress sent John Lamb, a Connecticut mule trader with some experience in the Mediterranean, to Paris in the spring of 1785. Lamb would not arrive in Paris until the fall and would not reach Algiers until the spring of 1786. By the time Jefferson and Adams realized that Lamb was incompetent, it was too late to find someone else. Jefferson did not think Lamb's ineptitude a problem; even an angel, Jefferson said, could not negotiate with Algiers. But while Adams and Jefferson waited for the tardy Lamb, Algiers declared war on the United States, and in September 1785 Jefferson learned that Algiers had captured two American ships.

Congress wanted to negotiate, and most Americans seemed to prefer paying tribute to waging war. Most Americans realized that the country, with no central government able to raise either money or a military force, was in no position to fight a war in the Mediterranean. John Page and Richard Henry Lee urged Jefferson to use flattery and presents to secure free trade in the Mediterranean, and Page was upset to learn that Morocco's Mawlay Muhammad had wanted peace with the Americans since 1778 but the United States had offended him by failing to send a negotiator. Jefferson disagreed. While he too was painfully aware of the country's military and financial weakness, he could not accept the idea of paying tribute to Algiers or Morocco. He told Page that he did not know how much a treaty with Morocco would cost, but was certain it would be more than Page imagined and certainly "more than a free people ought to pay." The "English" of Mawlay Muhammad's friendly overtures to the United States was "Plainly this. He is ready to receive us into the number of his tributaries." Algiers, the strongest Barbary power, would be next in line, followed by Tunis and Tripoli. European nations accepted the idea of paying tribute to the Barbary states, but Jefferson saw no reason for "laying the other hemisphere at their feet." Every American would feel this tribute when he paid taxes.

Jefferson did not think that buying peace with Algiers and the other regencies would be cheaper than fighting a war. "[O]ur Honour as well as our Avarice" was involved, and failure to establish a better national identity would "involve us soon in a naval war," if not with Algiers, then with England. America had to show strength and energy both to the Barbary states and to Europe. Buying peace, the short-term solution, could not prevent a war, which Jefferson considered the only long-term solution. Securing "a peace thro' the medium of war" would earn the newly independent nation the respect of Europe.[13]

The United States was not prepared for war, but Jefferson was confident that it would not have to fight this war alone. Spain's negotiations to release the *Betsey* reaffirmed for Jefferson the common interests of Spain and the United States. Each nation was threatened by the British presence north of the Ohio River and by British involvement in Central America. Jefferson hoped the Americans would recognize these common interests and join Spain's campaign against Algiers.[14] William Carmichael, the American chargé d'affaires in Spain, thought Spain was likely to cooperate with Naples and Venice against the Algerians. Since Spain had aided the Americans in Morocco, it would be fitting for the United States to join Spain in this multinational military enterprise. Congress had empowered Jefferson to negotiate, but he did not believe negotiations with Algiers were worthwhile. He summarized a letter he wrote to his friend in Italy, Philip Mazzei: "Query if ask peace with sword or money." To a Neapolitan diplomat in France, Jefferson asked if Naples would cooperate with the United States in joint actions against the Barbary states.[15] Jefferson imagined that the United States could help put together a multinational force of smaller European states such as Italy, the Scandinavian countries, and Portugal, as well as Spain. It would not have the support of either Britain or France.

War, Jefferson believed before a shot had been fired, was the only practical and honorable policy in dealing with Algiers and the other Barbary states. But as a diplomat he was bound to follow Congress's instructions. By the fall of 1785, when Algiers had already declared war and Patrick Henry was worried about an Algerian invasion, Jefferson still had not received the official word from Congress. Lamb, "this tardy servant," slowly made his way to Europe, though private correspondents had already told Jefferson and Adams what the instructions said. But Jefferson and Adams could do nothing without the official word.

The wait grew more frustrating. Jefferson learned in mid-September that the *Polly* and *Dauphin* had been taken by Algiers and that Spain and Algiers were negotiating. Spain, Jefferson heard, would give Algiers the equivalent of a million dollars, though details had not been worked out. It seemed that Portugal and Naples might also sign treaties with Algiers, thus destroying Jefferson's hope for a multinational alliance. Clearly, time was running out for the Americans. If Lamb did not arrive on the next packet, Jefferson would send Thomas Barclay to Algiers immediately.[16]

John Paul Jones, the American naval hero, was not surprised when he heard Algiers had declared war; he was only surprised it had not happened sooner. Jones hoped this war would jolt the Americans to unite "in measures consistent with their national honour and interest," and rouse them "from that illjudged security which the intoxication of Success has produced since the Revolution." This was precisely what Jefferson wanted to hear, and he shared Jones's hope that Americans would take action "as will make us respected as a great People who deserve to be Free."[17]

Jefferson shared Jones's sentiments, but Congress had decided to negotiate, and it was not up to Jefferson or Jones to make war against Congress's intentions. Jefferson felt "suspended between indignation and impotence." John Jay joined Jefferson in preferring war to tribute, but most Americans did not. While some Americans wanted war, according to the French consul in New York, many more were willing to pay tribute to secure a peaceful Mediterranean trade. Even those who wanted war recognized the country's weakness. Ezra Stiles, president of Yale, asked "Must we also Subsidize Algiers?" He told Jefferson, "Delenda est carthago. Algiers must be subdu[ed]." But until the United States was ready to subdue Algiers by force, "we must expend £200,000 and subsid[ize] that piratical State," since peaceful Mediterranean trade could bring the United States that amount every year. [18]

John Adams, American minister to London, agreed with those who preferred tribute to war. Adams did not think it good economics to sacrifice "a Million annually" in trade just "to Save one Gift of two hundred Thousand Pounds." If the Americans paid up like everyone else, Adams thought, they could at that moment have 200 ships in the Mediterranean, with freight alone worth £200,000. A simple gift to the Dey of Algiers would open the Mediterranean and raise the price of American grain. Instead, American reluctance to pay a few bribes meant the Mediterranean was closed, and American farmers and planters suffered. Adams joined Jefferson and the other bellicose statesmen in lamenting that the "Policy of Christendom has made Cowards of all their Sailors before the Standard of Mahomet," and agreed that it "would be heroical and glorious in Us, to restore Courage to ours." But Adams knew too much of American character, and human nature, to think that his countrymen would be any different. Of course, if the American people set their minds to fighting the Algerians, and, more importantly, committed their money to the cause, they could do it. "But the Difficulty of bringing our

People to agree upon it, has ever discouraged me."[19] Could Jefferson persuade the planters of Virginia and South Carolina to support a navy? Adams knew that people from Pennsylvania and all the states north would gladly do so, and he himself thought this would be a good time to build a navy. But Adams spent most of his time in Europe trying to borrow money to pay American debts. He had a keen idea of how little money the United States had or could raise.

The Americans neither prepared for war nor negotiated a peace. Algiers declared war on the United States, Spain made peace with Algiers, and it was likely that Naples and Portugal would do the same, completely freeing the Algerians to attack American ships in the Atlantic. William Carmichael lamented that the United States had not seized its opportunity and either joined a Spanish assault on Algiers or paid Spain to attack Algiers. "You see sir," he wrote to Jefferson, "the ruinous consequences of an ill-timed attention to Parsimony."[20]

Jefferson renewed his contacts with the foreign ministers of Naples and other Mediterranean states, urging joint actions against Algiers. He studied the history of France's sixteenth- and seventeenth-century attacks on Algiers, particularly the French blockade carried out by just two frigates and one battleship. He stayed in close contact with John Paul Jones, whom he thought should be sent to Algiers when Lamb's negotiation failed, as Jefferson knew it would. And in consultation with Lafayette, who acted as Jefferson's front man, he planned his multinational alliance against the Barbary powers. He wrote to Virginia Congressman James Monroe that peace with the Barbary states might cost 250,000 guineas but would last only as long as those states believed the Americans had strength to enforce it. Congress, Jefferson said, should weigh this cost against the "expence and probable success of compelling a peace by arms." A blockade would only cost 3000 guineas a month and would work in a short time.[21] Jefferson had Lafayette write to Henry Knox and other American officials, proposing a blockade. Lafayette acted for Jefferson, who did not want to draw attention to his differences either with Adams or with the Congress. Lafayette told his American friends that a successful blockade could turn the Barbary states from "a nation of pirates" into "a commercial people," and he broached the idea of sending John Paul Jones to negotiate, thus implicitly backing up diplomacy with the threat of military force. "The sooner He goes, the better," Lafayette wrote. [22]

While Jefferson, Lafayette, and Jones discussed this military option in Paris, in London John Adams pursued a diplomatic solution. In February 1786 an ambassador from Tripoli, Abdurrahman, arrived in London. He had three meetings with Adams, who thought him "either a consummate politician" or a truly "benevolent and wise man." If Abdurrahman really was as disinterested as he pretended to be, then "Providence seems to have opened to us an opportunity of conducting this thorny business to a happy conclusion."[23] Adams told Jefferson to come to London at once. Nothing they could do was half as important as establishing peace with the Barbary states. Though Adams feared that Tripoli would demand more than the Americans could pay, he was ready to go to Holland to borrow more. He did not want to waste this opportunity to prevent "a universal and horrible War with these Barbary states, which will continue for many years." He told Jefferson that they must persuade Congress to act. Adams himself was so "impressed and distressed" that he personally would go to New York and Algiers to resolve the problem.[24]

Though Jefferson expected nothing from negotiating with Abdurrahman, he arrived in London in early March. But they accomplished nothing with Abdurrahman. Peace with Tripoli would cost 30,000 guineas, which meant Tunis would demand the same; Morocco 60,000; and Algiers, the strongest of the Barbary states, 120,000. Jefferson returned to Paris more committed than ever to a blockade and military action. But still, the United States had no more resources to launch an attack than it had to pay expensive tribute. In America, George Washington recognized that the federal government in 1786 had no power either to pay tribute or to make credible threats, and he did not foresee this situation changing unless the Americans created a stronger central government with the power to tax.[25]

In the summer of 1786 the situation improved. Thomas Barclay, an American businessman and consul in France, arrived in Morocco, where Jefferson and Adams had sent him to negotiate a treaty with Mawlay Muhammad. Barclay and the emperor agreed on a treaty within a week, and astonishingly, the treaty did not require the United States to pay any tribute to Morocco, while Morocco pledged to keep Algerian ships out of the Atlantic. Lafayette told Jefferson that all of Europe was amazed at this treaty, which did not require tribute, and marveled at the diplomatic skill of the Americans. Mawlay Muhammad further showed his good faith by delivering up James Mercier, a shipwrecked Virginian held captive by a desert tribe. Jefferson paid Mercier's passage back to Virginia.[26]

More good news came when Portugal and Naples did not follow Spain to make peace with Algiers. Portugal, in fact, decided to protect American ships from the Algerians. A Rhode Island delegate to Congress thought the queen of Portugal's gesture "worthy of imitation, and demands our grateful acknowledgements, as we have nothing better to offer her in payment." And though Naples would not lead the alliance against Algiers, she would support it.[27]

In July 1786 Algiers captured a Russian ship. Jefferson thought this might bring Catherine the Great into his multinational alliance against Algiers, and when her foreign minister demanded that Turkey intervene to free the ship, America's ambassador to Spain thought the empress would "be pleased to see one of her Ministers writing in a haughty State to a Power that all Europe courts at present" but added, "When shall we be in a position to do this?" George Washington was confident that Catherine would not forget that Algiers had supported the Ottomans against her, and she would "take some leisure moment, just to keep her fleets in exercise, for exterminating those nests of Miscreants."[28] But Jefferson was anxious for the United States to be able to stand up and not rely on Catherine the Great to solve its international problems. While he waited impatiently for his nation to stand up to the Turks and Algerians, he tried to build an alliance of nations for mutual support against the Barbary states. Jefferson thought Russia and Portugal would join, and in fact he believed these two nations would provide most of the force.[29]

John Paul Jones left for Russia in August. The Algerian capture and other matters had brought Russia to the verge of war with Turkey, and Jones offered his services to Catherine the Great. In October, Jefferson and Lafayette perfected their antipiracy convention, which they hoped Naples, Rome, Venice, Portugal, the German towns, and the United States would support. The convention forces might be able to use a harbor in Sicily, should get the support of Malta, and Lafayette thought the King of Naples would lend them a regiment if they needed one. With two or three fifty-gun ships and six large frigates, the united powers could blockade the Algerians. Lafayette communicated the idea to influential Americans—George Washington, Henry Knox, and James McHenry—confident in their support. The real problem, Lafayette knew, would be his own government. "The devil of it will Be to make it Agreeable to this ministry that I should meddle with the War."[30]

Lafayette was right. Vergennes summoned Lafayette to his private office at Versailles, and told him the project would not succeed. Furthermore, Vergennes had been commanded to tell Lafayette to abandon it. Jefferson and Lafayette had not expected England or France to support the convention; they had not expected that these countries would not allow anyone else to do so. Vergennes told Lafayette that the English and French governments both profited from Barbary piracy and would not permit anyone to stop it. Though his convention went against the policies of the world's two most powerful countries, and though Lafayette had to drop out, Jefferson was not dissuaded. He wrote to the Russian and Portuguese ambassadors and knew John Paul Jones was presenting his idea to Catherine the Great. Meanwhile the Moroccan treaty meant the Atlantic was safe, as long as Portugal patrolled the straits of Gibraltar.[31] The Mediterranean, too, was made safer, not by European politicians, but by an outbreak of the plague. Hundreds died in Algiers each day between January and August, hitting dock workers and sailors the hardest. Eighteen thousand died, including some of the American captives, and the Algerian navy was stranded in the diseased port.[32]

In September 1787 Russia prepared to invade Turkey, and Jefferson thought Catherine the Great might drive the Turks from Europe. Two years earlier, when Austria had fought the Turks, Jefferson had not thought an Ottoman defeat desirable. He had agreed with his philosophical friends at home that it was a pity that Greece was in the hands of Muslims, whose religion excluded arts and sciences from the land that had created them. But an Austrian victory would merely have substituted one set of barbarians for another; it would not restore the land and language of Demosthenes and Aristotle.[33] But in 1787, when Russia prepared to attack the Turks, Jefferson was more optimistic.

Jefferson was not alone among libertarian intellectuals in cheering on the Russians. The Abbe Constantin de Chassebouef Volney, an outspoken opponent of every kind of intellectual tyranny, saw Turkey as the epitome of despotism and wrote a pamphlet endorsing Russia's war against the Ottomans, for which the Czarina Catherine rewarded him with a gold medal. Jefferson saw an opportunity for America in the widening European war, as Russia's war against Turkey had kindled "the flames of war completely" in "two distinct parts of this quarter of the globe," and though England and France were not yet involved, they soon would be. England would be too busy to use Algiers against the Americans, and Catherine would remember that Algiers had supported Turkey against her, while John Paul Jones served in the Russian Navy. Both Jones and Jefferson saw this as a great moment for the Americans to make an alliance with Russia, and Jones thought the Americans and the Russians could earn Europe's respect if together they drove the Turks from the Black Sea. After that, Jones thought the Americans and Russians could drive the Algerians from the Mediterranean.[34]

Jefferson saw in Turkey's fate a lesson for Americans. The Americans, like the Ottoman Turks, had tried to remove themselves from the tangled affairs of Europe. To an extent, it was a wise policy "not to entangle ourselves with the affairs of Europe," but the Turks had carried it too far, and Jefferson feared the Americans would make the same mistake. The Turks, in distancing themselves from the affairs of Europe, had "unwisely chosen to be ignorant of them also," and now because of this ignorance, European interests and alliances threatened to annihilate the Ottoman empire. Jefferson wanted the Americans to follow a course of informed neutrality, to form a network of neutral nations against the entangled diplomatic network of Europe.[35]

While Jefferson dealt on this level with theory and international alliances, he still had to deal with the practical matter of American hostages. John Lamb's 1786 mission failed. Lamb proved incompetent, and David Humphreys informed Jefferson from Connecticut that people there found it extraordinary that Lamb had been given the assignment, as "his character is perhaps much lower here than we could have conceived." Another correspondent told Jefferson that the failed diplomat had resumed his career as a mule trader. "Mr. Lamb is about to embark from Minorca with a load of Jack-asses for America. *Sic transit gloria mundi*."[36]

Jefferson could not find another agent, and knew that negotiations would be fruitless as long as the United States had neither a navy nor lavish tribute to offer. Richard O'Brien and twenty other Americans still were captive in Algiers, and Jefferson was their main contact. He advised O'Brien to be discreet and not to tell the Algerians what strategy Jefferson was pursuing for their release. In truth, O'Brien would have had very little to tell. To discourage the Algerians from capturing any more Americans, Jefferson feigned indifference to the captives' fate. If the United States offered large ransoms, Jefferson reasoned, or seemed overanxious to redeem the hostages, the Algerians would go out and capture more Americans. What seemed cruel to the men in captivity, Jefferson explained, was a kindness to those still free. It was for the ultimate good of the captives, and the United States, to bring down the price.[37]

Making the Algerians think the United States would not redeem its citizens was more than, or less than, a stratagem to prevent future captures. Jefferson and Adams knew that the United States had no money; its citizens were reluctant to give it any. The Congress had tried to get the states to allow it to raise money through a tax on imports—unsuccessfully. Massachusetts tried to raise taxes to pay off its war debts, provoking an armed rebellion in the winter of 1786–1787. Jefferson knew the American people wanted rigid economy in government. He thought war would be more economical against Algiers than tribute, and that a blockade would be the most effective as well as the least expensive military tactic. Knowing the general public's aversion to taxes, Jefferson suggested a special tax on goods imported from the Mediterranean: The merchants who profited there should pay the expense of keeping it open. If only those who would benefit were taxed, most of the people would never feel this burden.

Jefferson also knew that the central government needed some coercive power. He knew a standing army would always threaten the people's liberty, but a navy could not be used against them. A navy would prove to Europe and Algiers that the Americans were a strong and independent people, a people to be reckoned with, a people who, as Jones had said, deserved to be free. But none of these things came about while Jefferson was in France. The United States did reorganize its government, giving it more coercive power, but it did not yet decide to build a navy, nor did it tax the Mediterranean merchants. Jefferson returned home from France in 1789, leaving behind the problems of the Americans in Algiers and the Mediterranean trade. But these problems followed him: On arriving in Virginia, Jefferson learned that President Washington had appointed him secretary of state.

When Jefferson took office as the first secretary of state under the new Constitution in 1790, he faced once again the problem of American relations with the Barbary states. The surviving Americans in Algiers, now in their fifth year of captivity, had petitioned this new government, asking what was being done for them. President Washington submitted their petition to Congress and asked that body to define American policy in the Mediterranean. To help them, he asked Jefferson to report to Congress on the negotiations with

Algiers and on American trade in the Mediterranean. Jefferson had been waiting for someone to listen to his ideas and now found himself in a position to recommend policy. His report laid out three available options, the same options he had noted in 1786. First, the United States could ransom the captives and pay tribute to the Barbary states, as all the nations of Europe did. Second, American merchants could abandon the Mediterranean. Or, finally, the United States could use military force. Though he left the decision to Congress, it was clear which of the three options Jefferson preferred: He put his favored option last, confident Congress would reject the first two.[38]

But Congress had other ideas. The Senate agreed with Jefferson and Washington that the Mediterranean trade could not be protected except by a navy, but they wanted to strengthen public finances before building one. They promised to turn their attention to a navy as soon as public finances allowed it, and meanwhile authorized President Washington to spend $40,000 to redeem the American captives in Algiers and another $100,000 annually on tribute to Algiers, Tripoli, and Tunis.[39]

Congress had voted for peace, but Jefferson did not want the Algerians to think the Americans were unprepared for war. Congress had authorized him to send an agent to negotiate a treaty: Jefferson decided to send John Paul Jones. Jones had just finished his service in the Russian war against Turkey, and Jefferson knew his mission to Algiers would convince the Algerians that the United States would go to war if necessary. In June 1792 Jefferson notified Jones of his assignment, repeating for Jones the history of American relations with Algiers. Once Jones had established peace and ransomed the Americans, he would remain in Algiers as American consul. But Jefferson did not expect peace to last. He told Jones that "we look forward to the necessity of coercion" against Algiers, and Jones should "be pleased to inform" himself in detail of everything that might help future military operations on the Barbary coast.[40]

Jefferson must have been pleased to see his schemes of 1786 becoming public policy. But before Jones received his commission or his instructions, he was dead. Jefferson's next choice was Thomas Barclay, who had negotiated the treaty without tribute in Morocco and had just returned to Tangier to reaffirm that treaty with the new emperor. Jefferson told Barclay to cross out Jones's name on the commission and fill in his own. But before Barclay could do this, he died.

Nearly two years after he had been authorized to send an agent, Jefferson still had not found a living one. Finally, in the spring of 1793 he commissioned David Humphreys, American minister to Portugal, to negotiate. Humphreys, a poet and Revolutionary aide to Washington, had been secretary to Jefferson and Adams when they had first wrestled with the Barbary problem in Paris. Though Humphreys was the third choice, he was as good a choice as Jones or Barclay.[41]

By the time Humphreys was designated to go to Algiers, Washington and Jefferson had problems that seemed more pressing than the plight of the thirteen Americans in Algiers. Britain was supplying Indians in the Ohio river valley and encouraging them to attack American settlers who had pushed across the Alleghenies to settle on the frontier. France had abolished its monarchy and was encouraging other nations to join in a war against the established order. Spain now feared American settlement in the Ohio and Mississippi basins, and was encouraging American settlers in Kentucky, Tennessee, and the southwest territory (now Alabama and Mississippi) to believe that the Spanish crown offered more protection from the Indians than did the weak and distant government of the United States. On the island of St. Domingue the slaves drove out their masters, and white refugees to American cities brought their fears of slave revolts with them. The Washington administration itself had become divided on issues of finance and international policy: Secretary of the Treasury Alexander Hamilton pushed for a national bank, internal taxes on whiskey, high tariffs, and close relations with England; Secretary of State Jefferson opposed banks, taxes, and tariffs, and though he supported revolutionary France, he pushed for American neutrality in the European war. By the time

Humphreys arrived in Algiers late in 1793, Jefferson had resigned as secretary of state. He was replaced first by Edmund Randolph and then by a series of men loyal to Treasury Secretary Alexander Hamilton who were more interested in conciliating the British than in an independent American policy.

In October 1793, as Humphreys was on his way to Algiers, the British arranged a truce between Algiers and Portugal. Lisbon disavowed this truce as soon as it heard about it two weeks later, but in the meantime, Algerian cruisers managed to slip through the Portuguese fleet patrolling the Straits of Gibraltar. By the time Lisbon denounced the treaty, Algiers had captured eleven more American ships and over 100 sailors. The United States now prepared to build the navy Jefferson and others had proposed eight years earlier. But now the political climate was dramatically different: Jefferson was out of power, siding with the Republican opposition, who saw Washington's Federalist administration as both too friendly with England and too anxious to establish a British-style government in America. Republicans saw the proposed navy as another Federalist ploy to augment the government's power and asked why the Federalists did not turn against America's real enemy, the British. Instead of a navy to fight Algiers, the Republicans proposed a complicated tariff system that would hurt British trade in America. The Federalists refused to believe that Britain was behind the Algerian attacks and thought the Republicans were themselves tools of the French. Every issue became loaded with symbolism far greater than its immediate political importance and took on the dimensions of the deepening struggle between Federalists and Republicans, a struggle not only over political power, but over how much political power any men could hold.

In December 1793, President Washington submitted a message to Congress on the negotiations with Morocco, and though Washington may have expected this to be a routine message, particularly since Secretary of State Jefferson had prepared it before leaving office, it became instead a focal point for this increasingly bitter partisan debate. The message, a report on relations with the Barbary powers, produced a stormy reaction completely unrelated to the subject at hand. In submitting the report Washington mentioned that he had withheld one letter, which he said contained a confidential diplomatic conversation, and he also informed Congress that he believed the government should keep secret the amounts it was prepared to pay for peace and ransom. He thought it important that the American people know that their government was doing something but did not feel the people needed to know every single detail, and he thought that some details, such as diplomatic conversations and how much money the government was willing to spend, should remain secret.[42]

James Madison, Virginia congressman and leader of the Republican opposition, reminded the House that "secrecy in a Republican Government wounds the majesty of the sovereign people; that this Government is in the hands of the people; and that they have a right to know all the transactions relative to their own affairs." Madison moved for an open debate and warned that secrecy would not protect the government's international position but would weaken the government by destroying the American people's confidence in it. A Republican government, Madison said, was not to be conducted in secrecy. How could the people govern themselves if they did not know everything their government was doing?

The Federalists disagreed: Even a Republican government could have secrets. Though the people had a right to govern themselves, they also had "a right to be well governed," and in addition to having rights, the Federalists said, the people had interests. The government was responsible for protecting the people's interests as well as their rights, and diplomatic secrecy sometimes was necessary to do this. The Federalists won this round, though their assertion of the need for secrecy gave their opponents grounds to charge that the Federalists were not protectors of the people's liberty.[43]

This debate over self-government versus good government arose every time the Federalist administration proposed a policy. When Washington suggested that the United States build six frigates to sail against Algiers, Republican critics took it as an attempt to expand government power at the expense of liberty. Virginia Congressman William Branch Giles said that navies were "very foolish things," that the French monarchy had collapsed under the weight of naval expenditures, and that England "groaned under a great part of her immense load of taxes from the same cause."[44] Madison thought that instead of building its own navy, the United States could pay Portugal to cruise against the Algerians. New Jersey Congressman Abraham Clark feared that these six frigates would be merely the beginning of an uncontrolled military expansion. Build six frigates this year, he warned, and "we should next year find it necessary to build six more, and so on." This swelling navy would require people to run it— a secretary of the navy, clerks, aides, and "a swarm of other people in office, at a monstrous expence."[45] Jefferson had once been confident that a navy could be a safe military tool in a republic. Now, after the Federalist administration had created a national bank and had raised an army to suppress the Whiskey Rebellion, Republicans were not so sure. Allow the Federalists to create a navy to fight Algiers, and there was no guarantee that they would not turn it against the American people.

Though the Republicans opposed building the frigates, the Federalists controlled Congress. The United States began building a navy, and Washington's administration sent new agents to negotiate with Algiers. Joseph Donaldson, a businessman and American consul in France, and Joel Barlow, a poet and intellectual living in France, were sent to Algiers in 1795 and negotiated a treaty with the Dey. The United States promised to pay $800,000 to Algiers and to send him $20,000 worth of naval supplies every year. Barlow stayed in Algiers to work out the details of the treaty and to appease the Dey when the tribute failed to arrive. He sent Richard O'Brien, one of the hostages, to Europe to borrow the money the United States promised to pay. In the course of his travels O'Brien's ship was captured by Tripoli, but he used his time there to negotiate a treaty with Pacha Yusuf Qaramanli and then stopped in Tunis to begin negotiations with that regency.

By 1796, the United States was at peace with the Barbary states.

But still none of the prisoners had been released, and though the frigates were not finished, Washington pushed ahead with their construction. Congress had approved spending $688,888.82 on the frigates in 1794; by 1796, they had cost over $1,152,160 and still were not finished. The Bank of the United States, which Hamilton had pushed as an essential institution that would allow the government to borrow money, had refused to lend the government the $800,000 required by the Algerian treaty. Instead, the bank had issued bonds, which the government could sell in Europe. Instead of bringing in their face value, though, the bonds sold poorly, and the sale left the government $100,000 short, a sum that would have to be made up through more borrowing or increased taxes. The shortfall would wind up costing the United States an extra $300,000 and delay the captives' return until 1797. Republicans charged the administration with incompetence, financial misconduct, and spending too much on the military.[46]

Secretary of State Timothy Pickering issued a new warning to American merchants that delays in the Algerian treaty made the Mediterranean unsafe for American trade. The Republicans were outraged. Had any of the money reached Algiers? Who had gotten the money? The Republican press had "no doubt it has or will fall into good hands," and while the taxpayers lost money, "some folks will be the better." The whole episode demonstrated the "folly and imbecility" of Washington's "'six years *glorious* administration.'"[47]

John Adams became president in 1797 and found that France, not Algiers, was the greatest threat to American security. Adams went ahead with the frigates begun under Washington, and the navy completed under his administration fought an undeclared war against France. In addition, the United States built a frigate for the Dey of Algiers, the *Crescent*, as an apology for American tardiness in paying tribute. Algiers was allied with England against France, and Adams wanted to keep Algiers on the American side. Adams briefly planned to send an ambassador to Turkey, which was also at war with France, but called it off because of the changing nature of the European war.

Adams did send consuls to Algiers, Tunis, and Tripoli (Richard

O'Brien went to Algiers, William Eaton to Tunis, and James Leander Cathcart to Tripoli), but his administration was preoccupied with the war against France and with its own political problems, and so was chronically late in sending the tribute promised to those regencies. The consuls, as we will see in a subsequent chapter, had varying degrees of success in appeasing the Barbary rulers. Pacha Yusuf Qaramanli of Tripoli proved the most impatient, and the American consul in Tripoli, James Leander Cathcart, proved the least able to mollify him. By the end of 1800, Yusuf Qaramanli was threatening war against the United States. He could not have anticipated that Thomas Jefferson, the most persistent advocate for military force in the Mediterranean, was about to become president of the United States.

Few men have assumed the presidency with as clear an agenda as Thomas Jefferson. His was more than a political program: Jefferson saw his election in 1800 as a revolution, as a return to the ideals of 1776, as Jefferson understood those ideals. "Kindly separated by nature and a wide ocean from the exterminating havoc of one quarter of the globe," the American republic, Jefferson believed, had room for generations of citizens to live in peace and prosperity. But though peaceful, the Americans were "too high-minded to endure the degradations of others," and when Secretary of State James Madison found dispatches from Tripoli warning that Pacha Yusuf Qaramanli was threatening war with the United States, Jefferson acted quickly. In his first annual message in December 1801, he told Congress that Tripoli "had come forward with demands unfounded either in right or in compact" and that the "style of the demand admitted but one answer."

The answer was the one Jefferson had been proposing since 1785. He sent the U.S. navy to the Mediterranean. Jefferson acknowledged that the previous administration had allowed the United States to lag in its tribute payments, but he quickly moved to pay what the Americans owed, and so "vindicate to ourselves the right of considering the effect of departure from stipulation on their side." The

United States would not be accused of failing to honor its obligations. Jefferson proposed to pay up and fight.[48]

Jefferson's diplomatic experience in the 1780s had convinced him that military force was the only way to deal with the Barbary states. But his political experience in the 1790s had reinforced his fear of government power and made him wary of using that force. So in plunging once again into Barbary affairs, Jefferson was setting out to do a number of things. He was as determined as ever not to submit to the demands of the Barbary powers, anxious to prove both to the North Africans and to the Europeans that the Americans were not going to play the same power games other nations did. But Jefferson was also determined not to create a military machine in the United States, and his administration was committed to reducing the federal debt. Some extreme Republicans, like William Branch Giles, wanted to abolish the navy altogether. Jefferson was not so dogmatic, though he would insist on extensive cuts in the navy budget. He would also insist that the navy—that any military branch—be strictly subservient to civil power, that the military not become an independent interest, but that it be completely under the control of elected officials.

Jefferson also revived the idea of an international alliance. Tripoli had threatened Sweden as well as the United States. Jefferson did not know that Adams had rebuffed Swedish overtures in 1800. Jefferson ordered the American fleet to cooperate with Sweden or any other nation at war with Tripoli, and if Yusuf Qaramanli had declared war on the United States Jefferson ordered the fleet to blockade Tripoli.[49]

Jefferson's seemingly contradictory policies—reducing government spending and sending the navy halfway around the world—were in fact directed to the same goal. He had taken part in a revolution against a large, abusive government. That revolution, as Jefferson saw it, was fought to free the people's energies. By closing the Mediterranean to the people's entrepreneurial spirit, the Barbary states imposed a barrier that was just as effective as the British Navigation Acts. By engaging in official piracy, the Barbary states placed themselves outside the accepted bounds of international law.

That the British used Algiers to attack Americans did not excuse the Algerians, any more than British instigation of Indian atrocities on the frontiers excused the Indians. By refusing to play the European game of bribery, by standing up to the Barbary powers and removing them from the European arsenal of weapons against the New World, Jefferson would convince Europe that his was a new kind of nation, one that would not follow the corrupt practices of the old world.

By December 1801 Jefferson could report success. Lt. Andrew Sterrett and the schooner *Enterprise* had engaged a Tripolitan ship in a day-long sea battle, killing twenty Tripolitans and wounding thirty others without losing a single American. In an early draft of his message, Jefferson wanted to cite this as the first example of American bravery; he was advised that others had given examples of courage during the Adams administration's war with France. Jefferson did tell Congress that Sterrett's victory should convince Europe that Americans were willing to fight. Jefferson wanted Sterrett's victory to be a lesson to Europe as well as to Tripoli. And though he said that Americans would fight, they only did so to secure peace, preferring to "direct the energies of our nation to the multiplication of the human race, and not to its destruction."[50]

Jefferson meant to prove that the Americans were going to behave differently from the Europeans, that they would not make war and peace articles of commerce, and that they could fight a war without creating a military machine or sacrificing republican values. Jefferson told Congress that he had sent the *Enterprise* to the Mediterranean for purely defensive reasons. The decision to wage war or not would be left up to the Congress. The following week Congress debated the issue, considering whether to allow Jefferson "further and more fully and effectually to protect" American commerce. Maryland Republican Joseph Nicholson objected. The words "further and more," Nicholson said, should be stricken since Jefferson plainly did not want more power. In fact, Nicholson pointed out, Jefferson's administration was making drastic reductions in the army and navy. Why would he, on the one hand, want to reduce the military and, on the other, want more military power? This "would be in the same breath, to say one thing and mean another." The Federalists knew this and wanted to put the Republicans on record as saying one thing—promising to cut government spending—while doing another—actually increasing spending. The Federalists wanted to demonstrate the illogic of Republican policies and the contradictions in Jefferson's statecraft. The Federalists saw Jefferson as a master politician, as a confident man perpetrating fraud on the American people, who would ignore his inconsistencies as he gave them "a smile, a nod, and a squeeze of the hand."[51]

Though Congress granted Jefferson more power to protect commerce, in 1802 it did not seem that he would need it. The Swedish–American blockade, and a hard winter in North Africa, threatened Tripoli with starvation. Neither Algiers nor Tunis came to Tripoli's aid. In December 1802 Jefferson, committed to protecting commerce without a military build-up, reaffirmed his blockade of Tripoli as a way to secure American commerce "with the smallest force competent" to the task.[52]

Jefferson could also report that Morocco would not go to war with the United States, thanks to Consul James Simpson's "temperate and correct course" and Commodore Edward Preble's "promptitude and energy." The *National Intelligencer* exulted that Jefferson "had commanded peace" with Morocco "on his own terms," without either blood or tribute. What did the Federalists, who not long ago had exclaimed "*Millions for defence, but not a cent for tribute*" say about this? The *Intelligencer* reminded its readers that President Washington, "imitating the example of Europe," had bought peace from Algiers with naval stores and a frigate. Jefferson had done more with less money and "without a dollar's tribute"! The same day, the *Intelligencer* published an excerpt from John Rodgers's journal giving details of his June victory over a Tripolitan frigate, which ended when the Tripolitan captain blew up his own ship rather than surrender it. Tripoli saw how hopelessly outmatched it was, and Jefferson took pleasure in relating the "honorable facts" of Rodgers's "gallant enterprise" to Congress.[53]

The administration was so confident in its policies that when

27

William Eaton, consul to Tunis, suggested more military force in the Mediterranean, he was brushed aside with "predictions of a political millennium" about to be ushered in "as the irresistable consequence of the goodness of heart, integrity of mind, and correctness of disposition of Mr. Jefferson." Eaton was assured that "All nations, even pirates and savages, were to be moved by the influence of his [Jefferson's] persuasive virtue and masterly skill in diplomacy."[54]

Each dispatch ended with a promise that the next one would bring news of victory and peace. Then, in October 1803, the *U.S.S. Philadelphia*, the navy's second largest ship, ran aground off Tripoli and was captured, along with 300 sailors. The men were imprisoned, and the ship was refitted for use against the United States. When news of this disaster struck in March 1804, the Federalists finally had a concrete example of Jefferson's ineptitude to use against him. They had long tried to note the contradiction between Jefferson's cutting of the military budget and promises to maintain sufficient force, but as long as Jefferson and the navy succeeded, this was an empty charge. Now, though, the Federalists could say that if Jefferson had sent more ships to the Mediterranean, the *Philadelphia* would not have been captured. Had there been another frigate, or even a smaller ship accompanying it, Captain William Bainbridge would not have had to strike his colors and submit to the Tripolitans. Now that Jefferson's parsimony had cost the nation a frigate, the Federalist attacks seemed to have been proven right.

Jefferson immediately called for an increased force in the Mediterranean. This prompted the New York *Evening Post* to quote Swift:

> Behold a proof of Irish sense,
>> Where Irish wit is seen;
> When nothing's left that's worth defence,
>> We build a Magazine.[55]

But though Jefferson now called for more force, he was as determined as ever not to let the military grow unchecked. He would not borrow money to rebuild the navy, nor would his administration take money they meant to use to repay the national debt. Instead, Jefferson and Treasury Secretary Albert Gallatin revived the idea that Jefferson had broached in the 1780s for a special tax on merchants trading in the Mediterranean. This import tax of 2.5 percent would last only as long as the war with Tripoli. The administration feared the prospect of "increasing taxes, encroaching government, temptations to offensive wars, &c" more than it feared Tripoli. Preparing for contingent wars, Gallatin and Jefferson agreed, encouraged war. The administration insisted that the war be fought with money raised specifically for the war, that the country not be constantly ready to fight.[56]

The Federalists did not think much of either Jefferson's economics or his plan to prevent a permanent military establishment supported by permanent taxes. They took the Mediterranean fund to be another ploy by Jefferson to increase his own popularity. He had cut the navy, the *Charleston* (South Carolina) *Courier* insisted, to secure his reelection, and now that his promises of frugality had yielded a harvest of "smut and chaff," his "farce of penury with which the public was cajoled, vanishes from the stage." The New York *Evening Post,* Alexander Hamilton's paper, called the loss of the *Philadelphia* "a practical lesson in Jefferson's economy" and the Mediterranean fund "the most audacious attempt" ever seen "to impose an oppressive burden on the commercial states." The *Post* saw through the "persecuting, oppressive, insincere" tricks of these "political jugglers," noting that the United States owed $800,000 in yearly interest on the money borrowed to buy Louisiana: Was it only a coincidence that the Mediterranean fund would raise $792,000 every year? Jefferson was taxing New England merchants to buy more land for southern farmers, trying to "increase the revenue without loss of popularity." Merchants needed the navy to protect their trade; Jefferson would scrap the navy, then tax the merchants under the pretense of protecting them, and use the proceeds to buy Louisiana. The administration would not tax farmers and laborers, whose votes they needed. Gallatin would not think it proper to raise money "by laying on the *southern whiskey* the tax from which the *mouth of labour* has been so pleasantly relieved."[57]

Jefferson's plan to reduce naval spending by building small gunboats to defend harbors and rivers, boats that would not cross the ocean to fight Tripoli or carry out an offensive war, also came in for Federalist ridicule. When a hurricane flung one of the gunboats out of the Savannah River and dropped it into a cornfield, the *Post* suggested that "in imitation of her gallant Lord High Admiral," she was defending the agricultural interest. "If our gun boats are of no use upon the water," an anonymous Bostonian said, "may they at least be the best upon earth."[58]

The Federalists had always supported the navy and regarded the Republicans as the its enemies. "May its strength protect our commerce," one Federalist toasted, "and its glory confound its enemies at *Washington* and Tripoli." Jefferson and his Republican administration, Federalists charged, cared more about buying the swamps and salt licks of Louisiana than about protecting American commerce and sailors in the Mediterranean.[59] Had the administration sent more than the "smallest force competent" to the Mediterranean the *Philadelphia* would not have been captured. But Jefferson had concluded that since one frigate cost less than two, it would be more economical to have one frigate off Tripoli. This foolish economy had cost the nation one frigate, and now Jefferson saw that he needed to build more frigates. New Hampshire Senator William Plumer conceded that the Adams and Washington administrations had spent too much on the navy, more than $2,000,000 each year compared with Jefferson's $600,000 annual navy budget. But Plumer thought Jefferson's $600,000 naval budget too little, that it was "*bad policy, & base wickedness*" to send men to fight without adequate force. A sufficient navy would have been expensive, Plumer wrote, and might have hurt Jefferson's "reputation for economy & lessened his popularity with the rabble," but it would have saved lives.[60]

The Federalists might have won the argument, but Stephen Decatur, a second-generation naval officer, put a stop to the partisan bickering by sneaking into Tripoli's harbor with a select crew and setting fire to the *Philadelphia*. It is impossible to overestimate the impact this news had when it reached America. In Salem, William Bentley had gone to bed despondent on May 15, 1804. A contentious town meeting that day had chosen mediocre men for local offices: Salem's best men refused to serve. Bentley worried about the fate of Salem. But the next morning his spirits lifted. "We receive the news of the destruction of the *Philadelphia* in the harbour of Tripoli just in season to relieve us from the events of yesterday," he wrote. Across the country, Decatur's raid stirred patriotic emotions, changing a disastrous defeat into a glorious victory.[61]

Valorous as Decatur's action was, it did not change the situation in Tripoli. In August and September 1804 the navy increased its blockade of that city and then bombarded it. The actions were not successful and were called off until the spring of 1805, when they resumed, as William Eaton began his own march from Egypt across the Libyan desert to the town of Derne. The navy besieged Tripoli, Eaton besieged Derne, and Tobias Lear negotiated a peace treaty. In June 1805, the United States agreed to pay a $60,000 ransom for the 300 prisoners, and the war ended.[62]

The *Post* asked "our boasting, blustering ministerial sycophants who tell us of Mr. Jefferson's feats in bringing the war with Tripoli to a glorious termination" to read about a French action against Algiers, which resulted in the release of French captives within twenty-four hours. This "mere show of respectable force, and a proper tone" accomplished in a day what took Jefferson four years. The *Post* thought the Republicans should keep quiet about the "stupid manner in which we have carried on a four years war."[63]

The Philadelphia *Aurora* responded that the Federalists would rather have left the officers and crew of the *Philadelphia* "consigned to eternal chains" than see Jefferson have "the merit of emancipating them, and humbling the Tripoline barbarian." When the war ended, and the prisoners and victorious American fleet arrived home, the *Aurora* wrote that "Events speak for themselves"; the "wise and prudent" administration had won the war, despite Federalist carping. A Richmond dinner toasted the administration, "The success of its measures the best proof of its energy."[64] And, the Republicans claimed, all measures had been successful. Even the Mediterranean fund, which the Federalists had charged was a scheme to get New England merchants to pay for Louisiana, the Republicans now claimed had been an important weapon. Yusuf Qaramanli, had reportedly read American newspapers and been "particularly struck with...the report of the secretary of the treasury" that the Mediterranean fund would raise more than half a million dollars every year. Treasury Secretary Gallatin had filled the Pacha with "surprise and apprehension," and in the American treasurer's reports Yusuf "saw that the spirit of the American nation was yet unbroken" and he knew he was impotent against a nation "which would thus contribute 'millions for defence but not a cent for tribute.'"[65]

In fact, though most contemporary Americans dismissed the Federalists as partisan malcontents, subsequent historians have followed their condemnation of Jefferson's handling of the Tripolitan war as inept or inconsistent, and that only luck and Decatur's bravery saved the day. But the Federalists, and subsequent historians, have missed the point. Jefferson had advocated using force against the Barbary powers since 1785, but he perceived that war was a limited instrument, one that must be completely under the control of civilian authorities. Jefferson, more perhaps than any of his contemporaries, feared the consequences of excessive power. He had to fight Tripoli without invoking the war powers, which he thought would lead inexorably to an expanded government and the potential for executive tyranny. William Plumer, the New Hampshire Federalist, called on Jefferson as the Senate considered the Tripolitan treaty. Plumer told Jefferson that the U. S. government seemed more suited to domestic than international affairs. "Your observation is perfectly correct," Jefferson told him. "Our constitution is a peace establishment—It is not calculated for war. War would endanger its existence."[66] In the war against Tripoli, Jefferson kept the military strictly subservient to civil power and had used the Mediterranean fund to ensure that those who benefited from the war would also pay for it. But Jefferson also knew that the benefits of this war would extend far beyond safer commerce in the Mediterranean. By proving themselves able to use power without abusing it, or without being absorbed into it, the Americans had proven themselves, as John Paul Jones had written twenty years earlier, a people who deserved to be free.

Twenty years earlier, visitors from North Africa had roused fear and suspicion. Now, in 1805, such visitors were harmless objects of curiosity. Seven Tripolitan prisoners of war, captured at sea, were brought to New York on the *John Adams* in March 1805. Their arrival was a boon to the local theaters, which competed for the Tripolitans' attendance. Though New York audiences had often seen "the personation of Turks and three-tailed Bashaws," this was the first appearance of "your real *bona fide* imported Turks" on any American stage. The seven Tripolitans drew such large crowds that one theater ran a benefit night for them at the end of March, and advertised that on April 5 "THE TURKS WILL VISIT THE THEATRE FOR POSITIVELY THE LAST TIME." By contrast, twenty years earlier, three Jews had been sent out of Virginia for fear that they might be Algerian spies. Now, seven Tripolitan sailors caught after a battle with an American ship, amused the public and boosted theater attendance.[67]

The contrast was even more striking in Richmond, Virginia. Doctor William Foushee, who had interviewed the Moroccan strangers in 1785, presided over a dinner for William Bainbridge and other returning captives in 1805. Perhaps Foushee remembered the dark winter days of 1785, when Patrick Henry had called on him to investigate the mysterious North Africans whose arrival so shook the commonwealth. What a contrast from those days of fear and uncertainty were these days of the nineteenth century! In 1785 there was no national government to speak of; the United States had title to land up to the Mississippi, but had to contest nearly every inch of it with Britain, France, Spain, and the fearsome indigenous people; and Americans were held captive in Algiers. Now, in 1805, the United States controlled the Mississippi and most of its headwaters; France had abandoned the New World; a benevolent federal government was pacifying the Indians; and Americans had returned in triumph from the Mediterranean, having humbled the ancient enemies of Christian civilization, asserting their role as Americans in defending freedom. The victory over Tripoli, which Foushee celebrated in 1805, had made the Americans the equals of any other people, not because of military power, but because that power was guided by a spirit of justice, and its goal was not conquest but freedom. The Americans, statesmen and sailors, leaders and common folk, were different from the "the plundering vassals of the tyrannical Bashaw," as one poet had described the Tripolitans, and the European nations that countenanced the Bashaw's plunder and tyranny. Foushee may have reflected on the changes twenty years had brought as he presided over this celebratory dinner. The Americans were not only people to respect, people who, as John Paul Jones had said, deserved to be free; they had become people to emulate. As one celebrant at the Richmond dinner proclaimed, the Barbary states would not disgrace the civilized world if the cabinets of Europe were inspired by "an American spirit."[68]

CHAPTER TWO

The United States and the Specter of Islam

Americans and Europeans had distorted ideas about Islam, but they found these ideas useful. Enlightenment writers created a picture of the Muslim world that served as a sober warning about the dangers of submitting to despotism, about the dangers of suppressing public debate, and about the twin evils of tyranny and anarchy. The European image of Islam remained unchanged throughout the eighteenth century, but it was useful to Europeans and Americans with dramatically different political ideas. During the American Revolution, patriots could use the image of Turkish janizzaries to warn their countrymen about the dangers of submitting to British tyranny. Tories could draw on Western images of Muhammad to warn their countrymen of the dangers of upsetting the established order and following passionate advocates of new ideas. During the debate over the Constitution, Federalists could warn of the dangers of anarchy and instability, pointing to the Ottoman empire, which had no control over its distant provinces, while anti-Federalists repeated the Revolutionary warnings of centralized power, pointing to the absolute tyranny of Muslim sultans. Americans of different political philosophies disagreed on the particular lessons drawn from Muslim history. But all of them, Tories and Patriots, Republicans and Federalists, agreed that Islam fostered religious and political oppression.[1]

The American and European image of the Islamic world is most clearly seen in an anonymous Englishman's biography of Muhammad written at the end of the eighteenth century and reprinted in America in 1802. This book's long title sets its tone: *The*

Life of Mahomet; or, the History of that Imposture which was begun, carried on, and finally established by him in Arabia: and which has Subjugated a Larger Portion of the Globe, than the Religion of Jesus has yet set at Liberty. The author's "Philanthropic heart" ached at the sight of rational men "degraded to the rank of brutes" by Muhammad's "artifice and wickedness." Muslims were so debased by fraud and violence that this author saw no other way to save them than by conquering them. Only conquest by the West would free Muslims from "that system of blasphemy and iniquity by which they are at present enslaved." No peaceful invasion by missionaries or teachers could enlighten the Muslims, whose rulers supported their own beliefs with "carnal weapons" and respected no argument but force. Heathens and savages were easier to convert than Muslims.[2]

Religious differences between Islam and Christianity were only part of the problem. As this biography of Muhammad makes clear, Islam established a tyranny over the minds of men, which created a political tyranny just as wicked as Muhammad's religious imposture. At the end of the volume, the publisher advertised two books that he knew would appeal to readers of this biography of Muhammad. One was a series of essays on Christ's redemption and other religious ideas. The other was Montesquieu's *Spirit of the Laws*, the eighteenth-century's most influential work of political theory, which set out liberal ideas on government and political organization. This *Life of Mahomet* was bound together with an "Account of Egypt," which concluded with a warning on the evils of absolute monarchy, which was just as much a "slaughterhouse for the people" as it was for their rulers. Absolute power for the prince "places the lives of millions on the footing of a lottery" and tempts the king to a wickedness he cannot resist. If an absolute ruler, such as Islam permitted, acted to the full extent of his powers, "there is little probability that he will die in his bed." The author granted that the ancient Egyptians had some degree of civilization and even happiness under their absolute rulers, but "let none admire it upon that account, and hope to be equally happy by trying the experiment."[3]

The anonymous author of the *Life of Mahomet* acknowledged his debt to the only other English biography of Muhammad, one written in 1697 by Humphrey Prideaux, an English clergyman. While acknowledging Prideaux, the author found his book severely wanting in style, arrangement, and that "sine qua non of a good history, which is better felt than described." Prideaux had failed to raise moral and philosophical points, and was not critical enough in evaluating evidence. Though the anonymous Englishman was not an objective writer, Prideaux was even less so. Prideaux had written his *The True Nature of Imposture, Fully displayed in the Life of Mahomet* as a warning to young people who were becoming indifferent to religion and were even flirting with dangerous ideas like deism, a belief that God may have created the world but did not require man's complete attention. Prideaux was a religious scholar and had planned to write a great historical work on Constantinople's fall to the Muslims. But a rising tide of religious indifference so horrified him he decided to write a biography of Muhammad to warn off young people who seemed more interested in fashion and the trivialities of life than in their souls. Proponents of deism and free thought pretended they were freeing men's minds from the chains of ignorance and superstition; Prideaux saw in the story of Islam that the consequences of this religious indifference would be religious slavery. That is, once people stopped taking religion seriously, believing instead that each man could follow his own heart to whatever God he chose, they would not recognize a religious fraud like Muhammad until it was too late. A false prophet could attract enough converts to enslave the nation. Prideaux, like his radical cousin Walter Moyle, whose 1690s pamphlets attacked the idea of the monarch's unlimited power, was trying to prevent tyranny from taking root in England. Prideaux believed that the way to prevent tyranny was to prevent the social apathy that would allow it. Muhammad's religious fanaticism would have found no outlet had the Arabian people been more attached to their own religion. Muhammad's lust and ambition drove him to become a tyrant, but the people's religious apathy allowed him to succeed. Prideaux hoped this story would warn Englishmen of the 1690s, just as the later author hoped to warn Englishmen of the 1790s about the evils of atheism, deism, and religious indifference.[4]

According to Prideaux, Muhammad had come from a prominent family, though the death of his parents had deprived him of a rich inheritance. Prideaux dismissed other accounts that gave Muhammad a "mean and vile" origin. Ambition and avarice were most dangerous in someone like Prideaux's Muhammad, who was well born but had lost his standing. Muhammad sought ways to advance himself with his "subtile and crafty" mind. Meccans worshipped many different gods and tolerated the religious doctrines of their neighbors. These diverse religions were regarded as relative truths; none was considered absolute truth. Muhammad exploited this toleration and relativism, and thought that by creating a religion of his own, he could suppress all others and secure his own power.[5]

Prideaux was not merely a Christian writer upset that Muhammad had set himself up as a prophet, or that Muhammad had denied the divinity of Christ. Prideaux's Muhammad was a religious heretic, but his real sin was his ambition. Prideaux noted that Muhammad's "imposture" began at about the same time that Gregory I had become Pope and claimed supremacy over the entire Christian church. Muhammad and Gregory I, "having conspired to found themselves an empire in imposture," urged their followers to use fire and sword to achieve it. Prideaux, an Anglican minister, saw Islam and Catholicism as the two feet of the Antichrist, set on Christendom in the East and West. Both Catholicism and Islam permitted religious and political tyranny, but more important than their inherent evil was that both were allowed to grow because good men were indifferent to their consequences.[6]

Prideaux hoped his picture of Muhammad would awaken those tempted by deism or indifferent to it. Muhammad had succeeded because people stopped taking their true religion seriously and had begun to question the tenets of their faith. Muhammad had exploited religious indifference to create religious and ultimately political tyranny. He had used revelations as a cynical cover for political ambition, an ambition that he would achieve by persuasion if possible but by the sword if necessary. When people demanded proof of Muhammad's divine mission and asked to see miracles, Muhammad answered that God had wearied of showing proof and had sent his last prophet to secure the faith with the sword. For this reason, Prideaux wrote, Muslim clerics preached their sermons with a sword by their side.

A century after English religious and political schisms had moved Prideaux to write his *True Nature of Imposture*, political and religious schisms prompted two American editions of his book. These two separate publications show the immediate political use a biography of Muhammad, even a century-old one, could have in America. Stewart & Cochran of Philadelphia, publishers of religious books, issued the first American edition of Prideaux's *True Nature of Imposture* in 1796. Stewart & Cochran included Prideaux's original introduction, with its attack on the "great prevailing of infidelity in the present age" and its plea to every Christian minister to fight deism, apostasy, and their horrible consequences. Prideaux in 1697 had been frightened by the "giddy humour" into which too many people, particularly the young, had fallen, blindly accepting whatever was in "fashion and vogue." This could have been written in 1796 by an American alarmed at the age that had produced Thomas Paine, the French Revolution, and other assaults on Christianity and order. Prideaux had warned that many influential people were flirting with deism, leading the "unthinking people" into calling "christianity a cheat and an imposture" without considering what an imposture truly is. His *True Nature of Imposture* clearly defined imposture. He hoped to convince a skeptical people of the difference between Christianity and Islam or other false beliefs. A decline in piety would lead not to religious liberty but to tyranny.

This dark vision was sobering to those who witnessed the revolutionary turmoil in France, which upset the established order in Europe and even threatened the security of America. Vice President John Adams was so worried by events in France that in 1790 he wrote a series of essays, "Discourses on Davila," warning that "If all decorum, discipline, and subordination are to be destroyed," replaced by skepticism, "anarchy, and insecurity of property," people would "soon wish their books in ashes, seek for darkness and ignorance, superstition and fanaticism, as blessings, and follow the standard of the first mad despot, who, with the enthusiasm of another Mahomet, will endeavor to obtain them." For Adams, as for Prideaux, tyranny would be the ultimate consequence of too much liberty. Ultimately, Napoleon would prove Adams right, but in 1790 and 1791 the cause of republican France was so popular in the United States that even Federalist newspaper editors refused to publish Adams's essays. Adams opposed the revolution in France because he thought it would end in military despotism. But because he opposed a revolution that promised democracy and equality, his critics thought he was against those principles. In 1791, Thomas Paine, in France as a member of the National Assembly, defended the French Revolution and the right of the French people to tear down social, political, and religious hierarchies in his book, *The Rights of Man*. Secretary of State Thomas Jefferson praised *The Rights of Man*, and said he hoped Paine's book would counter "political heresies" that were arising in America. Though Jefferson did not mention any names, few Americans doubted that John Adams was the heretic Jefferson had in mind. Adams's son John Quincy responded by comparing Jefferson with "the Arabian prophet" who called on "all true believers in the Islam of democracy to draw their swords." Paraphrasing the Muslim creed, "There is no God but Allah, and Muhammad is his Prophet," the younger Adams had Jefferson and his zealous supporters shouting, "There is but one Goddess of Liberty, and Common Sense is her prophet." Jefferson was a well-born, respectable man like Prideaux's Muhammad, but by countenancing the free thought of Thomas Paine and others, he would ultimately destroy the liberty he pretended to defend. Like Prideaux, John and John Quincy Adams saw in Muhammad a lesson not only to the orthodox but also to the religiously or politically indifferent.[7]

For defenders of the established order, Prideaux's *True Nature of Imposture* carried a powerful message. But theirs was not the only possible reading. In 1798 a second American edition of Prideaux's *True Nature of Imposture* appeared in Fairhaven, Vermont.[8] This edition omitted Prideaux's original preface, which had warned against infidelity and unbelief. This 1798 edition was less worried about the possible social causes of tyranny than about tyranny itself. The threat of tyranny implicit in Muhammad's career was perhaps more clear to the publisher of this edition than it had been to any other. James Lyon of Fairhaven, a printer trained in his trade by Benjamin Franklin, published Prideaux's *True Nature of Imposture* while his father, Congressman Mathew Lyon, was in jail for violating the Sedition Act of 1798. Mathew Lyon, a Republican and a harsh critic of Federalists, specifically of President John Adams, was in jail for charging Adams with using "the sacred name of religion" as a "State engine to make mankind hate and persecute one another." For this and other statements, made both in Congress and in letters to his constituents, Lyon was convicted of being a "notorious and seditious person, and of a depraved mind, and wicked and diabolical disposition." In *True Nature of Imposture*, false religion and the power of the state combined to enslave the people. Lyon saw the same forces at work in 1798. Direct criticism of the political establishment sent him to jail, so Mathew Lyon made an indirect attack by publishing Prideaux's *True Nature of Imposture*.[9]

Prideaux's book was heaven-sent for Lyon. Its message was clear on the dangers of indifference; it also showed the pernicious effects of enforced orthodoxy. According to Prideaux, Muhammad had been "teazed and perplexed" when his audiences either asked tough questions or laughed at him. Finally, Prideaux said, Muhammad had become so upset that he forbade "all manner of disputing about his religion" and threatened death to any who doubted or opposed him. "And certainly," Prideaux had written, "there could not be a wiser way devised for upholding of so absurd an imposture than by thus silencing, under so severe a penalty, all manner of opposition and disputes concerning it."[10]

Matthew Lyon could not have said it better. Though the Federalists had not executed Lyon or other political opponents, they had found in the Sedition Act an effective way to silence them. For Lyon, this first step was the most important. Once it was accepted that a ruler, whether a Muhammad or an Adams, could not be questioned, the consequence would be the same. It did not even matter if the punishment was prison or the sword; the effect would be the same. Muhammad could not endure the well-deserved ridicule of his audience and so had resorted to force. John Adams and his Federalist administration had done the same. The *True Nature of Imposture* showed the consequences of suppression. The Sedition Act showed that even a former Revolutionary like Adams could become enraptured with his own power.[11]

In addition to Prideaux's book, James Lyon, Mathew's son, published *A Republican Magazine* in 1798. All four issues detailed the elder Lyon's trial and imprisonment. The title page of *A Republican Magazine* carried an invocation from Daniel Defoe:

> Nature has left this tincture in the blood,
> That all Men would be TYRANTS, if they cou'd—
> If they forbear their Neighbors to devour,
> 'Tis not for want of WILL, but want of POWER.
> [Jure Divino][12]

The leaders of the American republic, like men in power anywhere, had both the will and the power to be tyrants, a fact plain to Mathew and James Lyon.

Prideaux's *True Nature of Imposture* allowed two seemingly contradictory interpretations. In the first, and most likely the interpretation favored by the author himself, the lesson was that too much liberty would lead ultimately to tyranny. When people lose their faith, when they question every value, when they no longer respect one another or the tenets of their society or religion, they open the way for a demagogue like Muhammad to establish a religious or political despotism. Mathew Lyon saw the second interpretation, that all men can be tyrants. Lyon warned that by refusing to tolerate public questioning of leaders, by insisting that established social and political forms be rigid and not yield to the forces of reason or common sense, even honorable men, like John Adams, can become tyrants. Never mind that neither interpretation had much to do with the historical person of Muhammad: Each one used a fictionalized Muhammad to make a point about eighteenth-century America.

Voltaire also used Muhammad to make a point about religion. From Muhammad's life Voltaire drew a warning about religious intolerance, not the dangers of religious liberty. In 1742 Voltaire had written a play, *Le fanatisme ou Mahomet le Prophete*, as a thinly veiled meditation on the evils of religious intolerance. Of course, Voltaire's Mahomet is the villain, but the pagans of Mecca turn out to be the play's secular humanist heroes. Shortly after Voltaire wrote his play, James Miller, an English clergyman and also a writer of plays, translated it, keeping its praise of the secular humanists of Mecca but turning it into a play about the evils of fanaticism and blind devotion to men in power. A nineteenth-century biographer described Miller as a "political writer, who refused a large bribe, to abandon his opinions, and favour ministers of the state."

Miller's translation of *Mahomet* carried a powerful message. A Dublin audience was so aroused by one character's lines, which they thought were critical of the government, that they demanded he repeat them and cheered wildly at the encore. The theater manager feared the government would shut the theater down if he allowed such displays the next night, so he forbade the actor to repeat the controversial lines. The audience on the second night listened for the lines and their chance to show opposition to the government. Again they applauded, stamped, and cheered, demanding to hear the speech repeated. But under orders from the management, the actor kept silent. The audience pressed, calling for the lines, drowning out any attempt to continue the play. The show could not go on. When the audience realized the manager was preventing the encore, they burned down his theater. [13]

It is hard to recover the immediate political meaning that provoked this response. We can conjecture about the play's subsequent popularity and sustained relevance over the last half of the eighteenth century in England and America. In Voltaire and Miller's play, Mahomet is a charismatic charlatan, a cult leader. He has brainwashed two impressionable, idealistic young people, Zaphna and Palmira, to join him in overthrowing Alcanor, the pagan leader of Mecca. Palmira and Zaphna zealously agree to kill Alcanor, in return for which Mahomet promises to sanction their marriage. But Palmira and Zaphna do not know that they are sister and brother, that Alcanor is their father, or that Mahomet plans to kill Zaphna, as he has his own lustful designs on Palmira. Caught up in their religious zeal, they follow Mahomet's orders and kill their father, Alcanor, discovering his true identity too late.

Zaphna and Palmira kill themselves, realizing that the blessings Mahomet had promised are "the sword, the pestilence, the famine," and dying, they ask him, "How could'st thou damn us thus?" A glimmer of conscience awakens in Mahomet, who realizes that despite his conquests, he remains a slave to his own passions and ambitions. "In vain are glory, worship, and dominion! All conq'ror as I am, I am a slave. . . . I might deceive the world; myself I cannot." For the first time praying sincerely, he begs to be shrouded from the horrors he has created. The play closes with the warning:

> Here let the mad enthusiast turn his eyes,
> And see from bigotry what horrors rise,
> Here in the blackest colours let him read
> That zeal, by craft misled, may act a deed
> By which both innocence and virtue bleed.[14]

Mahomet is a slave to his own ambitions and passions, and enslaves others to them as well. He cannot restrain the passions of his followers because his own are out of control. Enthusiasm, bigotry, lust, and ambition are the lessons of his mad career. Mahomet uses his charismatic gifts to destroy innocence and virtue, persuading Zaphna and Palmira to reject their own father and follow his false doctrines.

We do not know what political events or personalities provoked the 1744 audience to destroy the theater. But we can imagine the reaction of this play's audience when *Mahomet, the Imposter* was first performed in America. The play premiered in New York in 1780. Like Mecca in the play, New York then was a city besieged. British troops controlled the city, Americans, the country surrounding. The cast for this first American production of *Mahomet, the Imposter* were all British soldiers. British soldiers and New Yorkers loyal to the king sat in the audience. New York was an enclave against the growing tide of revolution, and this audience and cast, like Alcanor and the tolerant pagans of Mecca, may have felt under siege by passionate zealots who were rousing the innocent colonists to kill their symbolic father, George III. Sent to America to preserve the British empire, the soldier actors may have seen in *Mahomet, the Imposter* a vindication of their role as protectors of the established order, as they tried to prevent the ambitious zealots and mad enthusiasts from destroying the traditional bonds of family, community, and empire.[15]

But New York, like Mecca, would fall. After 1777, *Mahomet, the Imposter*, which had been reprinted in England every year since 1745, would go out of print. It would not reappear until 1795, a year when all of Europe was at war over the doctrines of the French Revolution. In 1795 the dangers posed by demagogues and killers of kings were even more clear. Four London publishers issued *Mahomet, the Imposter* in 1795, and in 1796 it was performed in Philadelphia. Voltaire, now dead, might have wondered at his play's transformation from rejection of religious intolerance to support of the *status quo*, just as Muhammad might have wondered at his own transformation into a metaphor applicable to almost any ideology or situation. This metaphorical Muhammad carried a powerful message about the consequences of unbridled power and blind devotion. The images of Muhammad differed in detail, but all taught the same lesson, a lesson about tyranny and power that Americans never tired of hearing.

In the 1780s and 1790s in America, as the generation that had won the Revolution set out to create a new government and define that government's power, as the dangers of despotism and anarchy were plainly displayed by events in France, the full importance of the Islamic image came into focus. Americans regarded Muhammad as a dangerous false prophet and as the creator of an evil religious and political system. But these systems were not wrong merely for being non-Christian or despotic. The full danger of religious despotism or political tyranny was not the immediate evil these would do, but their ultimate consequences. This generation of Americans did not act just for themselves, but for all time. They set out to establish a political system not just for their own benefit, but for the benefit of future generations. Islamic despotism was wrong not merely for preventing men and women from enjoying liberty, but also because it prevented men and women and their offspring from enjoying the benefits of liberty. Islam prevented men and women from developing to their fullest potential. Islam, as the Americans saw it, was against liberty, and being against liberty, it stopped progress. Both Republicans like Mathew Lyon and Thomas Jefferson, who welcomed the progressive libertarianism of the French Revolution, and Federalists like John Adams, who feared the consequences of unchecked democracy, agreed that liberty and human progress were good things and that the unbridled despotism of the Muslim world was a bad thing for preventing it. Americans, though they disagreed on how much liberty a society could tolerate, agreed that the Muslim states did not tolerate even that much. For this reason, the once flourishing societies of Egypt, Syria, Turkey, and North Africa had stopped growing, and their lethargic and indolent people and rulers had allowed their once fertile lands to become desert wastes. This was a potent lesson for a people at work building their own political society. Americans could easily suffer the same fate.

Mathew Lyon and other Republicans saw that submitting to despotism was the first step, and the most dangerous one. John Adams and other Federalists thought that countenancing heretical doctrines would inevitably destroy true doctrines. The resulting evil, for both, would not be merely a false religion or even political tyranny. Instead, Americans of every political persuasion saw political and religious tyranny as symptoms of deeper social ills. Muhammad's "imposture" not only stifled religious and intellectual freedom, it killed the spirit of enterprise by which societies could flourish.

John Trenchard and Thomas Gordon's *Cato's Letters* (1723), perhaps the most influential English political tract of the eighteenth century and certainly the most important one to the Revolutionary generation of Americans, argued that tyrants like Muhammad feared that "common sense might get the better of Violence" and so prevented the free expression of ideas. Muhammad had made it a capital offense to reason freely on the Koran, and subsequent rulers of the Turkish empire and other Muslim states frowned on printing and other forms of mass communication. This had made the Muslims bigots as well as slaves. "No man can shew me a Bigot who is not an ignorant Slave," Trenchard and Gordon had observed, and they defined bigotry as "a Slavery of the Soul" to religious doctrines or tales that did not bear investigating. Cotton Mather, the Massachusetts clergyman and rigorous Calvinist, agreed completely with the English libertarians. In his treatise *The Christian Philosopher*, written just a year or two after Trenchard and Gordon's *Cato's Letters*, Mather incorporated modern science into his own rigid religious doctrine and contrasted his own intellectual freedom with the limited scope of Muslim philosophers. According to Mather's understanding of Muslim natural philosophy, all the wonders of nature had been explained fully to Muhammad, and "none of his Followers" dared question the prophet's explanations. If it was revealed to the "thick-skull'd Prophet" that an angel moving his wings caused the wind, an angel stepping in the sea caused tides, an angel cracking a whip made thunder, no Muslim scientist could ask for more explanation. In contrast, even staunch Calvinists were permitted to inquire closely into the workings of the natural world. Mather dismissed Islam as both a religion and a scientific tool: "*May our Devotion exceed the* Mahometan *as much as our Philosophy!*" John Foss, an American sailor held captive in Algiers in the 1790s, noted that "the Turks possess the greatest contempt for Learning." Under Ottoman domination, Greece, which was "the native country of genius, arts, and sciences," now produced only Turks and ignorant "Christian Bishops, priests, and monks." In the West, books and pamphlets allowed all issues to be discussed freely, and all shades of opinion could be expressed in print. But in Turkey only one book had been printed in the eighteenth century, in 1730. No one bought a copy, so none had been printed since.[16]

Islam did not encourage inquiry and reason, but relied on received doctrine to answer questions. This defied the spirit of progress being spread by Europeans and Americans. Abbé Constantin François de Chasseboeuf Volney, a French *philosophe*, traveled throughout the Muslim world in the 1780s. In his *Travels through Egypt and Syria*, he explained that the Egyptian port of Alexandria had fallen into disrepair because "in Turkey, they destroy everything, and repair nothing....The spirit of the Turkish government is, to ruin the labours of past ages, and destroy the hopes of future times, because the barbarity of ignorant despotism never considers to-morrow." Volney saw in the Islamic idea of predestination, in the Muslim's willingness to accept everything and anything that happened as the will of God, a tendency toward apathy. The Turks had no reason to change, for their very despotism, since it existed, was mandated by God. This fatalism led to indolence. Men and women would amuse themselves by bathing, drinking coffee, and smoking their pipes. "We shall be no longer astonished that their whole character partakes of the monotony of their private life, and of the state of society in which they live." While the vicious spirit of despotism destroyed all monuments to past glory, Islam's spirit of indolence made people passively resist any attempt to improve tomorrow.[17]

People who passively submitted to tyranny were not worthy of being free. Volney saw this proved by the Greek Christians, who were so used to being slaves to the Muslims that they had taken on "the character perpetually ascribed to them" and had become slaves in attitude. Too weak to challenge their masters openly, they were cunning, dissembling, flattering, and treacherous. Volney wrote that slaves in the Muslim world, unlike slaves in America, could rise to positions of power through such tricks or through faithful service. Yet, however high they rose, they still had the character of slaves. Volney thought that these Christians who rose to power were the worst sort of rulers. Once in power, they feared losing it and falling back into slavery. This constant unease made them anxious "to make all the profits they can" while they had power. Their hands, having been "continually employed in beating cotton," were good at catching bribes but not at governing.

In contrast to these debased and degraded Christians, Volney thought their Muslim rulers, though "haughty even to insolence," were good-hearted, humane, and just. They were accustomed to power and knew how to use it wisely. Christians who had never been free feared losing what few benefits they had; they constantly sought new riches to exploit and were tormented by their failures. Thus, the inspiration that had propelled Western Europe's progress, its spirit of enterprise, had been distorted by submission to tyranny.

Curiously enough, the Muslim sense of fatalism, which prevented social advance, also made Muslim rulers less avaricious, less tormented by the prospect of losing power. God had decided long ago what would happen, so there was no reason to regret the past or provide for the future. Volney marveled that Muslims calmly said, "It is written," and without complaint submitted "to the most unexpected transition from opulence to poverty." The Turks had no reason to change either their government or their society, because Islam encouraged them to believe that everything was ordained by God. Muslims would accept despotism calmly: As it existed, God must want it to exist. This spirit of submission made them unable to change the government they had or to create a new government that might prevent the catastrophe looming over such an apathetic people.[18]

Two news items juxtaposed in the Philadelphia *Aurora* in December 1806 clearly set out the contrast between Muslim lethargy and American enterprise. The first item, hardly news, noted that in Morocco "the state of despotism" was such that in 300 years "not a village has been built, a city enlarged, a bridge erected, or a harbour formed in the whole kingdom." The writer did not need to explain why this was so. Immediately below the news from Morocco was a headline, "American Genius," and the story that inventor Robert Fulton had returned to America. Fulton was precisely the kind of genius produced by a dynamic American society. His parents were artisans, and Fulton had trained as a locksmith and gunsmith, as a painter and draftsman. He was a skilled workingman with a gift for perfecting the ideas of others, an American tinkerer who could turn abstract scientific principles into useful machines. Fulton had not yet built the *Steamboat*, but he was famous for his submarine, an underwater boat that Fulton, Volney, and others thought would make navies obsolete and war impossible. Moroccan despotism prevented ordinary artisans like Fulton, with a talent for innovation, from flourishing, and so discouraged the useful creativity American society encouraged.[19]

This discrepancy between a flourishing society and a stagnant one inspired Volney to write *The Ruins, or a Survey of the Revolutions of Empires*. In Egypt and Syria, cradles of world civilizations, Volney saw nothing but desolation and poverty. What had happened? he asked. His answer: Religious intolerance had stifled free inquiry and prevented men from rising out of their misery. Men were taught to believe that whatever was, was right, and so had no reason to aspire beyond their fathers' poverty. *The Ruins* was first translated into English in 1792; by the end of the decade, there were two more English translations and two American editions. While he was president, Thomas Jefferson decided that *The Ruins* needed a more faithful translation. The president himself, with Joel Barlow, translated it, and their edition appeared in Paris in 1802. *The Ruins* was more than a meditation on Islam: Volney, like Prideaux and Voltaire, saw in the Muslim world a lesson for Europe. The decay of the Egyptian and Syrian civilizations warned Europeans and Americans of their own potential for decline. If men accepted religious or political tyranny, they would inevitably decline into barbarism. In America, men could think and speak freely, and native geniuses like Fulton could rise by their talents, and by their talents push society ahead. On the other hand, if America allowed the religious fanaticism Volney warned of in *The Ruins*, it too would slide into indolence, and America would become a desert like Morocco.[20]

The point was perhaps most eloquently stated by French historian and economist Jean Charles Leonard Simonde de Sismondi in an essay on Arabian literature that appeared in the *American Register* in 1817. Sismondi surveyed the literary and poetic works of the Muslim golden age, in the eighth and ninth centuries of the Christian era, when Europe "was plunged into barbarism; population and wealth had disappeared," but Muslim rulers like Al-Mansur (caliph of Baghdad, 754–775) and Harun al-Rashid (caliph of Baghdad, 786–809) fostered a period of enlightenment, humanity, and progress. Sismondi's survey ended on a somber note. All these once flourishing homes of the arts and progress now were intellectual deserts, barren of any science, art, or learning. "The rich plains of Fez and Morocco," Sismondi wrote, once home to academies, libraries, and universities, "are now nothing but deserts of burning sand, for which tyrants contend with tygers." The once "gay and fertile" coast of Mauritania now was home only to pirates, "who spread terror over the seas, and who relax from their toils in vile debaucheries, till the plague...comes to mark out its victims." Egypt was lost in the sands it had once cultivated, and wandering Bedouins desolated the empty lands of Syria and Palestine. No enemy had conquered these lands; no stranger had robbed them or destroyed their people's heritage. "The poison was within them, it developed itself, and has annihilated all."[21]

"Who knows," Sismondi concluded, "if some centuries hence, this same Europe, to which the reign of literature and sciences is now transported, which shines with so great lustre, which judges so well of times past, which compares so well the successive influence of ancient literature and morals, may not be deserted, and wild as the hills of Mauritania, the sands of Egypt, and the valleys of Anatolia?" When Europe had become a desert, perhaps a new civilization would emerge, "in country entirely new, perhaps in the highlands whence flow the Oronoko and the Amazon," and with new morals, languages, and ideas these new people would regenerate the human race, and their scholars might recall "the Newtons, the Racines, the Tassos, as examples of the vain struggles of man, to attain an immortality of renown which fate denies him." Civilization was not moving west, but Sismondi warned that any society would decay if its people did not jealously protect their liberty and learning.

The poison that had destroyed the Muslim world was within it. Its people had allowed the disaster to happen. British writer Edward Stanley's *Observations on the City of Tunis, and the Adjacent Country* (1786) stated that the whole African coast from the Straits of Gibraltar to Tripoli was "one of the finest and most fertile countries in the world" and could be "a granary for Europe" if it were "in the hands of proper cultivators." Mathew Carey's *Short Account of Algiers* (1793) described the seven rivers of Algiers, which had neither bridges nor ferries, testifying to the "gross ignorance of the natives in whatever concerns domestic improvement." A traveler wandering for miles in search of a ford, in a land where ferries were unknown, might join the author in wishing that Algerians were "of a more intelligent and industrious a character." One wonders if President Jefferson ever read this account while traveling between Monticello and Washington, having to cross eight rivers, five of which had neither a bridge nor a boat. Though Americans could point with pride to Robert Fulton and other inventors, their own country remained a wilderness, and the lesson of Algiers and other Muslim states warned them of the consequences of lethargy. What would prevent America, with so many opportunities to excel, from remaining a wilderness or becoming a desert?[22]

Penelope Aubin, a contemporary of Trenchard and Gordon, wrote a novel, *The Noble Slaves,* based on the captivity of some Spanish nobles in Algiers. Aubin praised "our excellent Constitution," which would keep the people "rich and free," in contrast to "Turkish policy," which made the prince great and the people wretched. But policy alone was not to blame for the people's misery: "it must be our own fault," Aubin said, "if we are enslaved or impoverished." The spirit of the people made the difference.[23] Muhammad had insisted on blind submission to his religious creed, and those who embraced Islam submitted both to the religion and, it seemed, to whatever outrage their rulers chose to perpetrate. Trenchard and Gordon quoted French traveler Jean Thevenot, who spoke of the "blind

Submission" of the Turkish people to the sultan's will, a submission enjoined by Islam. "His Will, that is to say, his Lust, his Maggots, or his Rage, is his only Law, and the only Bounds to the Authority of this Viceregent of God." Trenchard and Gordon, like Mathew Lyon, dismissed as an absurdity the idea that subjects could not judge their governors. An absurdity it was, but a "monstrous and mischievous" one, invented by "a few wretched and dreaming *Mahometan* and Christian Monks" who bewitched the world with their holy lies. No state power could oppress a people if priests and mullahs had not made "passive obedience" a religious principle. "Yes, *Turkish* Slavery is confirmed, and *Turkish* Tyranny defended by Religion!"[24]

Religious tyranny permitted extreme despotism and even encouraged it. Trenchard and Gordon made much of the seventeenth-century emperor of Morocco, Mawlay Isma'il (1672–1727), saying that he had personally killed 40,000 of his subjects. More alarming, his people clamored for the honor of being killed by him, believing death at his hands would send them to paradise. John Foss, an American sailor held captive in Algiers in the early 1790s, borrowed this image of Mawlay Isma'il killing his subjects and applied it to the dey of Algiers. "Everyone is amazed to find these people so submissive and patient under so excessive and cruel a tyranny," but there was no mystery in it. The people were "taught to believe, if they fall by the hand of their king," whom they thought to be "Mahomet's successor," that they would immediately go to heaven.[25]

European and American writers came to the same conclusion about why the Muslim world remained backward. A wicked religion had fostered bad government, and bad government thwarted social progress. Instead of encouraging industry and enterprise, these governments fostered ignorance, which bred indolence. William Eaton, American consul to Tunis (1799–1803), noted the desolation in Algiers. The Algerian cruisers that had once ranged into the English Channel now were confined to the Mediterranean. "Her spirit of enterprize is relaxed," Eaton wrote, and the Algerian fleet rotted away under poor management. "Her subjects have neither relish nor stimulus to ambition—Her religious system favors indolence by inspiring a reliance" on divine interposition, just as it closed their minds "to the Gift of reason."

Eaton prepared for his mission to Tunis by reading Volney, whose descriptions of the Turks, Eaton wrote, "exactly fit them *here*," except that the "insolence" of Barbary rulers increased as they grew more independent of the Ottoman empire. "Ignorance, exalted to a station of receiving tribute from every slave below him, from the wandering Bedouin to the sedentary monarch of Spain, feels none of those *manly* restraints of justice," which they would feel if the European powers did not pay tribute, but rather used force to reprimand these rulers. If the country, "naturally luxuriant and beautiful beyond description," were in the hands of "an enlightened and enterprising people," it would rival the Mediterranean's opposite shore "in every thing useful, rich, and elegant." But the Tunisians, abject slaves "to their despotic government," could not own property, so they had "no ambition to cultivate" the rich land. In addition to being subject to political tyranny, they were victims of "the worst of all tyrannies, the despotism of priestcraft," and lived in "solemn fear of the frowns of a bigot," Muhammad, "who has been dead and rotten above a thousand years." Indeed, the Tunisians were more afraid of the dead Muhammad than of the living pacha. "The country is indeed beautiful," Eaton wrote to his wife, "but the people are superlatively wretched. They are humbled by the double oppression of civil and religious tyranny; seem to have but little enterprize, and are grossly ignorant."[26]

Ten years later, another American consul, Mordecai Manuel Noah, saw Tunis in a remarkably similar way. Noah, though, was most struck by what he saw in Spain: the contrast between the remaining Moorish architecture and the more recent examples from the Christians who had displaced the Muslims. He wrote that "the reign of the Moors in Spain, was more glorious, more prosperous, and enlightened, than the present dynasty, that now wields the sceptre." Noah wrote that the Moors had brought to Spain a golden age but had not been able to maintain it, unable to conquer the problems of excessive religious zeal, government spending, or undisciplined troops. "Had the Mussulmen in Spain, established a government of laws, divested themselves of a portion of their Religious zeal, disciplined their troops, and economised their expenditures, the Mahomedan Religion, at this day, would have spread itself over all Europe, as it had over Asia," Noah wrote. The Muslim rulers of Spain, like Sismondi's caliphs of Baghdad, had enjoyed a golden age, but their religious zeal and unrestrained passions had destroyed them.[27]

A failure to restrain passions, either in the people or in their rulers, would lead to disaster. Though Algiers, according to Mathew Carey's *Short Account of Algiers,* was called a kingdom ("an epithet which might, without regret, be expunged from every human vocabulary"), it was actually a "military republic, though it certainly can reflect no lustre on that species of government." The dey was chosen by the resident Turkish janizzaries, and he "seldom secures his office, without tumult and bloodshed." Usually he lost it the same way. A "Concise History of the Algerines," published in the *Massachusetts Magazine* in 1789, said that though Algiers was a province of the grand seignior, the nominally dependent dey would more often than not "assume a despotick power and oppress the people. Nor do they feel much dependance upon their master at *Constantinople.* When they once get the power, they fear only the Turkish soldiers, by whom they are supported, and who keep this dread upon their minds" by frequent military coups. These janizzaries represented military power unchecked by civil government and were mercenaries drawn from the lowest orders of society. Any private soldier could murder the dey and assume the office himself. "When the dregs of the populace feel themselves important, we need not say how capricious, how cruel, how abusive and tyrannical they are!" This lesson the French were learning in the 1790s, as John Adams and other more conservative Americans would have noted. "How miserable the men who must needs be the sport of their passions!" The all-powerful rulers of Algiers, Morocco, and Turkey were no more than slaves to their own military, who were no more than slaves to their basest passions. "Had they not better crawl with the worms than be seated on high, where they are afraid to look, lest they should see a sword suspended over their heads!"[28]

This was as true at the center of the empire as it was in the provinces. The grand seignior, or sultan of Turkey, had the misfortune to sit atop a system of power he could not control. Trenchard and Gordon had written in 1723 that "Power does not glide there,...down an even and easy Channel with a gentle and regular Descent, but pours from a Precipice with dreadful Din, Rapidity, and Violence, upon the poor and passive Vallies below," smashing and laying waste all it encountered. This want of regular, orderly power meant that there were no checks from either below or above. Edward Gibbon had written of Algiers as a military government that "floats between the extremes of absolute monarchy and wild democracy." This image was so deeply engrained in the American consciousness that even when events in Algiers or Turkey did not conform to the image, they were reported as though they had. In 1798, for instance, Dey Hassan of Algiers died after a long illness and was succeeded by Mustafa Bobba. Despite the peaceful and orderly succession, the Western press reported that Hassan, all his court, and even the French consul had been beheaded. The Turkish sultan could not control the officials below him, or maintain order in his own dominion or in distant provinces. Thus the sultan of Turkey sat atop a world any Western leader, a Thomas Jefferson or a George III, an Alexander Hamilton or a Thomas Paine, would equally dread.[29]

This theme of political chaos was echoed in popular plays, in novels, and in travelers' accounts. Isaac Bickerstaff's play *The Sultan, or a Peep into the Seraglio* had Soliman II, the all-powerful sultan of Turkey, hesitating to reform the system for fear that the janizzaries would revolt. A traveler's account published in *New York Magazine* in 1795 called the sultan of Turkey "unquestionably the most absolute among the sovereigns of Europe," but said he was subject to the horrors of a military government, even degradation and death at the hands of janizzaries who were "as mercenary, turbulent, and as powerful" as Rome's Prætorian bands, though less enlightened. The sultan did not dare check the authority of the janizzaries. Lady Mary

Wortley Montagu, who lived in Constantinople in 1717 and 1718, wrote that the sultan, "with all his absolute power, is as much a slave as any of his subjects, and trembles at a janisary's frown." Lady Mary wrote sarcastically that Turkey lacked some of the unpleasantness of a free society: There were no "huzzaing mobs, senseless pamphlets, and tavern disputes about politics," no name calling or public slanders. A minister who displeased the janizzaries, Lady Mary wrote, would lose his head, and the sultan, "to whom they all profess an unlimited adoration," would tremble at the mob's fury, not daring to defend or avenge his aide. "This is the blessed condition of the most absolute monarch upon the earth, who owns no law but his will." Lady Mary wished that a shipload of "your passive obedient men," who supported the British government in all its errors, could be sent to Turkey, where "they might see arbitrary government in its clearest and strongest light" and judge who was most miserable under it: the people, the ministers, or the sultan.[30]

As the American people debated the Constitution in 1787 and 1788, anti-Federalist critics, not surprisingly, used the image of Turkish despotism to attack the proposed government. The government created by the Constitution, by giving the power to levy taxes and raise armies to the central government, did not provide enough safeguards to individual liberty, and the men chosen under the Constitution would quickly become tyrants. There was no provision against a standing army and no guarantee of religious freedom. What, the anti-Federalists asked, would prevent the new government from introducing hordes of jannizaries to prop it up or from establishing Islam as the state religion, replacing the Bible with the Koran? These fears may have been wildly exaggerated, but they were nonetheless part of the debate. Patrick Dollard, an Irish immigrant, tavern keeper, and political leader in South Carolina, warned that state's ratifying convention that if they did not accept the Constitution, then "your standing army, like Turkish Janizaries enforcing despotic laws, must ram it down their throats with the points of Bayonets." Noah Webster, writing as a "Citizen of America," rejected this whole idea as a ridiculous rhetorical trick, and said that the spirit of the American people was such that there was no necessity to prohibit either a standing army or the introduction "of the Mahometan religion." In America, Webster said, "no man will suffer his liberty to be abridged, or endangered." But this guarantee was not enough for the anti-Federalists. Patrick Henry asked the Virginia ratifying convention, "Who has enslaved France, Spain, Germany, Turkey…? They have been enslaved by the hands of their own people." The American people, Henry feared, were no different.[31]

Webster, Henry, and Dollard all agreed on the evils of Turkish despotism. Webster had no firm defense against the charge that the Constitution might establish just such a despotism in America. He could only rely on the character of the American people to prevent it. Alexander Hamilton, though, saw a way to use the image of despotic Turkey to bolster the case for a stronger central government. Hamilton saw two sides to the idea of Turkish despotism. On the one hand, the sultan, supported by his janizzaries and Islam's absolutism, was all-powerful. On the other hand, he could not restrain his people's avaricious violence or prevent any of his janizzaries from killing him. Most important for Hamilton's purposes, the sultan, who with a nod of his head could do away with his subjects' lives and property, "has no right to impose a new tax." In *Federalist* 30, Hamilton drew a comparison between the sultan and the U.S. government under the Confederation. The sultan could not tax his subjects, but he permitted the local governors or bashaws "to pillage the people without mercy," squeezing from them the necessary revenues to support the state.

In the United States, the central government under the Articles of Confederation could not tax the people. But instead of freeing them from the burden of taxation, the Articles of Confederation allowed individual states to impose oppressively high taxes on the people, while it gave the people no protection from economic chaos. The central government atrophied, while the states absorbed all power. "Who can doubt," Hamilton wrote, "that the happiness of the people in both countries would be promoted by competent authorities in the proper hands, to provide the revenues which the necessities of the public might require?"[32] Thus, if the central government had more power, it could protect the people from oppressive local governors. This argument defied those who thought that giving the central government more power would make it despotic. Instead, Hamilton saw despotism as a natural consequence of the sultan's weakness, just as Prideaux had seen despotism as a natural outgrowth of Mecca's unrestrained religious liberty.

The historical truth of this image is not the issue. Americans who used the Muslim world as a reference point for their own society were not concerned with historical truth or with an accurate description of Islam, but rather with this description's political convenience. The Muslim world was a remarkably useful rhetorical device that could be used by libertarians like Mathew Lyon and Thomas Paine and by conservatives like John Adams and Alexander Hamilton. With a popular image of Muhammad and the Muslim world firmly established in the public mind, it was enough to mention either one as a starting point for a political argument. Under this definition, Muslims submitted to religious despotism and were taught to accept political despotism. Initially, they may have submitted because they had been too ready to reject their true religious leaders or because those leaders were too ready to exploit an innocent people. In either case they submitted, and subsequent generations suffered for it. They lost not only liberty, but everything liberty made possible.

CHAPTER THREE

A Peek Into the Seraglio: Americans, Sex, and the Muslim World

Westerners saw the eighteenth-century Muslim world as a wicked mix of political tyranny and wild sex. The lustful appetites of Muslim rulers for political or sexual power were not restrained by either social or moral codes. In fact, sexual tyranny became the ultimate form of Muslim political tyranny, as Western magazines, newspapers, plays, and novels reported on the unrestrained sexual conquests of Muslim rulers, who supposedly kept large harems or seraglios filled with beautiful women, all slaves to the tyrant's lust, whose only function was to gratify his libidinous appetite. In the Muslim world, one novelist wrote, "the Monarch gives a loose to his passions, and thinks it no crime to keep as many women for his use, as his lustful appetite excited him to like."[1]

Certainly, images of unrestrained sexual activity gratified the prurient appetites of Western readers and may have been intended first to titillate a Western audience with descriptions of Muslim sexual conduct. But this image of unrestrained sex in the Muslim world carries a message on proper sexual relations. Further, the fictional Muslim world, the world of unrestrained sexual power, was also soberly reported in Western newspapers, magazines, and travelers' accounts. For instance, in 1798 a Philadelphia paper reprinted a news item from the Bombay *Courier*, which, in turn, claimed to have picked the item up from the Bagdad *Gazette*, reporting that the Russians had at last subdued the "ferocious, lawless, and predatory" people of Daghestan; these lawless people's main source of income came from kidnapping Circassian virgins to sell to the sultan of

Turkey. The Russians ended both the Daghestanis' "haughty independence" and the "rapes of Georgian and Circassian Maids to supply the Turkish Harems, and the Seraglio of the Grand Seignior." The Russians had performed a great service to humanity by ending this "infamous commerce in Circassian virgins," though the Philadelphia editor omitted the "ironical condolence" the original article had extended to the sultan on the loss that he "must sustain in this luxurious commerce."[2] By making women objects of lust, the sultan of Turkey had debased international commerce into a prostitution ring, and had extended the evils of his own ungoverned passions well beyond the walls of his own harem and beyond even the confines of his own empire.

The sultan was seen to be as much a slave to his unbridled passion as he was to his janizzaries. An American captive in Susanna Rowson's 1794 play *Slaves in Algiers, or a Struggle for Freedom* tells the dey of Algiers not to call his captives slaves, for he is the biggest slave of all, to his "rude, ungoverned passion" and to his pride, greed, and "lawless love." With no restraint on his sexual appetite, the sultan could not enjoy the true pleasure of consensual sexual relations.[3]

Sexual relations in the Muslim world, according to Western commentators, were founded in violence and completely dictated by power, and these relations defined the entire society. George Henry Rooke, an English visitor to Yemen in the 1780s, thought no Englishman could be happy in Arabia because property rights were too often violated and because "the intercourse with the *beau sexe* is founded on tyranny and compulsion, instead of that delicacy and sympathy of sentiment which forms those attachments with us." Muslim society lacked the two foundations of English liberty: property rights and female sexual autonomy. Jacques Grasset de Saint-Sauveur's 1796 *Encyclopédie des voyages* noted that "The Turks and Algerians, not anxious for large families, behave as true pirates on the marital bed. They ravage the fields of sensual delight without making any effort to have them bear fruit." Men sought only the gratification of their lust, not population, turning Franklin's admonition to "use venery" only for "health and offspring" on its head. In the

Muslim world, men did just what Franklin, and other American and Western counselors, said they should not do. With no respect for women, the men were quick to leave a partner once they had tired of her, seeking fresh conquests. Beauty became the measure of a woman's value in this society, which inverted all Western perceptions of worth.[4]

Islam, Westerners believed, permitted this sexual tyranny because it taught that women had no souls. "They believe the women have no souls," American captive John Foss wrote, "and are only formed for propagation; they are therefore not allowed to enter their mosques, because they esteem them incapable of being received into heaven: Yet the women say their prayers secretly at home." Women were not the spiritual equals of men, but mere objects of male lust. This made it impossible for men and women to associate in any other than a sexual way. The Abbé Volney wrote that Muslim men "have no idea how it is possible to see them [women], to talk with them, and touch them, without emotion, or to be alone with them without proceeding to the last extremities."[5] Having stripped women of any character other than a sexual one, Muslim men could not see women as anything but objects of desire.

To prevent sexual anarchy, Muslim society had to confine its women for their own protection. Montesquieu thought the sexual drive strongest in warm climates, where people were more passionate. Since Islam did not instill moral restraint in male believers, some other barriers had to be put in place. In these warm climates, "where the impulses of nature have such force that morality has almost none," Montesquieu wrote, when "a man be left with a woman, the temptation and the fall will be the same thing; the attack certain, the resistance none." Since social virtue and stability rested on female virtue, in all societies no matter what the climate, in these places where the danger was greatest, women had to be confined both for their own protection and for the good of society. Especially in despotic countries, Montesquieu wrote, where the rulers could not risk any revolt of public displeasure, where the slightest challenge to authority must result in bloodshed and anarchy, "where the extreme subordination calls for peace, it is absolutely necessary to shut up the women; for their intrigues would prove fatal to their husbands." If women were permitted to subvert their husbands' sexual authority, they would subvert political authority. Women's "slavery," Montesquieu wrote, was "perfectly conformable to the genius of despotic government, which delights in treating all with severity."[6]

Underlying this severity was a fundamental distrust. If moral restraint could not control men's and women's passions, then force must. But most observers argued that instead of solving the problem, sexual segregation made the problem worse. Volney wrote that where men and women were ignorant of love, as Westerners understood it, their "enjoyment [was] without delicacy," and wives became "merely courtezans, who think of nothing but to strip their lover before he quits them." Husbands had "to assume the tone of a despot, and from that moment he meets with nothing but the sentiments of slaves, the appearance of fondness, and real hatred." Turkish men and women held one another in contempt, and in this total depravity could not learn to control their passions.[7]

Confining the women, Westerners believed, only led to greater moral depravity. Denied any natural opportunities to meet, men and women constantly sought one another for the most carnal reasons, "always alert to seize the first opportunity, because it seldom happens, and is soon lost." Married women especially "give themselves up to pleasure with the more freedom" to make up for their strict confinement. To prevent single women from becoming immoral, Muslim society endorsed polygamy and encouraged marriage at the onset of puberty or before. But these solutions to the problem of female incontinence exacerbated the problem of moral depravity, and in fact created new moral problems for societies that tried to establish virtue through force. Volney blamed polygamy and early marriage for making Turkish men impotent by age thirty, even though he, like the best-informed observers, knew that polygamy was rare—no man could have more than four wives, and very few had more than one. But the fact that polygamy could exist gave

Western observers much to talk about, and the consensus was that a plurality of wives rendered men impotent.

Confinement of women led men to homosexuality, or, as Montesquieu said, "that passion which nature disallows." Richard O'Brien, American consul in Algiers, referred ironically to the dey of Algiers as "the all-potent," writing privately that "The Potent is in Leasure Hours friged by a boy . . . he that used to open assholes now has his own shut up." In Tunis, William Eaton was shocked that Bey Hamouda Pacha, though married to one of the most accomplished women in the kingdom, had "a lusty Turk of thirty-three" as his lover. This "lusty Turk," Sidi Jusuf Coggie, was also his closest political advisor. Despite Hamouda Pacha's good qualities, this blemish would make "the most *depraved* of nature's children blush." Depravity, impotence, and homosexuality all resulted from the Muslim world's strict separation of men and women. The sultan's sexual power over women, like his political power over his subjects, was a public pretense. [8]

Lady Mary Wortley Montagu, the wife of England's ambassador to Turkey, lived in Constantinople in 1717 and 1718 and challenged these Western notions of Muslim sexual confinement and depravity. She especially attacked Western travelers who came East with pre-conceived notions. It was "a particular pleasure to me here, to read the voyages to the Levant, which are generally so far removed from truth, and so full of absurdities, I am very well diverted with them." The travelers, she wrote, "never fail giving you an account of the women, whom 'tis certain they never saw, and talking very wisely of the genius of the men, into whose company they are never admitted; and very often describe mosques, which they dare not even peep into." Lady Mary, who adopted Turkish dress and visited women in their homes, in the harems, and even in the bath, had arrived with a certain ideological bias of her own. Daughter of a prominent Whig politician and wife of another, she was an intimate of such literary men as Alexander Pope and Joseph Addison, and she was trying to construct an independent life for herself as a woman of letters. She used the Muslim women she met in Belgrade and Constantinople as a contrast with her own status as a woman in English society.[9]

She thought it "pleasant to observe how tenderly" male travelers lamented "the miserable confinement of the Turkish ladies, who are perhaps more free than any ladies in the universe." Along with being the freest women in the world, they were the only free people in Turkey. The veil, for other Western observers the symbol of their oppression, allowed them to go where they pleased without being observed. When a Turkish woman cheated on her husband, no one knew. Turkish women had the unique pleasure of spending all of their time "in visiting, bathing, or the agreeable amusement of spending money."[10]

On her visit to a women's bath house in Adrianople [now the Turkish city of Edirne], she marveled at their grace, courtesy, and equality. Mistresses and slaves sat naked together "without any distinction of rank by their dress," their beauty and defects open for all to see, yet without the slightest "wanton smile or immodest gesture," or the "disdainful smiles" or "satirical whispers" so common among fully clothed gatherings of English women. This bath house, Lady Mary wrote, was the "women's coffee house, where all the news of the town is told, scandal invented, &c." She wished that Charles Jervas, an English painter famed for his portraits of women, could visit this bath, as it would improve his art "to see so many fine women naked, in different postures, some in conversation, some working, others drinking coffee or sherbet," others having their slave girls braiding their hair. The women urged Lady Mary to join them, but she showed them the stays on her corset. Though she merely wanted to indicate how difficult it would be for her to undress, the Turkish women thought her husband had locked her "up in that machine, that it was not in my power to open it." They misunderstood the purpose of her corset, but the episode underscored for Lady Mary her own confinement, her own constraint by fashion. In this visit to a bath house, she noted that the naked women could not be aware, as all gatherings of English women were, of differences in rank and status. Their loose clothing, which she adopted while in

Constantinople, was less confining than English fashions, and the veils both protected their privacy and made all women equal in public appearance. This made the Turkish women more free than their English counterparts, who were both confined in "machines" called corsets and ever conscious of their relative social rank. Behind their veils, the Turkish women had opulent privacy and freedom.[11]

Lady Mary, generally better informed than the men who visited Turkey, wrote about one Christian woman, "a very agreeable and sensible lady," who had accepted life as a Muslim's consort. A Spaniard, she had been captured at sea by a Turkish admiral. "The same accident happened to her that happened to the fair Lucretia," Lady Mary wrote. But unlike that literary victim of seduction, this woman was too much a Christian to kill herself. Her family sent £4000 for her ransom, but she told her Turkish captor that her liberty meant less to her than her honor, which only marriage could restore. Having been raped or seduced, she would have no chance to marry if she returned to Spain. Her family would send her to a nunnery. To save her from that fate, her captor married her, promised never to take another wife, and returned the ransom money to her family. She had managed to restore her honor by marriage in Turkey. She persuaded her captor to love her and used this love to negotiate a relationship on her own terms, or as close to her terms as an eighteenth-century woman could make. Her alternative would have been confinement in a Spanish convent. Had she exchanged her spiritual liberty for the opulent life as the wife of a Turkish admiral? Lady Mary did not think this woman had lost too much. As a lady of quality in Istambul, she lived in indolent leisure; how much she could spend was only "limited by her own fancy." Her husband would never question her expenses. "Tis his business to get money, and her's to spend it."[12]

Lady Mary's was a minority opinion. Americans could not accept this idea of freedom. Equality with one another in a bath house, a secret opulence, a veiled freedom were not enough. In Susanna Rowson's 1794 play *Slaves in Algiers,* ben Hassan asks the American captive, Rebecca, to be his wife. "Make me your wife!" she exclaims.

"Why, are you not already married?" Of course, he tells her, but as a Muslim he can have a "great many wives—our law gives liberty in love; you are an American and you must love liberty." Horrified at this play on words, she tells him to "prostitute not the sacred word by applying. it to licentiousness; the sons and daughters of liberty, take justice, truth, and mercy, for their leaders, when they list under glorious banners."[13] Americans did not condemn the restraints imposed on Muslim women for being restraints, but rather for being artificial. Americans believed that moral restraint was essential, and thought these imposed barriers prevented men and women from developing their own virtuous characters. Susanna Rowson was shocked to think that "liberty" might be taken to mean licentiousness or libertinism and condemned this prostitution of the sacred word.

While Western observers condemned the Muslim world's sexual tyranny that masked sexual depravity, not all were comfortable with what they considered, in contrast, to be excessive sexual liberty in America. Washington Irving wrote a series of letters from a fictional Tripolitan in New York in 1805 commenting on American society. In Mustapha Rub-a-Dub Kheli Khan's first letter from the New World, the Tripolitan comments on "the charms of these infidel women" whom he sees running "about the streets with bare arms and necks" and seeming to "belong to nobody." Their beauty so openly displayed makes him speculate with wonder about the beauty of "those who are shut up in the seraglios, and never permitted to go abroad!" Irving is not celebrating the freedom of American women; he is troubled at their flirtatious behavior. The Tripolitan, despite being attracted by the Americans' beauty, notes that they have a major flaw. "Wouldst thou believe it, Asem,…that at least one-fifth part of them—have souls!" One woman he had seen had enough soul "to box her husband's ears" in public. Irving was not entirely happy with the complete freedom enjoyed by these coquettish, domineering American women. [14]

Confining women, too, might lead to the debasement of manners, but it could also contribute to domestic peace and tranquility. William Eaton admired the Tunisians for their simplicity, temperance, and honesty. "They have no midnight revels, no assaults and batteries, and very seldom assassinations," in contrast to the New England society that Eaton had left. "The deplorable wretchedness which always attaches itself to seduction, and which so frequently wounds the eye of sensibility in every village in the Christian world, is unknown here: because they imprison their girls." That is, without chances for seduction, the women of the Muslim world were protected from becoming pregnant without being married. According to Eaton, then, Montesquieu was right in that confining women protected domestic peace and tranquility. The Tunisians averted the real tragedies of seduction and illegitimacy by locking up their women.[15]

Montesquieu had speculated about what would happen if French women, with their "levity of mind," their passions, caprices, and "active fire," and "full liberty" were taken to Turkey. He asked, "where would be the father of a family who could enjoy a moment's repose?" The men would become enemies, suspecting one another of sexual indiscretions, so that "the state would be overturned, and the kingdom overflowed with rivers of blood." In Isaac Bickerstaffe's play *The Sultan*, an English woman full of active fire appears in Turkey and overturns the state, though without the rivers of blood Montesquieu had predicted. Instead, Roxalana teaches the women self-respect, and once she wins the sultan's heart she insists on being his equal. The servile Osmyn, keeper of the sultan's seraglio, wonders "that a little cocked-up nose" could overturn "the customs of a mighty empire!"[16]

Roxalana was a British heroine, but the play was quickly adapted to the American stage. Its title was changed from *The Sultan* to *The American Captive*, making Roxalana, not Solyman, the central character. No copies survive of this American version, which was performed regularly from its premier in 1794 until 1840, so we cannot know what else was different about it. The new title, though, highlights Roxalana's national identity, the incongruity of being an American and being a captive, and the centrality of gender roles to political power.

Roxalana begins subverting the Ottoman order in the seraglio, teaching the women self-respect, dignity, and their proper political and sexual roles. The Persian slave Ismena, whose singing delights Solyman, entertains the sultan in the first act by singing of him as a "Blest hero, who, in peace and war / Triumph alike, and raise our wonder." But after Roxalana has begun shaking things up, Ismena sings a new song: "Let them say whate'er they will, / Woman, woman rules them still." Roxalana is able to transform these women because they are no longer content with their lives as courtesans, and she is able to win over the sultan both because he finds her independence fascinating and because he, too, feels empty inside. He is bored with the "mere caressing machines" of his seraglio, women whose love is dictated by fear or interest. He tells Osmyn, the man in charge of the women, to "quit this style of servitude; I am weary of it," and calls this servant his friend. But Osmyn cannot rise above his servile habits; he cannot become the sultan's friend. Roxalana, though, can, and she does, telling Solyman, "I am nothing but a poor slave, who is your friend." A friend can tell Solyman things a servant or a slave cannot. When Solyman asks Roxalana to be the first woman of the seraglio, telling her, "I here devote myself to you, and the whole empire shall pay you homage," she refuses. She reminds him that she is "a free-born woman, prouder of that than all the pomp and splendour eastern monarchs can bestow," from a nation where "every citizen is himself a king" and "the king is himself a citizen." As a free woman, Roxalana will never "ascend his bed at night, at whose feet I must fall in the morning." She will be Solyman's wife only if she shares political power. If the man she loved had only a cottage, she would share it. Since the man she loves has a throne, she must insist on sharing it.[17]

When Solyman objects that the "mufti, viziers, and the agas" will not allow this, Roxalana tells him that they are his slaves, that he must be despotic at times on the side of "virtue and reason," and tells him to "make the people happy, and they will not prevent your being so." With the pursuit of happiness the empire's new governing principle, the play ends with Roxalana becoming Solyman's "unrivalled partner," an acknowledged and recognized power on the throne. Her role will be to help the unfortunate, to relieve the distressed, and to "diffuse happiness through the palace," serving as a domestic and political partner to the sultan. Friendship and marital equality become the basis for the new political order. For Solyman to begin enjoying life, he must recognize Roxalana's equal power in the relationship. Roxalana rejects a role as a "mere caressing machine"; her personal autonomy must be respected. She is not the sultan's pleasurer but his partner.[18]

By establishing her role as the sultan's partner, Roxalana overturns Turkey's political despotism. An American or an English woman, independent, candid, and sincere, could overturn despotism by her very honesty. Roxalana wins power by having the sultan fall in love with her, which she does not through the duplicity and scheming, but by being herself. Roxalana, the outsider, overturns the customs of a society she does not understand. More often, in the stories of the Muslim world, it is up to women who grew up in the society to reform its institutions or subvert despotic authority.

The political despotism of Turkey, *The Sultan* suggests, is centered in the palace. When Roxalana turns Solyman into a benevolent man, with conjugal relations based on love, not on power, she overturns the whole basis of political power in Turkey. The idea that the national polity reflected domestic relations was a truism in the eighteenth century. Volney devoted a long footnote in *The Ruins* to the theme of household tyranny. "Paternal tyranny laid the foundation of political despotism," he wrote, and said he could easily "write a long and important chapter" on this single idea. In a simple barbarous state, Volney wrote, the father is a despot, the mother his slave, and children servants. Parental authority remained strongest in despotic countries such as Turkey, China, and India. In these societies, a tyrannical ruler exerted power through all the fathers in the land. "One would suppose that tyrants gave themselves accomplices, and interested subaltern despots to maintain their authority." Like the tyrannical local bashaws and beys, whose despotism was worse than that of the sultan, the head of each family was an unchecked tyrant.[19]

Americans had only recently freed themselves from the perceived parental tyranny of England. Throughout much American literature of the Revolutionary and early national period the theme of parental tyranny as a form of despotism, a staple of Oriental literature as well as of the emerging English novel, had a particular resonance. American and British magazines were filled with Oriental tales of young lovers uniting in spite of parental objections or fleeing rather than to be separated by paternal fiat. The "Story of Solyman and Almena," for example, is a series of variations on this theme, with young love resisting tyranny in three different ways in its seven short pages.[20] Solyman leaves his Persian home, and his kind father, to learn more about the world. In this he is successful as he travels from Persia to India, encountering on the way two young lovers about to be separated by the woman's greedy father; the lovers Zara and Abbas, forced to separate by Zara's military officer father; a captive on the island of Hormuz; and finally Almena, whom Solyman has to rescue from the despotic governor of Delhi.

The first lovers Solyman meets are about to be broken apart by the woman's greedy father, who has sold his daughter to the khan of Bokhara. The couple take refuge with Solyman's father and make good use of their freedom. When the woman's father dies she inherits his fortune. She and her husband make restitution to the many other people whom her father has oppressed. In this way, they free others from his economic dominance, just as Solyman has helped them become free of his personal tyranny. By freeing this woman from a forced marriage to a political despot, Solyman has allowed her and her chosen spouse to do good works. His act of generosity, sending the couple to live with his own wise father, was more than just an act of personal charity. It allowed them to be free, and they use their freedom for much more than their own happiness. By repaying those the woman's father has oppressed, the two lovers themselves finally enjoy happiness.

The next example of lovers trying to break free from parental tyranny, the story of Zara and Abbas, parallels the plot of one of the era's most popular plays, *The Mountaineers*. Zara is the daughter of a military officer, Abbas a soldier under his command. Against his wishes they fall in love, and the father flies into a "rage of jealousy." Zara disguises herself as a peasant to lead Abbas over the mountains, where robbers attack them and carry Zara away. Abbas returns to camp and implores Zara's father to join the search, but "the unnatural wretch...uttered the most dreadful imprecations on his only child" and refuses. Outraged and embittered against mankind, Abbas becomes a hermit. Solyman is the first visiter his mountain cave has seen in years. After listening to Abbas's story, Solyman, with "the rage of honest resentment," inveighs against human baseness. His traveling companion remarks that "From the complicated distresses of one person, you draw a partial image of the life of man." Zara's father, unreconciled to her choice, allows her to remain a captive of the mountain robbers. Solyman wonders if it is "possible that any thing can induce a parent to make his child miserable." The story of Zara and Abbas gives evidence of this incredible possibility.

Solyman cannot help Abbas find Zara. Nor can he help the captive he meets on the island of Hormuz, whose story haunts him as he goes on to Delhi. There he meets and falls in love with Almena, but still he cannot forget the captive of Hormuz. Almena, showing her own virtue, tells Solyman to "go where your virtue leads you." He returns to Hormuz and rescues the captive, only to discover back in Delhi that Almena has herself been imprisoned by the lusty governor, who has his own designs on her. The governor throws Solyman into prison as well. But Solyman escapes, rescues Almena from the "distressful horror" of the governor's embraces, and the two lovers go back to Persia, to "the happy valley" of Solyman's youth, where Solyman's aged father, "with a heart full of tenderness, conferred on both his paternal benediction."

This romantic story is typical of the Oriental literature popular in the eighteenth century. When Lady Montagu met Achmet Bey, an Arabic and Persian scholar in Belgrade, she was able to tell him so many Persian stories that he could not believe she did not read the language. These stories had been translated into French and English by the end of the seventeenth century, and the *Arabian Nights* had its first American edition in the 1790s. The story of Solyman and Almena is held together by Solyman's picaresque encounters with abusers of authority and their victims; the much more elaborate *Arabian Nights* stories are held together by Scherazade's nightly evasions of the sultan's despotic will. By creating a fictional world too fascinating for him to destroy, she manages to preserve her own life and that of a thousand other would-be consorts.[21]

Susanna Rowson's 1794 play *Slaves in Algiers* displays several forms of parental tyranny. Fetnah's father sells her to the dey. Zoriana, the dey's daughter, defies her father to help the American captives escape. And the whole plot is set in motion by an event revealed only in the final scene. Rebecca, one of the American captives, tells her story to the other captives: her son Augustus, the British captive Constant, and his daughter Olivia. It turns out that Rebecca and Constant were married, and Henry and Olivia were their children, and that the family has been separated for fifteen years. Rebecca, an American, was disowned by her father when she married Constant, a British officer. When Rebecca's father fell ill, he relented, and begged his daughter to return and forgive him. She had gone with her son Augustus, Constant and Olivia stayed with the British regiment. While Rebecca was away Constant was left for dead on a battlefield, and the family scatters. Rebecca and Augustus stay in America, cursing her father's bequest, asking, what good is money when she has lost her family? She thinks Constant is dead, and Constant has heard that she had died grieving for him. Constant and Olivia end up in India; Rebecca and Augustus stay in America. The family is reunited in Algiers, where all are captives, and Olivia has agreed to marry the dey in exchange for her father's freedom. But once the family is together, they defy the dey by refusing the marriage, just as Rebecca and Constant had defied her father by getting married. Rebecca, Augustus, and Constant vow to die to prevent Olivia's marriage. The dey relents at this display of family strength and agrees to be a better ruler and father in the future, promising to "reject all power but such as my united friends shall think me incapable of abusing."[21]

The rather tangled story of Rebecca and Constant comes out

only at the end. The play's real focus is Fetnah, the dey's "chosen favorite," who opens the play lamenting her imprisonment in the splendid palace, gardens, and clothes of her station. "I like them very well," she says of all the finery surrounding her, "but I don't like to be confined." Lady Mary Montagu had thought that this confinement covered a liberty unknown to English women, but for Susanna Rowson this kind of liberty, a luxurious isolation that permitted sexual libertinism, was not enough. Fetnah paraphrases English novelist Laurence Sterne, asking, "is the poor bird that is confined in a cage (because it is a favourite with its enslaver) consoled for the loss of freedom? No! tho' its prison is of golden wire, its food delicious, and it is overwhelmed with caresses, its little heart still pants for liberty: gladly would it seek the fields of air, and even perched upon a naked bough, exulting, carrol forth its song, nor once regret the splendid house of bondage." Fetnah's father, Ben Hassan, and her mother, who passively accepted his plan, "loved gold better than they did their child" and sold her to the dey. Ben Hassan is the play's real villain, as he betrays every trust in his pursuit of wealth. Born in England, he moved to Algiers and converted from Judaism to Islam, betraying not only his daughter but also his nation and his religion. Finally, to escape from an angry mob of slaves who storm his house, Ben Hassan even abandons his gender to save himself, taking refuge in his wife's clothes.[23]

Ben Hassan will do anything for money; his daughter Fetnah will do anything for freedom. Rebecca feeds Fetnah's natural love for freedom, teaching her that "woman was never formed to be the abject slave of man." Rebecca is "from that land where virtue in either sex is the only mark of superiority. —She was an American." Rebecca's teachings are now "engraven" on Fetnah's heart: "I feel that I was born free, and while I have life, I will struggle to remain so." Fetnah sings a song of a wild rose "bursting into bloom," dispensing beauty and perfume around it, until it is clipped, when it quickly fades before withering and dying. A woman, too, "when by nature drest," without artificial ornament, can "bid the soul to virtue rise," and stir brave men to glory, but she "sinks oppress'd, and drooping dies, when once she's made a slave." In contrast to her father, who tries to escape by dressing like a woman, Fetnah escapes the dey's palace dressed as a man. This is an obvious reversal of gender roles. Rowson also reverses the roles of Olivia, the teenage girl, and Augustus, the teenage boy. Olivia forms a plot to free her father, while Augustus laments throughout the play that he is unable to free his mother.[24]

Fetnah continues to subvert gender roles, refusing a marriage proposal from her American lover and Rebecca's offer to bring her to America. She will stay in Algiers to support her father. He had betrayed her, but she cannot betray him. She will stay in Algiers to teach him a lesson on familial faith. Wives and children are not merchandise, to be bought or sold. Women are not objects but people, with important roles to play in any family or society. The Americans teach the Algerians, Muslims and Jews, these lessons, and leave Algiers instructing the dey to "sink the name of subject in the endearing epithet of fellow-citizen," echoing Roxalana's declaration that in her country, every citizen is a king and the king himself is a citizen. The Americans tell the dey to prove by his conduct "how much you value the welfare of your fellow creatures" as they return to the land "where liberty has established her court," hoping for the day when "Freedom" will "spread her benign influence" through every nation.[25]

Solyman II in *The Sultan* fell in love with Roxalana, and she checked his tyrannical power. In Rowson's *Slaves in Algiers* the dey's power is checked by families held together by love, not by despotism. Scherezade undermined the sultan's despotic will by creating a fantasy world too fascinating for him to destroy. These women used intellect and imagination to do what physical beauty could not. Roxalana mocked Elmira's attempt to use a scented handkerchief to win back Solyman, rejecting the merely physical forms of courtship, just as Scherezade would not attempt to win over her sultan with physical or romantic charms. They resist established tyranny through wit, intellect, and imagination, and when they triumph, they establish a reign of virtue and benevolence. Susanna Rowson concludes her play with an epilogue in which she imagines the ladies in the audience saying:

> "She says that we should have supreme dominion,
>   And in good truth, we're all of her opinion.
>   Women were born for universal sway,
>   Men to adore, be silent, and obey."

This is not exactly the kind of dominion Mrs. Rowson had in mind for women. A woman rules through her heart, comforting the sorrowful and afflicted:

> To raise the fall'n—to pity and forgive,
>   This is our noblest, best prerogative.
> By these, pursuing nature's gentle plan,
> We hold in silken chains—the lordly tyrant man.[26]

One of the most popular elaborations of this theme had its nucleus in history and became an elaborated fiction, which then was accepted as history. The story was that of Khair al-Din, popularly known as Barbarossa, a Turkish sea captain who helped the Algerians drive out the Spanish in the early sixteenth century and then stayed to transform Algiers from an independent republic into a powerful military satellite of the Ottoman empire. Barbarossa's success against Spain led to nearly two centuries of Ottoman domination in Algiers. According to the brief histories printed in American magazines, the Algerians found the Turks more oppressive than the Spanish. Underlying this political lesson was a personal one. The center of the story, transformed from history into fiction, was the struggle of Algeria's Queen Zaphira, widow of King Selim, to maintain her own independence and virtue against Barbarossa's lustful advances.

In the "Concise History of the Algerines," printed in the *Massachusetts Magazine* in 1789, reprinted five years later in Newburyport's *Impartial Herald*, King Selim had invited Barbarossa to help him fight the Spanish. The "Turkish pirate," as Barbarossa was called, quickly killed Selim, took over the kingdom, and also tried to take Selim's widow, "the beautiful Zaphira." "With all his savage passions he could not resist her charms." But Zaphira was not "swayed by glory, greatness, and riches, more than reputation," and rejected his offer of a kingdom rather than make herself "an abomination to all true believers." Zaphira killed herself, retaining her virtue rather than submit to Barbarossa's lustful ambition.[27]

Zaphira's letters to Barbarossa, printed in the "Concise History," reveal a woman untempted by the splendor of power. She refuses Barbarossa's proposal by saying that "Any other, swayed by glory, greatness and riches, more than reputation, wherein true glory, supreme greatness, and the most valuable riches consist, would with transport give themselves up to you, to enjoy that shining fortune you so generously offer me." She acknowledges that "Few refuse a kingdom when within their reach," but she will. She accuses Barbarossa of complicity in her husband's death. Barbarossa responds with feigned shock, has some "suspects" arrested, and after confessions are tortured out of them, has them strangled. This, however, does not appease Zaphira. She refuses his offer, despite his pleas and threats, and when he demands to know what else he must do for her, she answers with a statement that must have struck a chord with an American audience: "my request to you is, death or liberty." Zaphira knows that liberty is not an option. When Barbarossa lunges for her, attempting to take by force what she would not give freely, she tries to stab him. He deflects the knife, which gashes his arm. While he has the wound dressed, Zaphira poisons herself. Her suicide Barbarossa takes as an insult, and to avenge himself, he has all her serving women strangled and buried along with her.[28]

In 1755 the English playwright John Brown turned this story into a play, *Barbarossa, the Tyrant of Algiers*. In the stage adaptation, Zaphira escapes both death and dishonor thanks to her son Selim's timely return. Selim kills Barbarossa and restores the rightful, benevolent monarchy to Algiers. The play has a subplot: Barbarossa's daughter Irene had been captured by the Spanish at Oran; she was rescued by none other than Prince Selim, who entreats her to "Go to Algiers" to protect his mother, to "be to her what Selim is to thee." Irene must choose between her father and the man she loves, and unlike Fetnah, she is never able to make this choice. When Barbarossa learns that Irene owes her freedom to Selim, he calls her a "false, faithless child," a "treacherous maid" who would "stoop to freedom from thy father's foe!"[29]

Despite her father's disowning her, calling her the "bane of all my joys," she remains faithful to him, even warning him of Selim's insurrection. But she tries to save Selim when her father sends him to the rack, and then tries to save her father when Selim escapes and leads the rebellion. To be true to her father, she must accept the death of her lover; to be true to her lover, she must accept the death of her father. Ultimately her father clears the way; as Selim kills him, Barbarossa entrusts Irene to his care. Zaphira, "Umov'd in virtue," tells Selim to marry Irene and make her queen so that her virtues can "atone for her father's guilt!"[30]

The virtue of these two women allows Selim to regain power, which he will use wisely. He has already proven his own virtue by rescuing Irene from her Spanish captors. The play hangs on the tension within these two women. Irene is torn between her father and her lover; Zaphira between resisting Barbarossa, which will certainly lead to her death, and marrying him, which might allow her to ameliorate the Algerian people's misery. Zaphira chooses. Irene, unable to be faithful to both her father and her lover, has the choice made for her. Zaphira is the play's heroine, Irene its tragic center.

This play remained a staple of the American stage until after the War of 1812. In the meantime, though, American literature created a Zaphira of its own in Mrs. Maria Martin. It is impossible to say that this is a true story; it is nearly as difficult to say that it is not. Though Maria Martin's book went through a dozen editions between 1807 and 1818, and was reprinted in Boston, Philadelphia, New York, New Haven, Trenton, Vermont, and Ohio, nothing is known of the author. The narrator is an English woman and the first American edition claims to be a reprint of an English book, but there is no record of the book's ever having been published in England. Since

Mrs. Martin was a captive in Algiers for six years, beginning in 1800, it seems impossible that there was an edition of the book before 1807, when the first extant copy was published in Boston.[31]

It is easy to understand why this book was so popular. It had all the elements of a Puritan captivity narrative, with the addition of lusty Turks and gruesome descriptions of torture and suffering.[32] Though Mrs. Martin claimed to be English, it is also easy to see an identification between her and female readers in America. Maria Martin was born in 1779, the daughter of "respectable and wealthy" parents. In the late 1790s she marries Captain Henry Martin of the British East India Company. Mrs. Martin has an urge to go to sea, and her husband finally takes her along on a voyage to Minorca in June 1800. Their ship, the *Unicorn*, carries 12 passengers, along with a crew of nearly 100 men. They run aground in a storm but manage to get the ship off the rocks by casting off its guns. This proves to be a dubious choice when a French frigate chases the unarmed boat, which nevertheless is able to escape. But the *Unicorn* runs aground again, this time on the North African coast. Two black sailors dive overboard and secure a rope between the ship and the shore, and Captain Martin, his wife, and the mate go ashore. Before any more of the crew or passengers can be rescued, the rope breaks. The party on shore is unable to find help, but listen to the desparate cries of the remaining crew and passengers, many of them children, trapped on the stranded ship. The *Unicorn* breaks apart in the surf.

The three survivors—Maria Martin, her husband, and the mate—spend a tormented night on shore. The two men have discovered no escape from their situation: To the south is an impenetrable forest, to the north a swamp. With no way out, the three face a hopeless situation the next morning. Mrs. Martin suggests that they begin the first day of their misery with prayer. Alone of the three, she remembers their helplessness before the omnipotent power of God.[33]

In the woods they meet men carrying spears, who direct them to Tenes, where they hope to send word to the British consul at Algiers. But instead, they are sold into slavery. The lustful Turkish governor buys Mrs. Martin and puts her to work in the kitchen.

Mrs. Martin hopes on being put under the authority of a woman and on seeing other women working in the kitchen, that she will not be abused and that she will be able to talk to other women. But she is quickly disappointed. The Moroccan woman running the kitchen is more of a despot than the dey of Algiers, and her fellow slaves, though sharing her condition and her gender, are Portuguese, and none speak English.[34]

So far, Mrs. Martin has lost every hope. Her husband, Captain Martin, could not prevent her from being enslaved. Having another woman as an overseer is worse than having a man, and none of the other women with whom she expects to share her feelings can talk to her. She does manage to make a connection with another slave. Malcome, her benefactor, has a tie stronger than gender or marriage. He is English and has been in Algiers long enough to speak the language.

The Turkish official who owns Mrs. Martin takes a fancy to her and makes advances to her through Malcome. Malcome is in a position to help Maria Martin, being both a translator and an interpreter of the Turk's proposition. If Maria agrees to be his concubine, the Turk will reward her with all the freedom his other wives and concubines enjoy. Malcome tells her, though, that she does not have to accept, that the local law will protect her from being forced into concubinage if she does not choose it. If the Turk uses force, Malcome tells Maria, he can be executed. She is free to choose either continued drudgery in the kitchen or the kind of veiled freedom Lady Mary Montagu said Turkish women enjoyed. Maria Martin's choice is obvious. She rejects the Turk, who becomes enraged and has her chained and thrown into a dungeon. Still, she does not relent. To weaken her further, he has her put in solitary confinement in an old castle, where she lingers for three years on a diet of moldy bread and dirty water.

After spending some time in prison, Maria's "fortitude began to revive," and she "glowed with the desire of convincing the world I was capable of suffering what man had never suffered before." She realizes that she is happier in her innocence than she would be had she accepted the Turk's terms, and so suffered the ignominy of men, the pangs of death, and "the horrors of internal guilt." Even in captivity, she enjoys the freedom of a pure conscience.[35]

Still hoping to destroy her spirit, the Turk cuts her meager rations. After eleven months of starvation, she has still not cracked. But when she is given good bread and clean water, she finds that her body cannot tolerate them. She gorges herself, but "Alas! my enjoyment was of short duration." She found that "excess is followed by pain and repentance." Her body swells and she becomes bloated, her body cramped and swollen, and she finds this new torment almost as unbearable as the months of fasting. "I began to pour out curses on those who seemed to refine on torture, and, after starving me so long, to invite me to gluttony."[36]

But in all this, she never questions God's omnipotence. She has a revelation one night as "the moon shone clear; I cast a wild distracted look up to heaven, fell on my knees, and, in the agony of my soul, sought comfort but no comfort could be found, nor religion nor philosophy had any to give." She seems lost and utterly helpless. But she "cursed not Providence, I feared not annihilation; I dared not Almighty vengeance; God the Creator was the disposer of my fate," and she knows God will not give her burdens she is unable to bear. In this moment, she is saved.

This is a classic conversion scene as Maria Martin realizes the sin of gluttony, that slaking her bodily hunger and thirst is not enough. She throws herself on God's mercy and immediately is released. The very next paragraph after this conversion scene begins, "Early one morning I heard the doors of my dungeon unbarring—the doors of my dungeon for the last time resounded—A gentleman in a Christian habit accompanied by the keeper entered." The man in the Christian habit does not represent the king of heaven but rather the king of England. He is the British consul, sent to free Mrs. Martin from her cruel and unjust bondage. Malcome, her fellow slave, had escaped to Algiers and informed the consul of her cruel treatment, and the consul has instructed the dey to release her.[37]

Mrs. Martin tells the consul her story of captivity and suffering, and wants to stay in Algiers to search for her husband. The consul advises her to go back to England and leave the search to him. She returns to England on a British ship, and the British captain hires a carriage to take her to her parents' home. Her own husband, Captain Martin, had been unable to protect her in Tenes; now she relies on the will of God and the kindness of strangers. Her own father faints when she arrives. He had not known of her captivity but had thought her drowned at sea, having heard nothing since she sailed for Minorca six years earlier.

Maria Martin has returned to her father, and six months later her husband returns to her. But she is a different woman from the one who longed for the sea in 1800. She has had a hard lesson of God's omnipotence but she has also learned of her own strength. Her husband could not protect her, her parents' wealth could not redeem her. Instead, she cast herself on God's mercy, and through His divine power and the intercession of the British consul, she was released. Free, she then persuaded the British consul to search for her husband, and Henry Martin was freed through his wife's efforts.

Zaphira, Roxalana, Rebecca, Olivia, and Maria Martin accepted only the choice between liberty or death; none would accept the slavery of confinement or unnatural relations. Death was preferred to that kind of dishonor. Other stories made it clear that those who chose slavery, opting to live as chattel rather than die as free women, would not be spared. *Solyman and Almena, The Sultan, Slaves in Algiers*, the *Arabian Nights*, and Maria Martin's *History of the Captivity and Sufferings* show that benevolence, virtue, and intelligence can overcome abusive authority. These stories conveyed ideas about despotism and power to a reading audience that likely would not have read Volney, Montesquieu, or Trenchard and Gordon. The women of these stories often have only their own virtue to defend themselves against the unlimited power of their husbands, fathers, or the state.

The moral of these tales from the Muslim world was that women who submitted to despotic power, hoping to preserve their lives by sacrificing their liberty, would not live long to enjoy their indolent luxury. Submission to another's despotic will more often than not meant sacrificing not only liberty, but life itself. This point is central to "The Story of Irene," which appeared in the *Rural Magazine* in May 1796. The story takes place in 1453, after the Ottoman ruler Muhammad the Great has conquered Constantinople, whose last Byzantine emperor chose to die defending his crown and faith rather than fall to the Muslims. "Dazzled by the charms of absolute power," the conqueror ordered all prisoners executed, "except the young and most beautiful of both sexes, whom he reserved for the abominations of his seraglio." One prisoner, Irene, a Greek girl of seventeen, melted his "fierce heart," and Muhammad neglected his army to spend all his time with her. This parallels the action in Bickerstaff's *The Sultan*, but "The Story of Irene" is more typical of the genre and is not a comedy. Irene cannot control Muhammad; she merely becomes the object of his lust.

Meanwhile, the idle army has neither Muhammad's iron discipline nor an outlet for its aggression. The restless soldiers whisper that their sultan's "ruling passion" is no longer war, and they hint at mutiny. Mustapha, Muhammad's loyal aide, warns the commander. After spending a "tender night" with Irene, Muhammad instructs her maids to dress her and adorn her as beautifully as they can, to add "if possible, new lustre to her beauty." She becomes a beautiful object, not a partner in power but a thing to be coveted. When she is ready, Muhammad leads her before the assembled army and, in an extraordinary public display, lifts her veil so that all can admire her. He demands to know if anyone has ever seen "such an accomplished beauty." The gathered sycophants all congratulate Muhammad "on his good fortune," enjoying this brief public glimpse of a desirable woman. While all are still admiring her, Muhammad takes Irene's hair in one hand, and with the other lifts his scimitar and cuts off her head. "This sword," he cries to the horrified crowd, "can cut, whenever I please, the bonds of love."[38]

The horrifying lesson is not lost on the members of the court. Each one "believed he saw that fatal weapon brandished over his own head." This fear is justified, as Muhammad has "the cruel satisfaction" of killing most of them, beginning with Mustapha, who is strangled in the seraglio. Muhammad's absolute power over his subjects, and his ability without remorse or hesitation to cut not only the bonds of love but also his lover's neck, show the consequences of submitting to this kind of tyranny. Irene had done what Zaphira, Roxalana, Maria Martin, and Scherezade would not: In return for being dressed in splendor and worshiped by the multitude, she had accepted Muhammad's unlimited dominion over her. She gave up her virtue for a kingdom. American women, who in Susanna Rowson's phrase came from a land where "virtue in either sex is the only mark of superiority," women like Maria Martin, Roxalana, Rebecca, and their counterparts Zaphira, Fetnah, and Scherezade, knew that no earthly kingdom was worth so much.

CHAPTER FOUR

American Slavery and the Muslim World

The Muslim world, with its political, religious, and sexual tyranny, had a profound interest for Americans, who were desperately afraid that despotic institutions might take root in their new world. Despotism had happened, Americans knew, because people let it happen. The Americans were determined not to make the mistake others had made. They could congratulate themselves on preventing political tyranny, on checking religious intolerance, and on restraining sexual subjugation. By avoiding these traps, the Americans seemed to have eluded the fate suffered by so many who had carelessly submitted to one form of tyranny or another. But the celebration could not last. Though Americans had avoided some forms of tyranny, they openly embraced another. When Algiers captured American ships in 1785 and 1793, and held as "slaves" some 120 sailors, Americans at home were outraged at this example of piracy and international lawlessness. But this moral outrage, like the civic celebration, could not survive a close look at American society. How could Americans condemn Algiers for enslaving Americans when Americans themselves were busily enslaving Africans? If slavery was wrong for white Americans, was it right for black Africans? Had Americans really escaped from tyranny, had they avoided the mistakes other people had made, if they forbade all forms of oppression except this one, which seemed to many the most severe?

Thomas Jefferson took a consistently hard line with the Barbary states. His ideas on slavery are more difficult to define, perhaps because he himself had so much trouble grappling with the issue. In

France, Jefferson spent much of his time seeing to the publication of his only book, *Notes on the State of Virginia*. He was reluctant to publish it, fearing that Americans at home, particularly in the Southern states, would be offended by his candid opinions on slavery. "The whole commerce between master and slave is a perpetual exercise of the most boisterous passions, the most unremitting despotism on the one part, and degrading submissions on the other." This described the relationship of master and slave in the United States but also the relationship, under despotic political systems, between ruler and subject. Jefferson saw that slavery brought to America the very tyranny he had led a revolution against, that slavery threatened to destroy the free society he had helped to create. The slave system so warped the personalities of master and slave, Jefferson wrote, that a man would have to be a prodigy to survive it unscathed. He asked, what kind of statesman could allow "one half the citizens thus to trample on the rights of the other" and what kind of republican system would make half the people despots, the other half their enemies? This indeed was a warped and dangerous system, one that Jefferson, in 1782, did not believe could survive. "Indeed I tremble for my country when I reflect that God is just: that his justice cannot sleep forever," Jefferson wrote.

John Adams, to whom Jefferson gave one of the first 200 copies of his book, thought the passages on slavery were "worth diamonds." Jefferson still was worried, both about what would happen when half the human race grew tired of being trampled on by the other and about what his friends in America would think of him for publishing these unpleasant but self-evident truths. Charles Thomson, secretary to Congress, tried to encourage Jefferson. Jefferson's blunt opinions on slavery might be disturbing to his countrymen, but they were just what they needed to hear. He had done his country a service by speaking his mind. If religion, reason, or philosophy did not convince the Americans that slavery must be abolished, Thomson said, then violence would. If Americans did not act in their own self-interest and end slavery peacefully, eventually the slaves themselves would act in their own self-interest violently. Neither Jefferson nor Thomson, close to the centers of American power, thought the American leaders they both knew so well were likely to take such farsighted action. "I confess," Thomson wrote, "I am more afraid of this than of the Algerine piracies...of which we hear so much of late."[1]

Jefferson's teenage daughter Martha, living in a Paris convent, knew how much these two issues, Algerian attacks on American commerce and slavery of Africans in America, troubled her father. As he traveled through the south of France in the spring of 1787 she wrote to him regularly, trying to keep him informed of public events, knowing how interested he was in these things, but not knowing that his own network of correspondents kept him better informed of world events than could a sixteen-year-old girl in a convent. She told him that Germany, Russia, and Venice had gone to war against Turkey and that Spain was suffering the plague. These distant events, she knew, must mean a lot to him, but they meant little to her, and she touched only briefly on them. But when she found a subject that touched her, she stayed with it. The story of a sea battle, which as far as can be determined never happened, piqued Martha's interest. "A virginia ship comming to spain met with [an Algerian] corser of the same strength," she wrote. "They fought And the battle lasted an hour and a quarter. The Americans gained and boarded the corser where they found chains that had been prepared for them. They took them and made use of them for the algerians themselves." Martha saw the irony in this turn of events. But instead of relishing the American victory, she saw only compounded tragedy. "They returned to virginia from whence they are to go back to algers to change the prisoners to which if the algerians will not consent the poor creatures will be sold as slaves." The Algerians, enemies determined to enslave Americans, now were poor creatures, as worthy of pity as the Americans might have been. But Martha took this concern a step further. The Virginians might enslave the Algerians, but she asked, "Good god have we not enough? I wish with all my soul that the poor negroes were all freed. It greives my heart when I think that these our fellow creatures should be treated so terribly as they are by many of our countrymen."[2] Martha Jefferson was

enraged by this story of a sea battle, which was not reported anywhere else. But the threat of slavery did not make her indignant
about inhumanity in Algiers or in Muslim harems, but instead
brought to mind the horrors of slavery in America. We cannot know
what her father thought, since he never mentioned this episode, or
Martha's comments on it, when he wrote back to her. Nor did he
mention it to anyone else.

The specter of American slavery continued to hang over the
American encounter with Algiers. A 1797 poem, "The American in
Algiers, or the Patriot of Seventy-Six in Captivity," told two stories.
The first canto is the story of a white American, a veteran of Bunker
Hill, forced by circumstances (some "daring villains with unfeeling
soul" had stolen his patrimony, and, as with other veterans of the
Revolutionary army, the certificates he had received in payment
were now worth "scarce one tenth" their value) to go to sea. The
economic dislocation of the 1780s deprives this man, as it did others,
of the security he had fought to establish. But his troubles are only
beginning. His ship is captured by an Algerian cruiser, and in an
Algerian prison this American veteran waits for his country to
redeem him. His story admonishes an American public that enjoys
freedom while forgetting those who have fought and suffered to
secure it.

The second canto turns the reader's attention away "From that
piratic coast where slavery reigns/And freedom's champions wear
despotic chains." Instead of viewing the horrors of that "piratic
coast," the poet wants the audience to "Turn to Columbia—cross
the western waves, and view her wide spread empire throng'd with
slaves." Lurid descriptions of slavery in Algiers, such as the first canto
offers, were common. But this canto tells a more horrifying tale, of a
veteran of Bunker Hill robbed of his freedom and enslaved by people who claim that all men are created equal. This speaker is a black
American who fought for independence, now a slave to the very
people he helped free. The Algerians had never proclaimed that all
men were created equal: Americans had. "By your own declaration
we are free," the speaker said, and asked Americans to stop boasting

of their freedom but to "Turn to your kitchens recognize your shame/And cease to stun our ears with freedom's name...." This "sable bard" is horrified that even heroes of liberty, such as George Washington, own slaves, making a mockery of American pretensions to liberty and morality.[3] The first canto chastises Americans for neglecting the men who had won their liberty; the second condemns Americans for neglecting the very freedom these men had fought to secure.

The *Rural Magazine or Vermont Repository* published a real-life version of the "Patriot of '76" during the debate over American captivity in March 1795. The newspapers at the time were filled with stories of American captives in Algiers, true stories very much like the one told by the first "Patriot of '76." The *Rural Magazine* reprinted one of them, under the heading "Curses of Slavery." John Burnham, whose story this was, had recently returned home from captivity in Algiers. But along with Burnham's story the editors reprinted another captivity tale, the story of Cato Mungo, an African prince who recently had returned to Ouidah, a West African port, after a long enslavement in America. Cato Mungo's story of suffering in America made John Burnham's tale seem insignificant, as he gave a "long and melancholy account of the treatment of the poor Africans in that land of cruelty." Just as Americans were debating ways to alleviate the suffering of Americans "enslaved" in Algiers, Cato Mungo suggested to Africans that "some measures" be taken to redeem "such of our brethren as it would be in our power to restore to their families and connections." He repeated with horror that "several of the Royal family of this kingdom" were now "doing drudgery in the kitchens of the *United States ! ! !*"[4]

The *Rural Magazine* also reprinted the story of Mawyaw, a free black man living in Connecticut, who had helped Cato Mungo escape to Massachusetts, where slavery had been abolished. Though slaves in Connecticut were treated better than they were in other states, Mawyaw said, they still were treated poorly. Connecticut's legislature had recently allowed "self-interest" to check its benevolence, rejecting an emancipation scheme. The legislature "did not think themselves justifiable in taking away the property of individuals," and so refused to grant liberty to other individuals. Though the legislature was then giving away a million dollars worth of public land, "their souls were not large enough" to free African slaves. But Mawyaw brought the issue of slavery back to Algiers, seeing both slavery in America and captivity in Algiers as symptoms of American moral indifference. Slaves in America had little reason to complain, Mawyaw said, since there were Americans "now in slavery in the kingdom of Algiers" whom "their countrymen could not find in themselves generosity enough" to redeem. Captivity in Algiers was a reproach to Americans for their lack of generosity; it was also a reproach for tolerating slavery in America.

Mathew Carey, one of the new republic's most prominent book publishers, issued a *Short Account of Algiers* in 1794, capitalizing on interest in the North African regency as the United States pondered its response to Algerian attacks on American ships. Carey condemned the Algerians for taking American hostages and selling them as slaves but noted, "For this practice of buying and selling slaves we are not entitled to charge the Algerines with any exclusive degree of barbarity." William Eaton, who arrived in Tunis as American consul in 1799, was appalled to find Europeans enslaved by the Tunisians. "'Slavery! thou *art* a bitter draught,'" he wrote in his journal, quoting Laurence Sterne's *Sentimental Journey*. If Eaton had the power, he would "shower for one dark moment, vengeance upon thy [slavery's] advocates hot[t]er than the blue wrath of presbyterian damnation— but halt! Alas, how many of my countrymen would be inveloped in the mighty ruin." He could not condemn Tunis without condemning America. "Barbary is hell—So, alas, is all America south of Pennsylvania; for oppression, and slavery, and misery, are there—!" Eaton, an official representative of the United States, could not ignore his own country's immorality. He wrote to his wife, "we boast of liberty and national justice. How frequently, in the southern states of my own country, have I seen weeping mothers leading the guiltless infant to the sales, with as deep anguish as if they led them to the slaughter; and yet felt my bosom tranquil in the view of these transgressions upon defenceless humanity." Eaton was appalled by the limits of his own humanity, cursing his own double standard, which made him curse the Tunisians for enslaving Europeans even though "the christian slaves among the barbarians of Africa are treated with more humanity than the African slaves among the professing Christians of civilized America; and yet here sensibility bleeds at every pore for the wretches whom fate has doomed to slavery." Eaton was troubled by his own failure to be as moved by the enslavement of blacks in America as he was by the enslavement of whites in Africa.[5]

Royall Tyler, a New England writer and lawyer, who almost married the daughter of John and Abigail Adams, wrote the most sophisticated novel on the American experience in Algiers, *The Algerine Captive, or the Life and Adventures of Doctor Updike Underhill, six years a prisoner among the Algerines* (1797). The novel begins as a satire on New England society, in which the classically educated physician, Updike Underhill, cannot find a secure place. He goes to sea and eventually becomes the doctor on a British slave ship. Dr. Underhill chooses to pursue wealth, not morality. Rough seas and disease kill the ship's human cargo, and Underhill finally convinces the captain to anchor on the African coast so that he can set up a hospital for the dying captives. On shore, he nurses the black captives back to health. He remains on shore with five recovering blacks when an Algerian cruiser drives away the slave ship. Four of the captives escape, to find their way home. Underhill and the remaining African are captured by the Algerians, who take on the black man as a sailor but lock Underhill in the hold. He is fed only the morsels his former captive can steal for him. This benevolence touches Underhill's conscience, and the first volume ends with him promising that if he ever returns to America, he will "fly to our fellow citizens in the southern states" and on his knees will "conjure them, in the name of humanity," to do away with the slave trade. If the name of humanity will not work, then "I will conjure them for the sake of consistency, to cease to deprive their fellow creatures of that freedom which their writers, their orators, representatives, senators, and even their constitutions of

government have declared to be the unalienable birthright of man."
Underhill apparently forgets this forthright declaration by the time
he is released by the Algerians in 1795. The book's second volume
ends with Underhill returning to America and enjoining his fellow
citizens to cherish their union, to remember that "BY UNITING
WE STAND, BY DIVIDING WE FALL."⁶ Underhill, like most
Americans, chooses union over liberty.

The idea of choosing remains central to Tyler's novel. One contemporary reviewer blasted the book for one chapter, in which
Underhill and a mullah argue over religion. The mullah, who is a
converted Greek, tells Underhill that his Christianity is the result of
birth and habit, not choice. If Underhill were born in India, he
would be a Hindu, but since he was born in New England, he is a
Christian. The reviewer, also a New England Christian, thought that
this chapter deserved "the most pointed reprehension," and that Tyler
had so "decidedly given the Mollah the best of the argument, that
the adherence of Updike to Christianity seems the effect rather of
obstinacy than of conviction."⁷

The mullah's most persuasive argument is that Muslims "never yet
forced a man to adopt their faith," but accepted as brothers all those
who did. Islam, the mullah told Underhill, freed all the slaves who
accepted it because "the souls of all true believers are bound up in
one fragrant bundle of eternal love. We leave it to the Christians of
the West Indies, and the Christians of your Southern plantations, to
baptize the unfortunate African into your faith, and then use your
brother Christians as brutes." Tyler puts this argument into the
mouth of a Muslim cleric, allowing the proponent of what many
Americans believed to be a false religion, a religion devoid of both
divinity and humanity, to lecture Americans on their moral duty.
Underhill could not help but admit that the mullah was right.⁸

Americans could not look too closely at the Muslim world without seeing a disturbing reflection. Another novel coming out of the
American encounter with Islam said, "Unconscious of our own
crimes, or unwilling the world should know them, we frequently
condemn in others the very practices we applaud in ourselves, and

wishing to pass for patterns of uprightness, or blinded by interest, pass sentence upon the conduct of others less culpable than ourselves." This 1801 novel, *Humanity in Algiers, or the Story of Azem,* is narrated by an American captive in Algiers who had been freed by the benevolent bequest of Azem, a merchant who left a generous bequest to free one captive each year. Azem's charity showed that there was, as the seemingly contradictory title said, humanity in Algiers. Azem was a black man from Senegal; he had been enslaved in Algiers, but was freed by his grateful master and established in business. He would not have had this opportunity in America had chance enslaved him there instead of in Algiers.

Humanity in Algiers is an antislavery novel, aimed not at the brutality of the Barbary states but at the inhumanity of the United States. The Algerians, who had made hostages of 120 American sailors, in fact were only repaying "us for similar barbarities." The Americans had to look at themselves honestly and acknowledge the sin of slavery in a Christian, republican land. "Taught and accustomed from infancy to think our own religious creed the only mark of civilization, we can scarcely think it possible that a Mahometan should possess a feeling heart, or perform a virtuous deed," the author declared. But Azem's story, "the authenticity of which may be relied on," proved that there was "HUMANITY in ALGIERS." By implication, there was no humanity in America. The white Christian American owed his freedom to the black Muslim African.[9]

Along with condemning slavery, *Humanity in Algiers* offered Americans a choice in redeeming their souls and nation. Omri, Azem's master, had chosen benevolence, freeing Azem when the faithful African prevents a lusty Arab from raping his daughter Narina. But Valachus, who owns Azem's sister Alzina, is "flushed with that self-importance which generally attends to wealth newly acquired." He refuses to be swayed from "what his passions seem to dictate, or his will determine," coveting the lovely Alzina for himself. His "independence of fortune" deafens him to both pity and reason. Valachus realizes his own sinfulness only when the plague strikes him, and he fears that his stubborn greed will keep him out of paradise. Americans were also in a position to choose. They could emulate Omri, motivated by gratitude and benevolence to free his servant and set him up in business, not as an act of charity but of good economy, since Azem is industrious and successful. Omri's son carries on Azem's benevolent work after Azem dies of the plague. The son of a successful merchant, he chooses charity, redeeming captives, over wealth. He works to abolish slavery. Or Americans could emulate Valachus, who is motivated by the desire for wealth and power and dies of the plague. American readers were warned. Accepting slavery offered worldly wealth, but only the work of freeing the slaves offered salvation.

As in Tyler's *Algerine Captive*, Islam, not Christianity, was the way to salvation. For American Christians certain of their moral superiority, this was a startling lesson to learn. Yet as long as some American Christians owned slaves and others tolerated their sinfulness, no Americans could preach to others from a position of virtuous complacency. Rather, it was left to an Algerian Muslim at the conclusion of *Humanity in Algiers,* to preach to Americans and the rest of the world. Omri calls for the light of Islam to shine throughout the world, for slave holders everywhere to remember "that important precept of the Alcoran—'Masters, treat your servants with kindness.'" More important were the words of Allah, "'Of one blood have I created all nations of men that dwell on the face of the earth.'"[10]

This novel, which circulated in upstate New York and western Vermont, was a pointed reminder to Americans that they did have it in their power to create the world anew, but that they must not congratulate themselves too soon for their success in doing so. The novel is a meditation on choosing, a point underscored by what might be an error in the beginning. The author, who claimed to have been a passenger on Richard O'Brien's ship, says he embarked with O'Brien on May 10, 1786. By then, O'Brien had already been a captive in Algiers for ten months. The author used O'Brien's name to give his novel a tinge of authenticity. But while this date shows the work to be fiction, it also suggests it to be more than just a sentimental tale. On May 10, 1775, the Second Continental Congress met, for the first time assembling in a nation at war. But they had not yet decided what the war would be about. Most delegates still hoped to resolve their differences within the British empire. One year later, on May 10, 1776, the same delegates faced a changing situation, and most were now ready to accept independence. On that date, they called on the colonies to set up new governments. This was not a declaration of independence, but it was the most important step toward independence, or, as one delegate said, it was a machine to fabricate independence. May 10 was an important date, though it still left up in the air the final choice, in Jefferson's words between, "submission and the sword." May 10 allowed the colonists to have a July 4 if they chose to have one. The narrator's voyage in *Humanity in Algiers* is a symbolic halfway voyage, much as the colonists' actions on May 10 had been. By 1801 American independence was secure. But the author of *Humanity in Algiers* wanted Americans to move further, to decide completely on freedom, not only for themselves but for all men. Like Tyler, this author tried to cajole his readers by having a Muslim lecture on brotherhood, showing Americans that people whom they considered moral degenerates were really their moral betters. These fictional Muslims showed American Christians the sinfulness of slavery in a land of liberty.[11]

We might dismiss this novel as the obscure and inconsequential work of a zealot. But it is striking how many Americans saw this same bitter lesson for themselves in Algiers. The consequences of submitting to tyranny, or allowing any form of tyranny to take root, were profound. Americans were accustomed to seeing in the Muslim world lessons for those who would accept tyranny. The despotic power of Turkey's sultan, the anarchic despotism of Algiers, the desolation of once prosperous societies in Mauritania, North Africa, Egypt, Arabia, Syria, and Iraq warned Americans of what could happen to them. The story of Azem concludes with one of the few positive statements about Islam found in early American literature. *Humanity in Algiers* suggested that Islam, not Christianity, offered freedom to all people. Something was wrong with either

Christianity or its adherents in allowing Islam to gain this moral advantage.

Could Americans really claim to be different from the failed people of the Old World if they tolerated slavery? It was in their power to choose what kind of people they would be. A "Copy of a letter from an English slave driver at Algiers to his Friend in England," published in New York and Salem in the 1790s, showed a man who had the choice between being a slave and being a slave driver in Algiers. He reconciled himself to his position of power, since the lot of slaves in Algiers was not much worse than that of English sailors or, indeed, of most English people. This was a chilling thought, perhaps as horrifying as the idea that slavery in America might be worse and more sinful than slavery in Algiers, since the Algerians did not leaven their slavery with the base alloy of hypocrisy. This English slave driver commanded twenty slaves, "some Spanish, some English, and some American." At first he found it hard to whip his own countrymen. But "custom, as the saying is, is second nature," and now he thought no more of whipping an Englishman than he would of whipping a horse. He hoped his friends at home would not condemn him for accepting the job of Algerian slave driver, but in his defense he said that the "infidels" of Algiers were no worse than the planters of Jamaica, who had ten times as many black slaves as the Algerians had whites. Furthermore, the English sailors captive in Algiers were "much better here than at home," where they had been no more than slaves. His friends, he reminded them, had been impressed into service on an English warship. He remembered one comrade who had fallen from the mast onto the captain's mistress's pet dog. The injured man had been severely flogged for the unfortunate landing. Compared to the way Englishmen treated black slaves and common sailors, the Algerian captives were treated mercifully. The captives in Algiers were forced to work, but at home they could either work or starve. This letter pointedly comments on English society and reminds the reader to look at his own society before condemning another. Could an American sailor choose to become a slave driver in Algiers, and whip American sailors as he would a horse? As long as Americans kept slaves at home or treated one another as less than human, this was a real possibility.[12]

As an American party system developed in the early 1790s, with Virginians taking an active role in supporting the ideas made popular in the French Revolution of universal equality and democracy, and condemning the Federalists, many of whom were New Englanders, for subscribing to ideas about hierarchy and social stability, some New Englanders responded by using the Algerian metaphor to blast the slaveholding Virginians for advancing ideas they did not practice. Under the heading *Profession versus Practice*, some New England papers reprinted "a most admirable satire on the *democratic professions*, and *despotic practices* of our ranting southern demagogues," who preached "*universal equality*" in Congress while they practiced "*piratical barbarity*" on their plantations. A satire on a fugitive slave ad, it promised a reward for the return of an "American slave" to his master, "Ibrahim Ali Bey" of Algiers. This American slave, an "ungrateful Villain" and "incorrigible infidel," could not be persuaded, punished, or disciplined into renouncing "his Christian errors," but instead had escaped by using a "borrowed" certificate of manumission. A freed slave, given such a document, could lend it to another slave, and through this "new invented species of *robbery*," half of the slaves in Algiers could be freed. The freed people, who had so defrauded their rightful owners, might consider their sharing of certificates as "*meritorious*. What strange, absurd ideas the Christians must have of *merit*."[13] So the Virginians, who professed liberty while owning slaves, were greater hypocrites than the New Englanders, who might not make pronouncements about equality but who did not own slaves. Mawyaw, the Connecticut man whose story appeared along with Cato Mungo's in the *Rural Magazine,* would have pointed out that all Americans were implicated in the slave system, that geographic position did not guarantee moral rectitude.

An 1812 play used a Barbary setting both to condemn slavery and to distance New England from the remaining slave states. In James Ellison's play, *The American Captive, or Siege of Tripoli,* Jack Binnacle, a captive sailor, tells the overseer, Hassan, that America is "a charming place, Mr. Overseer; no *slavery* there! All freeborn sons!" Hassan answers, "No Slavery, hey? Go where the Senegal winds its course, and ask the wretched mothers for their husbands and their sons! What will be their answer? *Doom'd to slavery, and in thy boasted country, too!*" At this moment the play's only black character, the ship's cook Juba, enters and assures Hassan that in Massachusetts "we brack gentlemen be all free!"[14] *The American Captive*, like *Profession versus Practice*, tried to distance New Englanders from the slave system. But as the mullah in Tyler's *Algerine Captive* had pointed out, all true believers were bound up in the same cloth. As the anonymous author of *Humanity in Algiers* had insisted, Americans in one section of the country could not distance themselves from the sins of another, evil in one part touched all Americans. All Americans had to choose which side they were on.

Humanity in Algiers circulated in a small area in Vermont and upstate New York. Tyler's *Algerine Captive* had three American editions in the decade after it was written but then disappeared. The other works cited may have had even less of an audience and less of an impact. So, how important was this whole Barbary theme? Did contemporaries really grasp the message these works were trying to convey about slavery and sinfulness? The fact that the message had to be repeated so often suggests that they did not. But other evidence suggests that at least some Americans did, and that those who did were in a position to act on their knowledge. One of the most influential books in the early republic, Caleb Bingham's *Columbian Orator*, was a collection of essays, poems, and speeches designed as a manual for young men ambitious to be statesmen, lawyers, or community leaders. One selection is a two-act play, *Slaves in Barbary*, which exploits the same themes of freedom, slavery, and national hypocrisy that the other authors found so compelling. The play's principal characters are three Venetian brothers, two of whom are captives in Tunis. But there is also an American captive named Kidnap, who has been kidnapped along with Sharp, his slave. Hamet, the "Bashaw of Tunis," learns from Sharp that Kidnap had been a cruel, drunken master. He orders the American sold to the highest bidder and has

Sharp put over him as overseer, to give Kidnap "the advantage of a whip-lecture from his former slave, whom he has treated so kindly." The Bashaw hopes that Kidnap will learn in slavery a lesson that "he could never learn in affluence, the lesson of humanity."[15]

The Columbian Orator remained an influential textbook for many years. In the early 1830s, when the other works considered in this chapter had disappeared completely, a young slave in Baltimore secretly taught himself to read and bought a copy of *The Columbian Orator*. Frederick Bailey did not need to read a book to find out that slavery was wrong, but from this book he learned that even some whites recognized that slavery contradicted their own professions of humanity and liberty. Bailey's keen mind grasped the point that white Americans, if they accepted liberty for themselves, had an uncomfortable feeling that it was wrong for others. He relished the way this short play took an idea all white Americans had to accept— that slavery was wrong for white Christians—and used it to make an argument they could not reject—that slavery was wrong for every- one. A few years later, Bailey escaped, changed his name to Frederick Douglass, and spent the rest of his life reminding Americans of truths they had once boldly declared to be self-evident.[16]

Frederick Douglass, like Martha Jefferson, Mr. Mawyaw, and the anonymous author of *Humanity in Algiers*, knew that all Americans, whether they owned slaves or not, were implicated in the crime of slavery. They knew that by being part of the same nation, all Americans were responsible for that nation's moral as well as political health. Complacency in the face of evil was almost as great a sin as the evil itself. The mullah in Tyler's *Algerine Captive* had said that all Muslims were bound up in one fragrant bundle of eternal love; Americans who were determined not only to create their own world anew, but to set their new world up as an example to the old, could not forget that every action was being judged both by God and by other men all over the world. Thus, though Americans could congratulate themselves on avoiding the tragic despotism that had desolated Turkey, Egypt, and Mauritania, and the sexual deviance that degraded Muslim women and corrupted the most personal relations, they could not look at slavery in the Muslim world without facing the grim truth that, in fact, they were no different from any other people in the world. They had not rooted out that germ in human nature that caused men to be tyrants; they had not created a society that would prevent a few from oppressing others; and they had not guaranteed that the many would reject oppression.

The dilemma of slavery lay just beneath the surface of the political and constitutional debates of the 1770s and 1780s. The wisest of the founders, like James Madison, knew that this problem ultimately would undo all of the compromises they had so carefully worked out. But even the wisest of them could find no way to resolve this problem. As Connecticut's Mr. Mawyay noted, American legislators, even in New England, preferred the property rights of slave owners to the human rights of slaves. In a nation founded to secure property rights, this was an ominous sign. In 1790 the tension between personal and property rights flared up in the U.S. Congress. A group of Pennsylvania Quakers petitioned Congress to abolish the slave trade. The Constitution had given Congress the power to do this, but not before 1808. The Quakers could see no virtue in waiting eighteen years to eliminate a sin. But representatives from South Carolina and Georgia, whose white constituents still needed to import slaves to cultivate their rice crops, protested. They still needed their slaves, they said; the Constitution would allow them to import slaves until 1808. Had the Constitution not given them this, they might not have accepted it.

The Quakers, like the author of *Humanity in Algiers*, might be dismissed as religious zealots determined to make others adhere to their own moral standard. Most members of Congress were ready to ignore the Quakers and concentrate on establishment of a national bank, assumption of state debts, internal taxes, and the site of a national capital, that were quickly dividing the new government into political parties. The simple argument that Congress could not interfere in states' institutions, and could not abolish the slave trade until 1808, was enough to dismiss the Quakers. But two days after Congress received the Quaker petition, it received another petition from a secular group, the Pennsylvania Society for the Abolition of Slavery. Instead of religious arguments, the Pennsylvania Society used political and ideological arguments that came from the heart of America's Revolutionary struggle. "From a persuasion that equal liberty was originally the portion, and is still the birthright of all men," the Pennsylvania Society was moved by the "strong ties of humanity" to "use all justifiable endeavors to loosen the bands of slavery." The society called on Congress to do the same, urging it to "step to the very verge" of its power to discourage "every species of traffic in the persons of our fellow-men."[17] This petition was signed by the Pennsylvania Society's president, Benjamin Franklin.

Though the Quakers were easily dismissed, Franklin was not. The protectors of slavery had to advance different arguments to use against a political antislavery movement which based its case on ideological precepts they shared. A congressman from South Carolina merely said that Franklin "ought to have known the Constitution better," and repeated that Congress had no power to interfere in a local institution or with the rights to property. But others knew that merely basing their argument on property rights or on state power would not be enough, that moral zeal combined with the ideals of the Revolution would destroy any legalistic property rights or states' rights argument. Georgia congressman James Jackson knew this, and knew that defenders of slavery must not grant their attackers' starting premise: that the institution was evil. If they did so, the battle was over. If they wanted slavery to survive attacks from Franklin and the Quakers, they must show that slavery was a good thing.

Jackson did this, blasting both Franklin and the Quakers as overzealous meddlers trying to destroy a valuable social institution. Those who attacked slavery, Jackson said, were ignorant. Religion, economics, politics, and history all justified slavery; Franklin and the Quakers were ignorant of all these things. Enslaved Africans, Jackson said, were taught the Christian virtues, and Georgians had done these slaves a great favor by lifting them out of barbarism. The slaves, then, had benefitted from the benevolent care of good Christian masters like Jackson. If the slaves were set free, Jackson asked, what would they do? Their freedom would ruin Georgia's economy. The slaves would not work unless they were forced to do so. If the freed blacks moved to the frontier, the Indians would kill them. So the only benevolent option was to keep these people as slaves, teach them Christianity, and allow them to cultivate Georgia's rice.

Jackson was a young and ambitious politician; Franklin an old man. Franklin may well have expected the petition on slavery to be his last public act: He was eighty-four years old and just a few weeks from the grave. But when he read Congressman Jackson's speech on slavery in the *Federal Gazette* in March 1790, Franklin launched one more missile. The stakes were too high to let Jackson go unchallenged, allowing the American republic, which Franklin had helped to create, go off into a morally corrupt future. Franklin also knew that moral indignation and direct attack were easy to ignore. Over his seventy years in public life, he had learned to use much more devastating weapons. He knew how to write satire and knew that no rhetorical device can be more effective than pretending to agree with an opponent, and pushing an argument based on a ridiculous premise to its inevitably absurd conclusion.

So, writing as "Historicus," Franklin praised Jackson's speech and said it reminded him of a similar speech he had read years earlier in *Martin's Account of his Consulship*, a book Franklin made up. The speech which Jackson's so closely echoed had been delivered in 1687 by Sidi Mehemet Ibrahim, the dey of Algiers.[18] A group of religious zealots, the Erika, or "Purists," had petitioned Sidi Mehemet to abolish Christian slavery and piracy. Slavery and piracy, the Erika said, were unjust and against the teachings of the Quran. Having set out the occasion, Franklin took Jackson's speech, defending African slavery in America, and made it a defense of Christian slavery in North Africa.

Slavery and piracy might be unjust, Sidi Mehemet agreed, but asked, "If we forbear to make slaves" of Christians, "who in this hot climate are to cultivate our lands?" Jackson had made this same point. Sidi Mehemet asked, if Algiers did not have Christian slaves, "Must we not then be our own slaves?" and what would happen to the slaves themselves if their Muslim masters set them free? "Must we maintain them as beggars in our streets, or suffer our properties to be the prey of their pillage?" Freed Christians could never be the equals of Muslims; they would not "embrace our holy religion; they will not adopt our manners; our people will not pollute themselves by intermarrying with them." Accustomed to slavery, they would not work unless they were forced to do so, and if they went out to the frontiers, they were too ignorant to establish a "good government" and would be massacred by wild Arabs. This ignorant weakness was not their fault: In their own countries these Christians—Spanish, Portuguese, French, and Italian—were all treated as slaves. Algerians had done them a favor by bringing them to work "where the sun of Islamism gives forth its light." To send them back to Europe would be to send them "out of light into darkness." Finally, if Algiers gave up slavery, piracy, and plunder, it would destroy its own economy merely to gratify "the whims of a whimsical sect."

The Algerians had found it impossible to say that plunder and slavery were wrong. After hearing Sidi Mehemet the Algerians decided that the moral argument was "at best *problematical*." Ending slavery would produce more problems than it would solve, and though some might think slavery a moral wrong, it was best for the majority's interest that it be left alone. The U.S Congress came to the same conclusion: Plunder and slavery, whether right or wrong, were in the states' interest.

Franklin fabricated the Erika, Sidi Mehemet, and *Martin's Account of his Consulship*. Unfortunately, he had not made up James Jackson. The similarities Franklin said he found between Jackson's speech and Sidi Mehemet's showed that "men's interests and intellects operate and are operated on with surprising similarity in all countries and climates, whenever they are under similar circumstances." Though Americans boasted of their own fidelity to the rights of man, they proved themselves no different from Turks or Algerians when those rights came into conflict with self-interest. Jefferson's blunt warning on slavery—that it would destroy the American republic by twisting American personalities—and the call delivered by *Humanity in Algiers* for Americans to awaken to their moral responsibilities were ignored. Americans pursued their immediate interests, leaving others to reckon with the consequences of their mistakes. Franklin, in the last essay published in his lifetime, came to the somber conclusion that Americans were no more likely than Algerians to be awakened to their moral responsibilities.

CHAPTER FIVE

American Captives in
the Muslim World

In 1800, nearly one million people of African origin were enslaved in the United States. Unlike the seven hundred Americans held captive in the Muslim states between 1785 and 1815, these million Africans and African-Americans could not expect their nations or families to redeem them, nor could they look forward to being returned to freedom. Compared with the suffering of slaves in America, the complaints of the 700 Americans who called themselves slaves in Barbary seem hyperbolic or hypocritical.

Slavery in America was lifelong, hereditary, and brutal. It was also defined by race. This was not the case in the Muslim states, which had slaves, but would not be considered slave societies. Slaves were held in the Muslim world for political not economic reasons. Children of slaves would be free, as would a slave himself on conversion to Islam. Slaves in the Muslim world could own property, testify in court, and even serve as ministers of state. James Leander Cathcart was an American captive, owned taverns and ships, and served as the dey's Christian secretary.

What kind of slavery was this? Why was slavery so different in Algiers than in America? The Western definition of slavery had changed since the fifteenth century, when Spanish writer Miguel de Cervantes Saavedra and others had been chained to the oars of Algerian galleys. Slavery in the fifteenth century did not mean loss of freedom. Few people in the fifteenth century had freedom to lose. Instead, slavery was a way to incorporate kinless strangers into society. These strangers might have been captured in war, displaced by a war in their homeland, or they might have broken their own society's legal code and so forfeited their right to membership. It was more humane to put criminals, infidels, or captured enemies to work (Spain and the Muslim world were at war when Cervantes was enslaved) than it was to kill them. Slavery as a temporary status gave these kinless strangers a place in society while their permanent fate was determined either by their families and government or by their own choice of Islam. [1]

Algiers and other Muslim states held on to this idea of slavery, while in the New World slavery took on a radically different meaning. Arabs, Italians, and Spanish had developed sugar plantations in the Mediterranean, using the forced labor of political captives: Moorish, Greek, Circassian, and Caucasian. The states of North Africa had found another source of captives in their dealings with the Muslim states of Songhai and Mali, which would enslave infidels from the forest societies south of the Sahara. Timbuctu became for Morocco, Algiers, and Tripoli a market for both gold and slaves by the fourteenth century. In 1433 the Portuguese rounded Cape Bojador and Timbuctu fell to the Tuaregs. At the very moment the caravan trade was disrupted in Muslim Africa, European Christians were poised to open their own trading posts on the African coast. Portugal found a way around the Muslim monopoly on the African slave trade, as well as islands in the Atlantic—Madeira, and Cape Verde—that were suited to sugar production. Twenty years after Portugal crossed Cape Bojador, the Ottomans wrested Constantinople away from the Christians, cutting access to the Black Sea slave trade.

All these complicated maneuvers and seemingly unrelated episodes in the century before Columbus sailed west changed the nature of the voyage he would make and the land he would find. By 1490 the Portuguese islands of Madeira and São Tomé were sugar islands, just as Sicily and Majorca had been and just as Cuba and Barbados would be. But these plantation economies had different sources of labor: All used slaves, but the Mediterranean slaves, for the most part, had been the spoils of war and conquest, put to work by the victors, while the Atlantic and Caribbean slaves were captured and then sold by their captors to Europeans. The Portuguese transferred this slave system to their colony in Brazil, and when the Spanish grew horrified at the death and destruction they had brought to the people of the New World, they too turned to Africa as a source of slaves. The English and Dutch, who followed the Portuguese to the coast of Africa and who followed the Spanish to the Americas would perfect this system of trading for slaves in Africa and selling slaves to American planters.

By 1800, slavery still meant political captivity in the Muslim world, and was still a means of incorporating kinless strangers into society. These Christian captives could become free on accepting Islam: Their slavery was a way station between heathenism and fidelity. But by 1800, slavery in the Americas meant lifetime hereditary servitude, and the slave, instead of being a potential convert and a member of society, was a chattel, a piece of property, having, in the words of an American chief justice, "no rights which a white man was bound to respect." The American captives knew what slaves were in America and knew that they did not want to be slaves. When these men wrote home of being slaves, Americans understood them to mean one thing, while the Algerians or Moroccans who enslaved them meant something else.

American captives who wrote accounts of their captivity followed a pattern already set in American literature, a pattern established by seventeenth-century Puritans captured by Indians. Those stories, mostly written in the aftermath of King Philip's War in the 1670s, were not meant to tell readers what the Algonquins or Iroquois were like, but to tell American readers what they were like. These Puritan captives had survived both the ordeal of captivity by Indians and often the far worse temptation to save themselves by joining the Indians' haughty allies, the French Catholics. The redeemed captives defied death and Catholicism to return to New England, and these captivity narratives were meant to shore up the faith of their countrymen. The narratives produced by American captives in the Muslim world had a similar function. Americans were reminded of the need for strength and courage, and of the rewards to those who would not give up. Thus in 1795 a reader recommended that others read Daniel Saunders's account of his shipwreck off the coast of Arabia. "How bitter is suffering, but how noble is generous courage, and ready invention. How soon is woe absorbed in sympathy," the reader said. "This rough path leads to our sublime pleasures."[2]

The captivity narratives, whether of suffering at the hands of Arabs, Algerians, or Algonquins, all showed the rough path and ended with a glimpse of the sublime pleasures. "We see woe," the reviewer concluded, "but we find how to relieve [it]. We pity the sufferer, but we resolve to [imitate] the benefactor."[3] These stories were meant to encourage Americans at home to behave in a certain way, by contrasting the brutality of Algerians and Arabs with the benevolence of individuals who came to the relief of the American captives. The captives themselves proved their virtue under the most brutal conditions. The rough path the Americans in captivity followed led them and their countrymen at home to life's sublime pleasures.

But the captives were not rhetorical devices or literary motifs. They were real men, and their experiences, whatever uses the reading or writing public made of them, were real. Between 1785 and 1815, some thirty-five American ships manned by over 700 sailors were captured by the Barbary states. These ships and men were captured at sea and were treated as political hostages. Their captors hoped to ransom the men and vessels back to either their friends or their government. Algiers captured twenty-two ships, Tripoli six, Morocco five, and Tunis two.[4] The Barbary states captured ships for political or diplomatic reasons. In 1778 Emperor Mawlay Muhammad recognized American independence, making Morocco second only to France in accepting the United States as an independent nation. Mawlay Muhammad announced his interest in forming a treaty with the new nation, and promised that American ships would not only be protected from attack by his cruisers, but would be welcome in Moroccan ports. The Americans were slow to respond to these gestures of good will; by 1785 Mawlay Muhammad was tired of waiting. He ordered a Moroccan cruiser to capture an

American ship and hold it hostage until the United States sent an ambassador. The merchant ship *Betsey* became a hostage to secure treaty negotiations; Mawlay Muhammad released the ship and its crew when the United States promised to send a negotiator, and the crew reported that they had been treated well by their captors. For good measure the emperor delivered up James Mercier, a ship-wrecked Virginian who had been held captive by Bedouins.[5]

Mercier's captivity was different from that experienced by the political prisoners in Algiers, Tunis, or Morocco. He was less fortunate. His ship had been wrecked on the desert coast south of Morocco. Other American ships wrecked on the Arabian or Mauritanian coasts, and the survivors, if they escaped from the wreckage and the surf, were almost certain to die of thirst. But if they survived, as a few like Mercier did, it was only because they were found by desert tribes that would strip the survivors of their clothes and valuables, and most likely keep or sell the men as slaves. In these cases, the men were not political prisoners, but actual slaves to the people who found them, though they would share with their masters a life of brutal nomadic egalitarianism very different from the life of an American slave. Some, like Mercier, might eventually find their way to areas under the control of a benevolent monarch like Mawlay Muhammad, who for his own political reasons would free them. A few others, like James Riley, whose ship the *Commerce* was wrecked off Morocco in 1815, would persuade their captors to take them to a port city, where they promised that a European consul would pay a large ransom.[6]

These, then, were the experiences of the captives. Some were prisoners of war, some political hostages. But all described their experience as slavery. "I am a slave to the Mahometans," John Foss wrote to his mother from Algiers. Captain James Taylor, also captive in Algiers, told his ship's owners that their vessel was lost, but "what I am sure is worse to your own feelings," he and the crew were confined in a "cruel slavery." An anonymous New Englander published a petition on behalf of the Americans in Algiers, calling on Americans at home to redeem their "fellow-citizens, chained to the gallies of the imposter Mahomet." Both the image of galley slaves and of Muhammad as an "imposter" were fundamental to American picture of the Muslim world, and the reality was irrelevant to this image. A 1795 poem, "American Captive in Algiers," had the American captive toiling and dying at the galley oar.[7]

These uses of anachronistic imagery, and of the word "slavery," were more than just hyperbole or an attempt to make their situation seem worse. Captives called themselves slaves even as they acknowledged that they were not treated badly. Slavery did not necessarily mean harsh treatment. William Knight, captured by Tripoli in 1803, wrote home that he was treated "well much better than I expected," but signed himself a "Slave to the Bashaw of Tripoli." William Ray, a marine captured by Tripoli, seems to have spent most of his time in captivity writing poetry, but he called his memoir of the experience *Horrors of Slavery*.[8]

These men may or may not have known about slavery's different meaning in America and in Africa. What they did know was that slavery, in whatever form, was not for them. It was not bad to be a slave because one was harshly treated. Instead, for these captive Americans, slavery was wrong because it denied them their liberty. For the Americans, freedom, not belonging, had become the opposite of slavery. Laurence Sterne's *Sentimental Journey through France and Italy,* a novel first published in 1768, provided this generation of Americans with its most compelling definition of slavery. "Disguise thyself as thou wilt, still slavery! said I—still thou art a bitter draught; and though thousands in all ages have been made to drink of thee, thou art no less bitter on that account." This sentence crops up over and over in the literature generated by Algerian captivity, quoted by David Humphreys, William Eaton, and the anonymous philanthropists who will be discussed in the next chapter.

Sterne's protagonist has made a lighthearted plan to escape his troubles by being imprisoned for debt in the Bastille, which he tells himself is only a tower, which is only a house you cannot leave. With pen and paper and patience, a man could happily pass a month or six weeks in such a house. But he quickly changes his mind when he hears a starling in a cage saying "I can't get out—I can't get out" as it tries to smash itself free. This starling, with its overwhelming desire for freedom, teaches a lesson in the meaning of captivity and the value of liberty. The author, chastened by the bird, tries to write about the "millions of my fellow creatures born to no inheritance but slavery," but their sheer numbers overwhelm him, and instead he writes a pathetic account of a single prisoner, his body wasted and his heart bleeding from "hope deferr'd." Slavery is not wrong because it is cruel, but because it is an unnatural state which denies a man his liberty. However it is disguised, whether it means chained labor on a West Indian plantation or life in a gilded cage, slavery is a bitter drink for free men.[9]

The Americans captured by Algiers in 1785 bear out this conception of slavery. Those put to work in the dey's garden, actually as slaves to the dey, complained that fourteen men were assigned to do the work that four might have done, and that "we had not a great deal to do" and suffered more from boredom than anything else. The three American captains taken prisoner—Richard O'Brien, Isaac Stephens, and Zachariah Coffin—were taken under the British consul's protection. They discovered that the consul's friendship was a pretense, that he had taken them in only to humiliate them. The men put to work in the dey's garden had it better than these men, on whom the British consul heaped "every indignity that inhumanity could devise to render their situation humiliating in the extreme." One of the dey's captives was shocked to find his superior officers hard at work in the British consul's garden, one planting a tree, another feeding pigs, and the third leading a mule carrying manure. Worse, to these men's sense of dignity, the British consul threw a dinner party for captains and officers from British ships and had the Americans serve at the table.[10]

Though the three captains were humiliated by the British consul, and though the captive from the dey's palace who was so shocked at their condition thought they suffered more than he did, in fact they were better off than the ordinary sailors, and they knew it. Eventually the Spanish ambassador, eager to do the Americans a favor, rented a house for the three captains. The common sailors put to work in the dey's palace, or on the waterfront, had both more physical labor to perform and more temptations to renounce their distant nation for a better life in Algiers.

James Leander Cathcart, one of the American sailors at work in the dey's garden, attracted the attention of Hassan, the minister of the marine. This attention brought Cathcart some opportunities he was able to exploit. With Hassan's patronage, Cathcart bought taverns that catered to thirsty Christian slaves and eventually even owned a few small trading vessels. His position greatly improved in 1793, when Hassan became dey and Cathcart became his chief Christian secretary, responsible for all Algerian correspondence with Christian nations. Though Cathcart never renounced Christianity to become a Muslim, his years of service to the dey of Algiers colored his personality. Years later, when Cathcart was the American consul to Tripoli and O'Brien was the American consul general at Algiers, William Eaton contrasted their personalities. O'Brien, Eaton said, "was a *Captive*, but O'Brien was never a *slave*." Unfortunately for Cathcart, Eaton wrote, his service to the dey made him fearful of all men in power, particularly the unrestrained despots of the Barbary states, and Cathcart trembled "under their frowns as he has smarted under their lash." Cathcart "would not shrink at the thunder of a Broadside of a man of war," but would "tremble at the Nod of a Turban...—such is the influence of habit, I may say education."[11]

Even though Cathcart had not renounced his status as an American, he had gone to work for the dey, and this made him less an American—more, in Eaton's phrase, a slave. Eaton understood Cathcart's reasons: He was barely seventeen when he was captured in 1785, and for most of his life he had been commanded by others. After a few childhood years in Ireland he had served as a cabin boy and ordinary seaman on merchant vessels, then joined the American navy. He spent two years as a British prisoner of war. He was not used to thinking or acting for himself. But still, Eaton thought, Cathcart made the wrong choice when he agreed to serve the dey. In 1803, when 300 American sailors were taken prisoner in Tripoli,

Commodore Edward Preble, U.S. commander of the Mediterranean fleet, wrote to remind them that "Altho' the fortune of War has made you prisoners to the Bashaw of Tripoly, it has not made you his Slaves—Whether you will be Slaves or not, depends on yourselves." Thus it was in their power, even when their situation seemed to deprive them of any choice, to refuse to be slaves. Preble warned the sailors that any who did willingly work for the pacha would be treated as traitors by the Americans. Preble's men, like O'Brien, were captives, but they would not be slaves. No American, Preble and Eaton agreed, could allow himself to be subjected to the arbitrary will of another.[12]

Though Eaton and Preble recognized that Americans might be compelled to serve their captors, this was different from submitting to their captors' arbitrary will. Slavery and freedom were intellectual concepts rather than physical conditions. Captivity became slavery only when the captive submitted to it. Slavery was not a life of toil or liberty a life of ease; rather, slavery and freedom were defined by a man's attitude toward work or ease. Independent Americans could no more reconcile themselves to captivity than Laurence Sterne's bird could reconcile itself to its cage. When James Harnette went mad in Algiers, O'Brien called it "a striking contrast of American Independency," suggesting that Harnette had lost his mind under the strain of being both an American and a captive, being both free and restrained by the will of another.[13]

The common sailors were treated differently from the officers, both by the regencies that captured them and by their home government. The sailors were put to work; the officers were not. The American captives in Algiers received a monthly allowance from their home government, with occasional gifts from the Spanish, Swedish, or Dutch consuls. The captains were given $8 each month, the mates $6, and the sailors $3.50. When the captives returned home, they found that charity also followed this hierarchical structure. The sum of $887.28, raised for the captives by a Boston theater in 1795, was kept in trust for them at the Union Bank. When twenty-four captives returned to New England in February 1797, the money was divided, with the sailors receiving $30 each, the mates $35, and the captains $50, except for Isaac Stephens, the senior member of the group, who received $65.[14]

In Tripoli, Pacha Yusuf kept the officers in his palace, while the men were put up in various empty buildings, including one bakery, throughout the city. But Captain William Bainbridge of the *Philadelphia* thought the men were more comfortable than the officers, and at least one officer wished he were with the men doing hard labor. Though the officers were treated better "than we had reason to expect from a Barbary Prince," it would have been better to be with the men "at hard labour" since then they could "feel the fresh air, which is so essential to human nature." The British consul in Tripoli reported that the men did not share this opinion. He said the American sailors he met in the streets "complain[ed] heavily of bad living & hard work." The officers finally got the benefit of fresh air without the hardship of labor when the pacha allowed them to take walks in the country "two or three times a week." But still, one American officer complained that the pacha's flower garden was "not laid out with any taste, and the flowers in it, are of the most common sort," though he found the pacha's orange grove to be "delightful beyond what you can imagine," and he reported to his friends at home that "we loll two or three hours under the shade of the orange trees, enjoying the cheerful fresh air, and feasting upon the most delicious fruits." This, indeed, was a peculiar kind of captivity.[15]

Jonathan Cowdery, the *Philadelphia*'s surgeon's mate, enjoyed an astonishing degree of freedom in Tripoli and became an intimate of the pacha's family, playing chess with the crown prince, visiting admiral Murad Reis's country estate, and dining with the royal family. One January day, Cowdery relaxed with the prince and the prime minister among the flowers and citrus trees at the pacha's country estate. He returned to the city after dark, noting in his diary, after his report on the day in the country, "John Hilliard died in the evening." Hilliard was an ordinary sailor; Cowdery, called in to treat him, was too late to save his life. William Ray, the captive marine, wrote an elegy for Hilliard when his comrade died. Years later, Ray exploded when he read the doctor's "laconic" comment in the diary published by Cowdery: If Doctor Cowdery had shown as much interest in the "languishing sailor, in a dreary cell" as he did in the prince in the flower garden, Ray said, John Hilliard would still be alive. When Ray published his own book of verse, he put Cowdery's terse comment—"John Hilliard died in the evening"—above his own elegy to Hilliard.[16]

Men and officers experienced very different lives in captivity. In May 1804, American newspapers published a letter from an officer in captivity in Tripoli. The letter describes a prison to which Yusuf Qaramanli banished the officers one morning after he heard that Tripolitan prisoners of war were mistreated by the Americans. To get even, Qaramanli ordered the American officers out of his palace. The officers were marched through streets packed with curious crowds anxious to catch a glimpse of the exotic Americans, to a "black and dreary" dungeon "more fit to be the abode of demons, than of mortals." The officer intended to create an effect. He may have been consciously echoing gothic fiction, with his descriptions of how "the sun gilded our prison windows" as the men rose from their "flinty couches" and were led past the mobs of "gaping people" brought out "by curiosity or the hope of plunder" to see the American officers. His descriptions of the prison itself seem to come directly from a gothic novel: Its walls were "entirely black and dripping with unwholesome damps, and the vaulted ceiling hung with cobwebs"; the floor was broken and crawling with vermin; the only light came from a small roof grate "which feebly glimmering served to make the darkness visible." As the officer's eyes adjusted to the visible darkness, he thought of the River Styx, the mythical river separating the living from the dead. The whole piece conveys a sense of horror and despair. But in the best novelistic tradition, the hero escapes from the abode of demons: Pacha Yusuf relents at the end of the day, perhaps having taught the prisoners a lesson, and has them all returned to his palace. The reader is as relieved as the officers at this narrow escape. But the whole effect is unintentionally changed when the officer mentions that the *Philadelphia's* sailors were already in the miserable dungeon, the abode of demons, and they stayed there when the officers were marched back to the palace.[17]

Despite the different status and accommodations of men and officers, and the impossibility of reconciling themselves to captivity, few Americans abandoned their nation or their comrades for Islam. Had they embraced Islam, or decided to serve Pacha Yusuf or the dey, the American prisoners might have enjoyed a prosperous life. Captain Bainbridge believed "there never was so depraved a set of mortals as Sailors are," and was shocked that some of the captive sailors stole their comrades' clothes to buy liquor. But they were not so depraved as to abandon their country. Only 5 of the 300 *Philadelphia* sailors "turned Turk," and William Ray was thankful that the "first one who disgraced our flag" in Tripoli by doing so was not really an American but a German, a "perfidious wretch" who had betrayed his comrades by spying on them even before he donned "the dress of a Turk."[18]

Renegades, or converts, could rise to prominence in the Barbary states. Tripoli's two most important officials after the pacha were immigrants, or renegades, who converted to Islam. The prime minister, Muhammad D'Ghies, was a Russian who had served as Tripoli's ambassador to England, France, Spain, and Naples before becoming prime minister. The admiral, Murad Reis, was a Scot named Peter Lisle, who had in fact arrived in Tripoli as a sailor on the American ship *Betsey*, which Tripoli had captured in 1796. Lisle stayed on to become Tripoli's chief admiral and to marry one of Yusuf Qaramanli's daughters.[19]

While this path was open to Americans as well, few took it. Richard O'Brien reported that the captives taken into the dey's palace in 1785 "were solicited to turn Mahometans" but refused, driving up their ransoms. One of those pressured to convert was Cathcart. The Irish Cathcart wrote of another Irishman, named Call, who arrived in Algiers in 1793, just as 100 more American captives were being brought into the city. Call went by the name Ibrahim and spent most of his time in Algiers in a brothel owned by Diggins, another Irishman. The story of these Irishmen may have touched a nerve in Cathcart, also born in Ireland, also an owner of taverns in

Algiers. He called Diggins and Call the "most complicated villains in the regency" and said they were hated "by Turks Moors Jews & Christ[ians]." Was Cathcart, the dey's Christian secretary and a competitor of Diggins, involved in the official raid on the brothel and the arrest of these two Irish renegades? He certainly was among the Christians happy to see them banished and warned not to return to Algiers if they valued their lives.[20]

Another American captive, John Foss, told the story of a French sailor who jumped ship in February 1795 and "through a mistaken zeal" converted to Islam. Though he was amply rewarded for renouncing his faith, his conscience troubled him. The renegade's "livid countenance, haggard form, and gloomy aspect" betrayed the "remorse...preying upon his mind." Tormented by his decision, the renegade spent many sleepless nights trying to find an escape. When a British warship came into port, this former citizen of the French republic tried to escape to it, hoping to find under the Union Jack the safety that had eluded him under the Crescent. He was caught, and on July 2, 1795, beheaded, an end the American captive thought fitting for a "wretch" who had exchanged the "true religion for Mahometanism." What significance should we attach to this story published during the quasi-war between the United States and France? How significant is it that the renegade, who cannot make up his mind what religion or nation he belongs to, has the choice made for him on July 2, the anniversary of the day Americans chose independence? This little story appears in the second edition of Foss's narrative;—it is not mentioned in the first edition. The story may have been an editorial embellishment of this American captivity narrative, pointing to the difference between the American captives, who remain true to their nation, and the faithless French. Whether this Frenchman was fictional or not, he came from a nation at war with Christian authority. He fled, first taking refuge beneath the Crescent, then seeking it under the Union Jack. Neither could protect him from his own conscience.[21]

Perhaps all this ideological and political freight is too much for this simple story to carry. Perhaps the only important fact is that the sailor was French not American. Americans did not renounce their nation or faith; when they did, or when other Americans wrote of their "turning Turk," the circumstances were extraordinary, and often another nation was to blame. Mordecai Manuel Noah, American consul in Tunis in 1813, learned of an American sailor named Walker who had been impressed into the British navy in 1810. Walker had a wife and children in Baltimore, but the "system of cruelty" inflicted on him by his British officers made him forget his American home and family. When the ship stopped in Algiers, Walker abandoned it, along with "his country, his family, and religion," to seek asylum "among a horde of barbarians!" British brutality had forced this man to renounce America for life in Algiers.[22]

Betraying one's conscience had severe consequences. Though it was easy to embrace Islam, it was difficult to change one's mind. William Ray remembered the end of the Tripolitan war, after Yusuf Qaramanli and the Americans agreed to a peace treaty. Five American prisoners who had betrayed their flag were called to the palace. The pacha asked if they wanted to remain in Tripoli or preferred to go back to America with their former comrades. Only one, John Wilson, the German who had been the first to "turn Turk," decided to stay; the others had had enough of Tripoli and wanted to go home. But they did not. Ray remembered the looks of horror on the four men's faces as they were led under guard out of the city, never to be seen again.[23]

These consequences were severe, but few Americans suffered them. Under the most dire circumstances, American sailors remained true to their nation, even when that nation seemed to abandon them. "O! America," Cathcart wrote, "could you see the miserable situation of your citizens in captivity, who have shed their blood to secure you the liberty you now possess." Cathcart saw his captivity as truly tragic, since he and the other captives had helped win American independence, and that independence had opened American shipping to attack by Algiers. While Americans at home enjoyed the benefits of independence, Cathcart and other men who had helped secure independence were "left the victims of arbitrary power and barbarous despotism."

Cathcart was especially grieved that while he and other Americans were "miserable exiles from the country for which we have fought," back in the United States "negroes have even had a share in your deliberations and have reaped the benefits arising from your wise and wholesome laws and regulations, and we, the very men who have assisted in all your laudable enterprises, are now cast off."[24] Black Americans had also fought for independence and had assisted in other laudable enterprises. This is a disturbing note to find in a captivity narrative. Cathcart did not feel that his captivity was wrong because he was a man entitled to liberty, but rather because he was a white man. Though other captives did not draw the color line as clearly as Cathcart did, the color line runs throughout American captivity narratives. Black Americans were taken captive in Algiers, Tripoli, Arabia, and Mauritania, but none of them, unfortunately, wrote about the experience. They do appear in the narratives of others and in the fictional accounts of captivity. While captives of all nations who sailed on American ships—German, Irish, English, and American—found common ground as captives in Algiers, this commonality did not cross the color line. Differences among captives in rank, or the place of capture, or the reasons for captivity are insignificant compared to the difference of race. Black captives had the additional burden of exclusion from the solidarity of other captives, of being treated differently not so much by their captors as by their fellow Americans. Cathcart may have been unique in contrasting his own suffering in Algiers with the good life enjoyed by blacks in America. But he was not unique in seeing an insuperable barrier between white and black, any more than Huckleberry Finn's father was unique in seeing it as an injustice that a black man could be a college professor and be able to vote.

Captivity did not break down the barrier of race, even as it reinforced for the white captives their common identity as Americans. When the ship *Commerce* was wrecked on the Arabian coast in 1792, only one of the thirty-four sailors was sold into slavery. He was Juba Hill of Boston, the only black man on the ship. Hill was immediately separated from the white sailors and segregated with thirteen East Indian sailors from the *Commerce*. When Hill called out "in the greatest distress" to his white friends and fellow Americans to rescue him, the Arabs were shocked that he spoke English and tied him up. Hill kept pleading with the whites to stand by him, but the white sailors, expecting at any moment to be tied up themselves "or to be instantly put to death if we made any resistance," were deaf to Hill's increasingly desperate calls for help. As they listened to him plead and shout, the whites resolved among themselves that if the Arabs "siezed on any one of us," the whites would either "rescue him, or die in the attempt."[25]

It turned out that the Arabs weren't interested in any of the white sailors. The Arabs carried on an extensive slave trade in East Africa and had no use for white slaves. Having stripped the white sailors of all their valuables, including, they thought, their "slave" Juba Hill, the Arabs left the whites to their fate in the desert. The Arabs eventually sold Hill to another desert band for sixty pieces of silver, and according to one of the white survivors, this "black man from Boston" remained "among the Arabs, probably as a slave." As a slave, he might have survived with his Bedouin captors. Only eight of the twenty whites survived. [26]

In 1807 a Tunisian ship stopped an American merchant brig in the Mediterranean, and the Tunisian captain ordered all the American seamen paraded on deck. He fixed his eye on two American sailors, both mulattoes, and demanded to know what country they were from. They were Americans, their captain said. But he had no proof, except that they had come with the rest of the crew from the United States. The Tunisian captain "had heard Americans played tricks," and said the two men looked like Muslims, even though they were clean-shaven. They were the same color as Muslims, and the Tunisian captain thought they only pretended not to understand Arabic. Algiers and Tunis were at war, and the bey of Tunis needed all of his children home to fight the Algerines. The Tunisian took the two Americans with him. The other American sailors could not prevent this impressment, and without the two men, the brig was so short-handed that it had to put in at Alicante. The American captain planned to bring the matter to his government's attention. Again, as with Juba Hill in Arabia, the white Americans protested, but would not defend a black American.[27]

When the merchant ship *Oswego* was wrecked off the Moroccan coast in 1800, Jack and Martin, two black American sailors, stayed with the Bedouins—"probably from choice," according to Consul William Simpson. Three years later, Simpson had accounted for all the other crew members, but not for these two. They may have stayed of their own free will, or they may have become slaves to the Bedouins. There is evidence to suggest either alternative but not enough to draw a conclusion. In 1801 Tripoli, then at war with the United States, captured the American brig *Franklin*. Most of the crew were not Americans and were released to their own governments. But four were Americans, whom President Jefferson identified to Congress as the "Captain, one American seaman, and two others of color." The Tripolitans did not distinguish between the Americans of different colors, the American President did.[28]

Scipio Jackson was a black man from New York captured by the Algerians in 1793. Like the other American sailors, he was put to work in the shipyard. John Foss wrote of Jackson's death as an example of Algerine cruelty. Jackson fell ill, and after some days in the Spanish hospital, an Algerine work master forced him back to the shipyard. Jackson worked as best he could for half an hour but was not working hard enough for the supervisor, who beat him to make him work harder. Jackson collapsed and died that afternoon.[29]

A happier day in Jackson's life was recorded under the heading "Anecdote of an American Black" in James Wilson Stevens's *Historical and Geographical Account of Algiers*. This episode was intended as comic relief from the picture drawn of Algerine cruelty, and to show how the captives amused themselves and used practical jokes to lighten their hard lives. One day, after the "Moors and slaves" had finished their work in the shipyard, they gathered around a caldron of couscous. The men pushed their way to the front of the crowd, where "one of the Americans took Scipio by the heels, and pitched him head foremost into the kettle." Scipio struggled in the porridge until a Moor dragged him out. He was "whitewashed" but otherwise unharmed, the men laughed, and some of the couscous was served at the dey's palace.[30] The practical joker might have tossed into the kettle any man who happened to be in front of him—the joke may have had no racial overtones. Perhaps captives played such tricks on one another frequently to relieve the boredom and tension of their lives. There are few practical jokes recorded in the captivity literature, and this episode, which makes Scipio the butt of the joke, is in stark contrast to the solidarity the white captives display against the hostile Muslim world. Scipio is called "An American Black," not an American captive. He is tossed into the kettle by a white American; he is pulled out by a Moor. The other captives all laugh; it is not recorded if Scipio did.

Black captives could also use humor to alleviate their misery. James Riley, whose ship the *Commerce* was wrecked off Mauritania in 1815, learned this at the hands of a black slave named Boireck. Every night, between evening prayers and midnight camel milking, as Riley and the Americans tried to rest, Boireck would entertain the Arab women and the camp slaves with a comedy show. Boireck "always had plenty of spectators to admire his wit, and laugh at his tricks and buffoonery," most of which were aimed at the American captives. Boireck showed his audience what pathetic creatures the Americans were, poking at their badly sunburned bodies with a stick, saying they "could not even bear the rays of the sun (the image of God, as they termed it) to shine upon us." Boireck maliciously addressed Riley as "rais," or captain, mocking the title of power once worn by this now naked and helpless shadow of a man. The Arab women, almost as powerless in this society as Boireck or the captive Americans, particularly enjoyed the black slave's "waggery," and they kept up "a constant roar of laughter until midnight," when it was time to milk the camels.

Riley understood what Boireck was doing, but the other

American captives did not. James Clark complained to Riley that it was bad enough to be "reduced to slavery by the savage Arabs," to be "stripped and skinned alive and mangled," but to have to bear the "scoffs and derisions of a d—d negro slave" was more than he could bear. Like Cathcart, Clark could not stand the idea that a black man had it better than he did. Riley told Clark to "let the negro laugh if he can take any pleasure in it; I am willing he should do so, even at my expense: he is a poor slave himself, naked and destitute, far from his family and friends, and is only trying to gain the favour of his masters and mistresses, by making sport of us, whom he considers as much inferior to him as he is to them."[31]

Boireck, Riley saw, was trying to survive in a way that made life bearable. Through his ridicule of the Americans, Boireck established his own superiority over them. Riley, too, would use any means he could to survive, and his ordeal gave him a deeper understanding of slavery and power. Riley's ordeal will be more fully explored in a subsequent chapter. He learned in his captivity a lesson that eluded Clark and Cathcart. As long as Americans owned slaves, they could not be free. Riley's ordeal in the desert tested his character, just as Maria Martin's captivity tested hers.

Americans held captive in the Muslim world were not slaves in the sense that Americans understood the word. Their Muslim captors understood slavery to mean one thing, whereas the Americans took it to mean something else. For the Americans, slavery was an arbitrary and permanent restraint on freedom. For the Moroccans, Algerians, or Arabs who captured American sailors, slavery was a temporary condition by which strangers could either be ransomed and returned to their own country or adopted into Muslim society. For the Americans, slavery represented shame and a denial of humanity: This definition held true in America. The American sailors could not accept slavery and continue to be Americans. Captivity in the Muslim world was thus a test for the character of the Americans who endured it.

The Muslim states, on the other hand, accepted former slaves into positions of power and influence. Any man who accepted Islam became a brother in the faith; by contrast, Americans drew sharp lines between those who could join their political society and those who could not. The bonds of American identity held, as men did not renounce their country. But in forming one set of political bonds Americans did not break the other stronger bonds of race and class. Captivity tightened those bonds. American officers maintained discipline over American men, and white sailors watched their black comrades carried off into slavery or laughed as they pitched them into pots of couscous.

Captivity in the Muslim world tested the characters of the men who endured it, but it also tested their nation's character. The individual captives were faced with the questions of how much they could endure and how much responsibility they had to their brothers. Would they steal their clothes to buy liquor, as some sailors on the *Philadelphia* did, or would they expend every ounce of energy to save one another from slavery and death? At home, the American people had to ask what kind of nation they were if they allowed their countrymen to remain captives, and what kind of government they had established if it would not redeem its citizens from Barbary captivity.

I · FIRST ENCOUNTERS

Captain John Smith, who would later found Jamestown, Virginia, began his career as a mercenary fighting the Turks in Eastern Europe. He was captured by the Muslim enemy and here is shown taken captive to the bashaw of Nalbrits. Smith, though, did not accept his captivity; he killed his captor, stole his horse, and escaped. Smith would remember the outcome of this encounter later, when he arrived in Virginia and signed a treaty with Powhatan.

Capt. SMITH led Captive to the BASHAW of NALBRITS in TARTARIA, Chap. 12 of *The True Travels, Adventures and Observations of Captaine John Smith, in Europe, Asia, Africke, and America...* ([London, 1629], Richmond, Va. 1819). Courtesy American Antiquarian Society.

Capt. SMITH Killeth the BASHAW of Nalbrits and on his horse escapeth. *The True Travels, Adventures and Observations of Captaine John Smith in Europe, Asia, Africke, and America...* ([London, 1629], Richmond, Va., 1819). Courtesy American Antiquarian Society.

Westerners came to see the Muslim world as a lawless place where man's savage nature could only be controlled by unrestrained power. This nineteenth-century watercolor shows the ruler of Tripoli, armed with three knives and a sword that looks curiously like a snake. His power to control his nation can ultimately destroy him. "Sidi Hassan, Bey of Tripoli" (unknown artist, after 1813). Courtesy Boston Public Library, Print Department, The Holt Collection.

This seventeenth-century Dutch or German portrait of a Moorish king could just as easily be a portrait of an American Indian ruler. Europeans often drew a parallel between the desert dwellers—Berbers and Tuaregs—and the Native Americans, seeing both as living simple lives, with a potential either for noble simplicity or savage barbarity. "Ein Konig der Mohren in Orient" (Caspar Luyken, n.d.). Courtesy Boston Public Library, Print Department, The Holt Collection.

These two nineteenth-century prints show the dual image Westerners had of Muslim women. Westerners lamented the repression of Muslim women, symbolized in the first print by this woman's complete concealment. In the second print, the concealment has given way to uninhibited sensuality as the Moorish dancer removes her layers of veils. The confinement of women, at least according to Western men who lamented it, might have been necessary to prevent these kinds of erotic displays.

(left) "Mauresque (en ville)" (unknown artist, ca. 1840). Courtesy Boston Public Library, Print Department, the Holt Collection.

(right) "Danseuse Mauresque" (unknown artist, n.d.). Courtesy Boston Public Library, Print Department, the Holt Collection.

The sultan grants the sultana and other women of the seraglio the privilege of walking in the gardens four or five times a year, according to this engraving. The white eunuchs make sure that no one is within 100 paces of the garden walls, and the black eunuchs accompany the ladies on their walk. Plate XX, Aubry de la Motraye. *Travels through Europe, Asia, and into Part of Africa* (London, 1723), Vol. 1. Courtesy Boston Athenaeum.

This scene shows a Circassian man (figure g) trying to sell his two daughters (figures e and f) to a Persian merchant (figure h). "Five Standing Muscovites." Detail, map of Caspian Sea, from Aubry de la Motraye, *Travels through Europe, Asia, and into Part of Africa* (London, 1723), Vol. 2. Courtesy Boston Athenaeum.

Stephen Decatur is seen at the lower right center, in mortal combat with the Tripolitan captain. The action occurred during the bombardment of Tripoli, 3 Aug. 1804. "Decatur Boarding the Tripolitan Gunboat," painting by Dennis Malone Carter. Courtesy The Naval Historical Foundation.

The Intrepid had been turned into a floating bomb which Captain Richard Somers and twelve men tried to bring secretly into Tripoli harbor. Discovered before they could reach the walls of the Pacha's castle, they preferred "Death and the Destruction of the Enemy, to Captivity and a Torturing Slavery," and detonated the ship themselves. Somers and his

men, all killed in the blast, were immortalized in Navy lore. Three years later Lieutenant Henry Wadsworth's sister, married to Stephen Longfellow, honored her heroic brother by naming her first son Henry Wadsworth Longfellow. *Blowing up the Fire Ship Intrepid.* Courtesy Beverly R. Robinson Collection, United States Naval Academy Museum.

In contrast to the Turkish, Circassian, Moorish, or black African women, who would accept life in the harem, the American/English Maria Martin resisted the advances of a Turkish ruler in Algiers and was put in solitary confinement.

CHAPTER SIX

The Muslim World and
American Benevolence

For eight years after 1785, two dozen Americans languished in Algiers, wondering when their country would redeem them. In 1793, when Algiers captured 100 more Americans, their country could no longer ignore the plight of the captives. Across the United States, individual citizens discussed the best way to bring the captives home, and some pressed their government to act with more vigor and dispatch. Their government insisted that it was doing all it could, and when individual citizens promised to take action on their own, the government rejected their offers of charity. The debate took on a meaning beyond how best to bring the captives home. George Washington's administration, believing it had been elected to conduct international policy, thought private citizens who tried to ransom the captives were interfering with the government's job. Some private citizens, believing it more important to comfort the afflicted than to protect presidential prerogative, asked what kind of people could leave their brothers in chains. For a time, humanitarians accepted the government's claim that it was doing all it could, having faith in President Washington's benevolent heart. But the humanitarians could not promise to remain complacent as they engaged in long, painful soul searching in 1794 and 1795, asking what would be the fate of a people who ignored the cries of the enslaved. In this debate, we can see the beginning of a struggle between complacency, or support for the status quo, and the benevolent zeal of humanitarians more concerned with doing right than with preserving peace or order. The benevolent spirit would ask, what good was peace or order for many if its price was slavery for some? In the debate over Algiers, the humanitarians knew that Washington, whatever his protests of presidential prerogative, was moving toward the same goal, though along a different path. But in the subsequent debate over American slavery, the humanitarians, asking the same moral questions, would see the nation's leaders moving not only on a different path but toward a different goal. Later humanitarians knew what fate lay in store for a people who ignored the cries of the enslaved. They would face not only the moral indifference and complacency that greeted the 1795 movement, but also public antagonism and hostility from men in power.

In early 1794, when news of the Algerian captures reached the United States, some Americans tried to help their fellow citizens. In Salem some concerned citizens formed "a Small Society" to raise money "for the relief of the known prisoners in the hands of the Algerines." In Philadelphia, Republican businessman Stephen Girard and others formed a committee to raise money to relieve the prisoners. These efforts, and others like them, raised small amounts of money that the contributors hoped would either alleviate the captives' suffering or purchase their freedom. While the focus of those giving and those organizing the charity was individual donation, some pushed in addition to have their government act more quickly. In April 1794, an anonymous citizen calling himself "Benevolence" wrote to Secretary of State Edmund Randolph, reporting that in New England "the Sufferings of our Citizens among the Algerines" was the universal topic of discussion, and that farmers all across New England were ready to contribute: No one pledged less than a dollar, and Benevolence himself promised ten guineas. Benevolence did not want to dictate policy to the president, but he thought that Washington could encourage a national contribution. This would merely be organizing the American people to do what they already wanted to do. If Washington issued a proclamation urging the people to contribute, and the proclamation was read in churches throughout the country, Benevolence was sure that a "Prodigious Sum" would be raised, and Washington would have the satisfaction of leading the American people in the right direction.[1]

Benevolence did not know that the president had already rejected this idea. Five years earlier, in 1789, shipping magnate Mathew Irwin, owner of the captive ship *Dauphin*, had proposed just such a public contribution to President Washington. Irwin had both a humanitarian concern for the captives and a financial interest in their redemption, but he also warned Washington about the stigma that would fall on a government unable to protect its citizens abroad. Irwin suggested that President Washington encourage merchants and others to give money to redeem the captives. But Washington did not like the idea of using his public office for what seemed a private benefit. He was even less comfortable with the idea of private citizens stepping in to do the government's job. Protecting American citizens, Washington agreed, was the government's responsibility. If individual Americans started redeeming the captives, it might hurt the United States's difficult negotiations with Algiers. He was "not satisfied that it would be proper" for him to propose or endorse "a subscription among the merchants and others…to raise a fund for delivering these unhappy men" from bondage. Though President Washington promised to "cheerfully give every aid" he could for the captives' release, he thought private subscriptions would hinder negotiations, which Secretary of State Jefferson was then conducting. Taking care of the captives was the new government's job, though Washington could not tell Irwin whether Jefferson's negotiations would succeed.[2]

Irwin had a financial stake in what the government did: He wanted the United States to get his ship back and to protect his other merchant ships in the Mediterranean. Others, like Stephen Girard, urged action for political reasons: Girard's benevolent committee actually was formed to counter pro-British American policies and to support republican France's war against England—the suffering captives were an afterthought. Girard and other republicans knew that England had instigated the Portuguese–Algerian truce, and this deed, letting loose the "barbarians of Africa, to plunder and enslave the citizens of the United States," became another grievance against Britain. These selfish or political motives made Washington distrust the motives of those like Benevolence, who supposedly had the suffering of the captives at heart. As to the question of what kind of government would allow its citizens to remain in slavery, Washington knew, as Jefferson had, that if the United States was too eager to redeem its captives, the Algerians would know that captured Americans were a valuable prize.[3]

Washington was in no mood in 1794 to let individual citizens dictate public policy. His administration had just suppressed a rebellion in western Pennsylvania, where citizens had decided that a federal excise tax on whiskey was wrong, had refused to pay it, and had prevented tax collectors from trying to get anyone else to do so. This episode of lawlessness, Washington thought, had been encouraged by private citizens who had formed Democratic-Republican Societies to debate political issues and press for particular government policies. Though the proponents of charity, and of speedy redemption of the captives, claimed to be moved by sympathy, they were still trying to tell elected officials what to do. As for their idea of raising money privately and sending it on their own to Algiers, that would be taking the law into their own hands, just as the western Pennsylvanians had decided they did not need to obey the excise tax law.

This charged political atmosphere prevented the national sympathy Benevolence hoped to see. In a message to Congress, Washington condemned "self-created societies" that tried to dictate policy to the government. Washington blasted the Democratic-Republican Societies and groups like the one Girard had helped form in Philadelphia, which set themselves up as an alternative government, organized in opposition to duly elected representatives. Though there were profound differences between the humanitarian New Englanders who wanted to raise money to relieve the prisoners in Algiers and the Democratic-Republicans who did not want to pay taxes on whiskey, both were groups of private citizens who did not have to answer to anyone but themselves, who organized to direct government policy. Washington was consistent enough to recognize the similarity, and he opposed the charity movement as an intolerable interference with government prerogative.[4]

But Washington's ringing silence on the issue was compromised in July. His former aide David Humphreys, now American minister to Portugal, had been commissioned to negotiate a new treaty with Algiers. Humphreys had been secretary to the American commissioners in Europe—Jefferson, Adams, and Franklin—when they had first taken up Barbary affairs in 1785. Jefferson, as secretary of state, turned to Humphreys to handle Algerian negotiations when his other agents, John Paul Jones and Thomas Barclay, both died in 1793. Humphreys was deeply moved by the plight of the American captives, and he thought it essential to rally American public opinion on their behalf. He sent a long message to be printed in American newspapers calling for a national lottery to raise money to redeem the captives.

This confused the issue. Everyone knew that Humphreys was in Washington's inner circle, and since Humphreys was supposed to negotiate with Algiers, his "Address" appeared to be official policy. Humphreys wrote that the United States did not need to negotiate a treaty before redeeming the captives;—the policy of making peace first and getting the captives later, he said, was wrong. It would actually help the treaty negotiations to have the hostage matter out of the way, and redeeming the captives for a few hundred thousand dollars would solve the problem. Meanwhile, Humphreys emphasized the humanitarian necessity for action. The plague, "that terrible scourge from Heaven," was raging in Algiers, "that city of human misery," and unless the captives were redeemed quickly, they would die in Algiers. Humphreys, a poet, reminded the American people that some of their "brave fellow citizens," who now were "crowded promiscuously into close prisons," had "fought the battles which established our independence." He might have embellished these images, but he knew that "Imagination can place before the mental eye the horror of such a situation, better than description."[5]

Another Washington aide, Benjamin Lincoln, was now customs collector in Boston, and was confused when he read Humphreys's Address. Lincoln knew what Washington's policy was, and he recognized that Humphreys was going against it. He therefore sent his copy to Secretary of State Edmund Randolph, asking for instructions. Lincoln knew that if a private citizen addressed such a letter to the American people, calling for a change in government policy, he, like most of the American people, would simply ignore it. But Humphreys was close to Washington, and he had been sent to handle the Algerian negotiations. Was he blurring the distinction between his humanitarian sentiments and his official duty?[6]

Secretary of State Randolph agreed with Lincoln. By the time Randolph received the Address from Lincoln, it had appeared in a number of American newspapers. People were stirred by Humphreys's description of the captives' plight, and thought he was speaking for their government. Randolph had the delicate task of reprimanding Humphreys while not alienating him, and refusing the American people's generosity while praising them for it. Randolph said the lottery Humphreys had proposed would be unnecessary since the government had already appropriated $800,000 to "soothe the Dey into a peace, and ransom." And though the government could not accept private contributions to conduct the public business, Randolph said he would forward any private contributions to the captives in Algiers for their temporary relief. Meanwhile, Randolph had to tell Humphreys to keep his private feelings from dictating his public course. His Address, Randolph went on to say, "has not been exempt from criticism." Some readers (Randolph did not mention Benjamin Lincoln or anyone else) felt that excessive humanity had prompted Humphreys to show his feelings publicly in a way that "resembles an appeal from the Government to the People." This was in direct opposition to government policy. The people had elected the government, and the people should trust the government to conduct its business. Having said this, and having corrected the humane ambassador, Randolph told Humphreys he still had full confidence in his abilities, and he had appointed J. F. Gabriels, a Mediterranean merchant, as consul to Algiers. But Gabriels would not be going since Randolph could not "discover where he is." So, Randolph said, he had commissioned a Danish captain named Heissel to carry on negotiations. Heissel would not go either—and that was a good thing since, unknown to Randolph, he was a British spy. Humphreys may have wondered, after reading of Randolph's problems in finding a reliable agent, how his own humanity had hindered negotiations.[7]

Just as Randolph and Lincoln had feared, Humphreys's Address gave the appearance of government sanction to private benevolence. Though no governments, state or federal, followed Humphreys's suggestion to hold lotteries, private citizens urged action. Over the next few months, newspapers were filled with various pleas from anonymous humanitarians, some of them probably clergymen, touched by the suffering in Algiers. The proposals advanced by these benevolent writers shared two features: All suggested ways to redeem American captives from their Algerian servitude, yet all reserved their strongest criticism for a morally complacent American public. These humanitarian calls to action condemn Algerian or British action less than they do American inaction. Though all agreed that Algiers has acted wrongly, the real crime, for these writers, was that individual Americans had not acted at all. What kind of people are we, the writers asked, to remain silent while our brothers are in chains?

In Boston, an anonymous writer calling himself "Heraclitus" asked in November 1794: Why did the Americans ignore the captives? Why did they "desire to remove, from our sight, their sufferings, our duty, and the wrongs which we do them?" How could Americans calmly sit "under the shade of the tree of liberty" and watch as "our brothers and friends" groan "under the yoke, and the lash of demons?" He did not know what to say about those "who can, unconcernedly, suffer their countrymen to remain in a state of slavery, worse than death."[8]

Heraclitus was shocked at the carefree, luxurious life Americans were enjoying while they ignored those less fortunate. Rich people sometimes spent as much on one dinner party as it would cost to redeem a captive and "restore us our friends." Theaters were packed on benefit nights for a favorite actor or actress, yet on a night set aside to raise money for the captives, "the house was not nearly full." Americans were more interested in stage players than in real-life sufferers, and they put their "own pleasures" before their duty, particularly their duty to alleviate "the miseries of others." Heraclitus contrasted the real sufferings of the American captives with the fictional suffering of the "prisoner of the pathetic STERNE." Laurence Sterne's *Sentimental Journey* had a profound influence on the slavery debate. "Disguise thyself as thou wilt, still slavery! said I,—still thou art a bitter draught; and though thousands have been made to drink of thee, thou art no less bitter on that account." Sterne had found it impossible to write effectively about the multitude of slaves, focusing instead on "a single captive," seeing him in the dungeon, drawing his pathetic picture "through the twilight of his grated door." Just as Sterne could not feel the powerful sympathy for the many that he could for an individual, Heraclitus feared that Americans could not feel for real captive Americans the same sympathy they felt for Sterne's fictional captive. Americans had become distracted by fiction, plays, the artificial gaiety of parties and the good life, and so had forgotten the real moral imperative of helping the less fortunate and of living by the golden rule.[9]

"The subject does not admit of moderation," Heraclitus warned. "To be cool, on such a subject, is to conspire with the tormentors of our countrymen." He was proud to be a zealot in the cause of liberty and urged others to join in the imperative duty of restoring their fellow citizens "from the depth of human woe, to the most contrasted state of happiness." No task would be more pleasing to God or man than to pluck fellow citizens from a place "where *tyranny* stalks in all its horrors, to the land, where *liberty* gives (or ought to give) a new character to man." But Heraclitus feared that liberty had not given Americans a new character; instead, it had made them indifferent to the misery of others. While Americans reveled in their liberty, they forgot that divine Providence had given it to them. Ignoring the captives was arrogant, and this indifference to misery suggested that Americans now vainly thought that their own efforts, not God's will, had made them free and prosperous. To forget the captives was to say that "*our hands have wrought this;*" our winds wafted us these riches; our own sun ripened these fruits; our understanding, which procured our wealth, is self-existent; and it is our power and wisdom, which subject the passions of men to government, and secure to us the quiet possession of property." The captives were a reproach to a people who could forget that they relied on God for the blessings of liberty. Heraclitus was aroused by the sufferings of Americans in Algiers, but more so by the prospective suffering of Americans in America if these attitudes prevailed. Like later antislavery zealots, Heraclitus exhorted his fellow citizens to end slavery to save their own souls.

Heraclitus chastised Americans for their indifference to suffering but singled out American women for their superior benevolence. American women, he said, were more interested than American men in the captives, and were more likely to be moved to take action to relieve their suffering. By endorsing a role for women in the work of benevolence, Heraclitus underscored the idea that the mass movement relied on individuals first, the government last. Women, after all, had no formal role in American politics. But they had a great role to play in this national public debate and an essential role in directing national policy toward humanitarian goals. It was imperative that women act both to redeem the captives—if Americans waited for their government to do something, Heraclitus feared, it would mean death for most of the captives— and to shape the character of the American people. By setting a humane example, by giving up "some of the ornaments of dress, for the beautiful and attractive ornament of an act of humanity," American women could not only free the hostages but restore the American republic's health. Their example would encourage American men to give up luxurious high living, "which saps the health of the constitution, and which probably pampers corrupting parasites," and instead show by their virtuous action the republic's robust moral health.

These philanthropic Americans could not accept the idea that their benevolence might interfere with the government's policies. By taking action themselves, Americans would actually make the government's job easier. Heraclitus followed Humphreys in arguing that the captives were an obstacle to a peace treaty, and their release did not need to be part of a general negotatiation. As for the idea that it would tarnish the government's dignity to rely on private charity, he thought it would be much more undignified for the American government to "stoop to the Algerine state." More important, it would be sinful for Americans to wait for the government to act, to defer to official policy makers, if that deference prevented Americans from performing their moral duties. It was blasphemous to think that state policy could prevent individuals from fulfilling their obligations to God. Heraclitus wanted to pierce his fellow citizens' "ears with the groans of the captives, and penetrate their hearts with anguish," to move them "to discharge their first duty to God, their first office to man, and to exercize the noblest prerogative of human nature."

In Marblehead, Massachusetts, "Essex" also knew the powerful effect Sterne's sentimental fiction had on his readers, but he did not condemn them for it. He quoted Sterne: "Disguise thyself as thou wilt, still, slavery!...still thou art a bitter draught; and though thousands in all ages have been made to drink of thee, thou art no less bitter on that account." But while Essex expected that most of his readers were familiar with this passage, and were equally moved by it, he was disappointed that so few shared his zeal for the captives in Algiers. News of their suffering, he said, had "set my soul on fire," but he had heard no one else talking about their ordeal and had seen no plans made for their redemption. "That a subject so important should be treated with so much tacit contempt, I lament, and conclude that it is as with eternity, which hath so often passed our lips that it hath forgot its way to our hearts." He rejoiced that he drenched his own pillow with tears shed for the captives, that he spent sleepless nights agitated by their suffering, thinking of their children and their "more than widowed spouses."

"Ye citizens of America," he asked, "who sit under your own vines and fig-trees, and have not to make you afraid—who repose in festive bowers—Can ye reconcile yourselves to give them up to a perpetual servitude, worse than death? Can ye forget the cause for which you and they mutually shed your blood?" Americans at home enjoyed the benefits of that Revolutionary suffering every day, while that shared suffering was a bitter memory to the captives since the independence they had bled for had led to their capture, and must add "another lash and lick to the Algerine whip and chain." The captives must "execrate the battles they have won" for their heartless and forgetful countrymen. "America," he asked, "can you...forget your sons, and leave them to beg bitter bread through realms their valour saved?" Did Americans want it said on their judgment day that the captives "were in Algiers, and ye righted them not?" Essex asked the Salem *Gazette's* editor to keep this issue alive, to carry in each paper "the lamentation of America, *O my Sons! My Sons!*" Essex, like Heraclitus, was moved by the sufferings of the captives but more shaken by the apathy of Americans. He asked what kind of people could forget their sons and brothers.[10]

In Philadelphia, "Humanitus" asked what had happened to Girard's committee, formed in the spring, to free the American captives. Their benevolence was "worthy of the American character," but Humanitus lamented that too many of his countrymen were complacent, "our minds only agitated now and then with a few perturbations," while the captives in Algiers were "hourly groaning under the chains of slavery, the stripes of cruelty, and the yoke of servitude." Like Essex and Heraclitus, he hoped to spur his countrymen to action.[11]

Washington would have no part in the charity movement, but the charity's promoters used him in spite of his opposition. On January 1, 1795, flushed with victory over the Whiskey rebels and pleased at the country's continued neutrality in the European war, Washington set aside February 19 as a day for the American people to thank God for "the manifold and signal mercies which distinguish our lot as a nation," in particular for the blessings of governments, "which by their union establish liberty and order"; for keeping the United States at peace, both at home and abroad; and for continued prosperity. Like Heraclitus, Washington wanted the American people to remember that God had bestowed these blessings; that the American people had a solemn duty to remember their source; and that God expected great things from a people to whom so much was given. Washington, like Heraclitus, wanted Americans to free themselves from the "arrogance of prosperity," to make their nation "a safe and propitious asylum for the unfortunate of other countries," and to prepare to extend American blessings to "the the whole family of mankind."[12]

Washington did not mention Algiers, an oversight ignored in New England, where Heraclitus and Essex had seen in the plight of the captives an indictment of the national character. These benevolent writers seized on the thanksgiving day as a time to raise money for the hostages. Though Washington intended the day as a time to reflect on the nation's peculiar character and on its safe deliverance from European problems, these New England humanitarians thought it impossible to consider Americans as exempt from the world's troubles, or blessed among nations, while some of their brothers were in chains. Within weeks of Washington's proclamation, New Englanders were campaigning to make February 19 a day to collect charity for the Algerian captives. President Washington had already rejected the idea of private charities doing the government's work. He was not given a chance to squelch this appropriation of his own Thanksgiving Day by people doing what their hearts dictated but what his policy rejected.

A Portsmouth, New Hampshire, writer issued a plan for a national contribution on February 19. This writer, like Heraclitus and George Washington, knew that Americans were waiting for divine judgment. Washington was the most confident of the group, though he worried about the arrogance of prosperity and the consequences of straying from the path of neutrality. The Portsmouth writer was not

so sanguine. He began his piece with Jesus's curse on the wicked—
"Sick, and in prison, and ye visited me not." (Matt. 25:43).
Americans needed to attend to the most degraded of their brothers
if all were to prosper.[13]

Again unaware of Washington's refusal to join in the charity
movement, the Portsmouth plan called on the "AUGUST PRESI-
DENT OF FREE-BORN MILLIONS" to urge the "ministers of
the benevolent Jesus" to use the thanksgiving day to raise money. At
a word from Washington, Americans would "heap the altars of
benevolence" with "free-will" offerings. Was it possible, the writer
asked, quoting the president, to *"review the calamities, which afflict so
many other nations"* and forget the greatest calamity of all, servitude
and death in slavery? "God forbid! This cannot be." If Americans
were "susceptible to the finest impressions of humanity," as he
believed they were, then the "sons of freedom" who had already
shown an unrivaled willingness "to relieve the wretched" would
surely "rise and redeem the solitary captive."

The Americans would make February 19 a blessed day, when four
million of them would devote themselves to charity, giving "LIFE a
second time to the dead." The redeemed captives were to be resur-
rected from two deaths, for in Algiers they were dead both "to themselves [and] to their country." The petitioner went on to connect
America's purpose with God's purpose. The "Patriots of seventy five"
were "heroes of both worlds," were "legislators giving freedom to an
universe," and their heirs were enjoined to carry on God's charitable
work, certain in the knowledge that God's will was "freedom to the
universe."

Though Americans were God's special messengers, it did not
speak well for them that they had to be goaded into carrying the
message. The petitioner was not as critical as Heraclitus had been of
Americans' social habits, but he was more critical of their moral
habits. He addressed different groups—Fathers, Husbands, Brethren!
Senators and Representatives of a Happy People! Governors of the
Several States! Ministers of Immanuel! Daughters of Columbia! In
each of these capacities, Americans had failed.

Did the "exemption from the scourge of foreign wars," cited by Washington in his proclamation, really furnish a cause for national gratitude? Could the captives join in the national rejoicing? Their fate was more horrible than a foreign war, since "the captive of the belligerent European, or American hostile powers, is the prisoner of HOPE," who waited to be exchanged under a treaty. But to the captives, "to us, to us alone, the hope of return is denied. We are prisoners in the prison of despair."

Congress came in for severe criticism: "What nation under heaven hath left her seamen in hopeless captivity? What power on the surface of the globe…hath not paid down the sums demanded for release?" Was the treasury empty? Had it been drained by fighting the "savage hordes on the frontiers" or by suppressing the Whiskey rebels? State governors were called on to issue their own proclamations so that the "individual republics" would join "in undivided fellowship of federal communion." The "land of our fathers, and we their sons as yet unsubdued by slavery, shall follow the standard of Massachusetts, if again it beams on the western mountains; or spread with the unfurled eagle of America, were…rebellion lifts the insolent head." Liberty for the captives was inseparable from the union of America. Suppressing the Whiskey rebels had not drained the treasury but was a necessary step toward America's greater role in restoring international order. The "all-potent energy of gold" might direct the rest of the world's policy, but Americans would be charitable.

Though critical, the writer did not despair. All money raised on February 19 should be forwarded to the U.S. Treasury, where "if a Hamilton still serves his country, he will faithfully register the utmost farthing." The nation would rise up, and the captives would live to see the day when "that heaven-born charity wings her flight to this palace of mammon, and by the all-potent energy of gold dissolves the wreathen chains of slavery, and unlocks the double-locked gate of the awful dungeon." The petitioner asked his readers to imagine themselves prisoners in Algiers, to feel their suffering, and then, "casting an eye towards your native country, whilst the bitter tear rolls down your cheek, and the agonizing sigh rends the tortured bosom, hold forth the PRESIDENT'S proclamation in your left hand" and stretch out the other homeward, to "the free-born sons of Columbia," who prepared to redeem them.

This Portsmouth plan, critical of Americans, was echoed by real and fictitious voices from Algiers. On January 26, Boston's *Federal Orrery* printed a "Petition of the American Captives, in SLAVERY, at ALGIERS" endorsing the idea of using February 19 to raise money for their release. Though the petition was signed "Richard O'Brien," it was most likely written by a New England clergyman.[14] This purported O'Brien petition was echoed by a real voice from captivity. Captain William Penrose had written to a friend in America in the fall of 1794; his letter was published throughout New England in February 1795, just before the thanksgiving day. Captain Penrose asked, "what in the name of GOD can our countrymen be about?" Dey Hassan, Penrose said, wanted to be on good terms with the United States, but the Americans were "too haughty to come to an understanding with him." The American failure to redeem the captives, or to provide them with food or clothing, "will remain a stigma on the American character." In contrast to Holland and Spain, which had redeemed their captives, America, "the freest country upon the earth," left its citizens, "who have fought and bled" for its liberty, languishing in chains, toiling from dawn to dark. The American prisoners could not stand much more. "Human nature must sink under the pressure of such accumulated misery," Penrose warned, and the captives were giving up the idea of liberty. He could not believe his country had forgotten them but wondered what the American people were doing.[15]

Organizers of the charity movement knew the human heart too well to rely solely on moral condemnation. Even while they condemned American indifference, the organizers praised American generosity. Weeks before the thanksgiving day, its promoters hailed it as a success, praising the American people for their exceptional generosity. Under the headline "Anticipated," Boston's *Federal Orrery* on January 29 reported that "a spark from the altar of charity had kindled the flame of benevolence throught the continent," and that

Boston had contributed far more than was expected, raising $20,000, enough to redeem one captain and eight seamen. The churches had never been so crowded, the paper reported three weeks before the churches opened their doors, and women who did not have cash cheerfully gave rings and jewelry. In Virginia, the Boston paper reported, the planters "did honor to themselves, by giving from 100 to 150 a-piece," even though only one Virginia ship was in Algiers. In Boston, a philanthropist who did not want to be outdone *put into the contribution box* 1000 DOLLARS, IN BANK BILLS." These tremendous contributions had "never been surpassed in ancient days, and perhaps will not be equalled again in the memory of man."[16]

Not to be outdone, Newburyport's *Impartial Herald* anticipated the thanksgiving day on February 3, mentioning the "benevolent liberality of a gentleman of this town, who, it is said, generously gave 'FOUR THOUSAND DOLLARS.'" Anticipated contributions added up as the paper reported that congregations throughout New England planned to join in. Reports from Marblehead and Maine said that people there planned to give "more than ever was given upon any charitable occasion." Hearing these anticipations from other states, "AN INHABITANT OF PORTSMOUTH" feared that New Hampshire was "ambitious of distinguishing itself" for inhumanity and injustice, and called on the people of his state to "rouse from their lethargy" and contribute. Fearing that people who could not afford to give $100 or $1000 contributions would stay home, he promised that "the widow's two mites, were accepted in ancient days, and will be accepted again."[17]

But the lack of official support hurt the cause. Washington had not mentioned the charity, though its promoters claimed him as an ally. Salem called a special town meeting to make plans for the contribution day but adjourned when it decided that the town could not legally direct the churches to do anything. A Connecticut writer signing himself "Ecclesiasticus" criticized the Portsmouth plan, as it was not "addressed to us from any existing authority" or "sanctioned by the name of an individual." He said that the government, not individual citizens, was responsible for the captives. Private citizens and churches should not "anticipate the measures of a government" that they had elected. Though Ecclesiasticus sympathized as much as anyone with the captives, he would wait for Congress and the president to act, and he was certain that when these elected officials set a policy, "all will be ready to hasten" to follow it. The recent example of "self-created societies" trying to hinder the government's actions was too fresh in Ecclesiasticus's mind to allow public benevolence to interfere with public policy. Ecclesiasticus had faith that the government would attend to the captives. But even if the government did nothing, if "they have not thought fit to adopt measures" to redeem the captives, he was sure they had good reasons for this failure. Ecclesiasticus trusted the men he had elected, even if writers like Heraclitus said that these men needed moral guidance. Maybe the government was waiting "until we are in a situation to prevent the increase of captures," and he predicted that the captures certainly would increase if Americans started sending large ransom payments for the men already already in captivity. This would be a result that "*Real charity*" would deprecate.[18]

Ecclesiasticus said he was just as sympathetic to the men in Algiers as any other writer, and he was just as concerned with the nation's moral character. By allowing their duly elected leaders to act wisely, Americans would show that they were guided not by personal sentiment but by rational leaders, and their "sensibility" would form a contrast both to the anarchic French, who were not governed by any order, and to "the cruelty of those who insidiously opened the gates and let loose upon us the Furies of Algiers," the British. Complacency was not a sin as long as Americans elected moral men to office and let those men fulfill their constitutional duties.

Though Washington did not comment on the charity movement, the administration did manage at the last minute to subvert it. On February 17, a Baltimore paper printed a story, which it claimed came "from government, which entirely superceded the necessity of carrying into execution the proposed plan for the rede . ption of our brothers in chains."

The papers reported that David Humphreys, whose plea for the captives had stirred Americans the previous fall, had arrived in Philadelphia to confer with President Washington. It was widely reported that "there are very favourable prospects, that a Peace with *Algiers* will be concluded." Though the paper later retracted its prediction and said that the original story had not come from the government after all, this timely publication may have dampened public enthusiasm for the contribution even as it allowed Washington's administration to reassert its role in public policy.[19]

For whatever reasons, the thanksgiving day did not raise the anticipated sums. In Salem, William Bentley reported that "the House was thin. The Contribution for the Poor exceeded 10£.... There was not a contribution in all the congregations, nor in such as contributed for the poor only." Portsmouth, New Hampshire, where the idea had originated, raised only $650. A Dutch reformed congregation in Albany gave $130. The church in Freeport, Maine, raised $90, and other Maine towns raised from $20 to $100 each. Brunswick promised to contribute when its minister returned from a trip.[20]

The Maine towns discovered that the lack of official sanction caused another problem: Having raised the money, they did not know what to do with it. When the Maine clergy initially had argued that they had no authority to raise money, one parishioner answered, "Do we wish for AUTHORITY to 'relieve the distressed and comfort those who mourn'[?] We have it, and from the hand too of an all merciful God!" But having found divine sanction, the Maine contributors discovered that they needed a worldly auditor. They asked the Boston papers where to send the money and who was to ensure that the captives got it. "At present we act in the dark—but are in weekly expectation of some communications from your press upon the subject."[21]

Though the thanksgiving day was a failure as a charity, it was a success in other ways. The Boston *Mercury* reported that "Federalists and Antifederalists, Jacobins and Republicans of all denominations" had joined together on the day to count their mutual blessings, and "the spirit of party lost much of its force" as they embraced one another. "Every heart palpitated with warm satisfaction, every face beamed the glow of pleasure, every tongue pronounced…gratitude for our unrivaled prosperity," but, as Heraclitus and Essex had feared, the captives were forgotten in the glow of national prosperity.[22]

The thanksgiving day sermons, as Washington had intended, focused on the American people's virtues, not on their moral short-comings. Virtually all the sermons elaborated on the themes Washington had suggested: that America had escaped from the turmoils of the Old World and that the American people had a special purpose. "Who is like unto thee?" Abiel Holmes asked his Cambridge, Massachusetts, congregation, and considering the world, he concluded that no one was. Africa, once home to flourishing commercial states, now "lies buried in profound ignorance and barbarism." The people of Asia, living in a vast and fruitful territory, were condemned by their governments never to see "the light of science, of true Religion, or of Liberty." In all of Asia, only the Tartars and Arabs were truly free, and Holmes did not think much of either their dignity or their happiness, comparing the Tartars to American Indians and saying that the Arabs were "thieves and pirates." In Virginia, Bishop James Madison, president of William and Mary College and cousin of the future president with the same name, spoke of how "our fore-fathers, amidst the wreck of human rights and the convulsive tempests which ambition had so often overwhelmed the nations of the east," still preserved a "small portion of that ethereal spirit, that ardent love of liberty, which glows in the American breast."[23]

In Marblehead, Reverend Isaac Story was an exception in focusing his thanksgiving sermon on the captives. Story preached a sermon the Sunday before the thanksgiving day encouraging his Congregationalist parishioners to open their hearts and pocketbooks on the following Thursday. He took Exodus 2:10 as his Sunday text: "And the child grew, and she brought him unto Pharoah's daughter, and he became her son. And she called his name Moses, and said, Because I drew him out of the water." Story ranged with this text over a number of profound issues: the captives (whom he hoped his congregation would help draw back across the water), American relations with England, the character of George Washington, and the nature of American society. Story reminded his parishioners that Pharoah had tried to suppress the Israelites, who had wanted to secure "the rights and the privileges of freemen." This was not the first time, nor would it be the last, that the story of Moses was appropriated by a people as a parable for their own struggle against oppression. Story compared Moses and Washington, who both had a "disinterested spirit, and esteemed the interest of his nation before any other consideration." Moses had renounced a position in Pharoah's court to espouse his country's cause, just as Washington had done. But Story took this comparison in a new direction, shifting the emphasis from Washington to others like Moses, "who have made the most distinguished figure on the pages of history," those "drawn from the water," with no advantages of birth, who had risen to lead nations. Moses had been educated to greatness, not born to it. Given a similar education, any child could grow to greatness, and Story told his parishioners that children of the town's poor, children of beggars, "by and by may rule the town" if the town saw to it that they were educated. Story told his congregation that they had a moral duty to educate the poor, to uplift the degraded and debased slave.[24]

Like Heraclitus and the other petitioners, Story worried that his congregation would fail to do their moral duty. Having told them to educate the poor, he asked them to imagine themselves prisoners in Algiers, chained to the oar and ignored by their countrymen. The abandoned captives must curse their heartless brothers at home, but the conscienceless Americans should most fear the wrath of God. The captives did not want to "rest as a constant burden upon you; only redeem them and they will help themselves, and may perhaps hereafter help you or yours." By educating Moses, Pharoah's daughter had done the world enormous good, a deed more glorious than "all the grandeur of the Court," more valuable "than all the jewels and ornaments of thy dress." The American people, like Pharoah's daughter, had it in their power to do great things. Their power went beyond teaching the children or freeing the captives. These acts were means to an end, enabling the American people to decide what kind of nation they were. Would they choose the jewels of the heart or the jewels of the court? Story's thanksgiving day message was that "a public spirit in a private sphere is a grateful spectacle" and a magnificent thing. This was the message Heraclitus and other proponents had hoped to get across on this day, though only Story rose to the occasion.[25]

Proponents of public charity, like Story, who wanted to see a public spirit in the private sphere, might have been surprised to hear their benevolent impulses compared with Whiskey rebels and French Jacobins. If they were surprised to see their humanitarian zeal attacked as a step toward anarchy, Samuel Seabury of New London, Connecticut, must have been amazed to see his benevolence attacked as a step toward monarchy. Seabury, the Episcopal bishop of Connecticut and Rhode Island, had learned too late about the Portsmouth plan. Nevertheless, he wanted to participate, and on February 19, the day of thanksgiving, he published a letter in the largest papers in his diocese calling for the Episcopal churches in Connecticut and Rhode Island to contribute on the third Sunday in March. He signed his letter "SAMUEL, Bp. of Connecticut and Rhode Island."[26]

Seabury was immediately condemned for assuming an "abusive title" by a writer who signed himself "Connecticut & Rhode Island," and who savaged Seabury for adopting a "courtly stile" and issuing a *"right reverend and right royal mandate"* from the "episcopal palace" in New London. This anonymous critic condemned Seabury's "pompous expression of priestly pride and charity," and on behalf of the "SOVEREIGN PEOPLE" blasted the bishop for using a title without either *"divine approbation"* or public consent. Neither the state nor the federal constitution, nor the "voice of the people," sanctioned bishops, and Seabury showed an "an alarming expression of aristocratic pride, and thirst for domination" by calling himself Biship of Connecticut and Rhode Island instead of the *"would be* Bishop of Connecticut and Rhode Island," or Bishop of the three dozen churches that recognized him as such.[27]

This anonymous writer remembered that Samuel Seabury, as an Anglican minister in New York in the early 1770s, had opposed the move toward independence and had engaged in a pamphlet war with young Alexander Hamilton in the years before the Revolution. Now, this critic charged, Seabury was an "arrogant citizen of a nation whose freedom he opposed," ignorant that in the new land "formed of the Cardinal virtues" there was no need for "those gaudy tinsels the mitre or crown." Seabury's simple gesture of benevolence had stirred issues far more urgent than the fate of 100 men in Algiers. This anonymous critic remembered the fear before the Revolution that England was preparing to impose an established Anglican church, complete with bishops and trappings of Catholicism, on Congregationalist colonies. The tension between church and state had not been resolved. Virginia had passed its act granting religious freedom only ten years earlier; few other states had followed.

In Connecticut, where the Congregational church dominated society, the thanksgiving day had been virtually ignored, since it fell during Lent. A writer calling himself "Plain Truth" accused the Congregationalists of insulting the people and government of the United States by failing to honor Washington's proclamation. In defense of the Congregationalists, a "Churchman" turned the issue into one of separation of church and state, of obedience to government or obedience to God. "We live in a time which boasts of its light, especially in the rights of man," the Churchman said, "and in a country which boasts of its candour and liberality of sentiments— where the rights of conscience are equal and secure." This Churchman said that Washington had proclaimed a day of thanksgiving during the church's season of fasting, and the Congregationalists had been left with the choice of obeying their religious obligations or their secular duties. The Congregationalists had disregarded a political act that ran against their religious tenets. Ecclesiasticus had warned his readers not to let their religious zeal overwhelm their sense of political decorum. The Churchman also argued for the separation of political and religious obligations, but for him this meant that government should leave religion alone, not that religious men

and women should not meddle in government. These arguments—
about church and state, about government's responsibility, about people's rights and duties—all emerged from the suffering of American
captives in Algiers. The captives were lost in the argument, as their
countrymen seemed to forget their distant suffering in the storm of
debate about the present and future prospects for the nation the captives had left behind.[28]

Three days after the thanksgiving day, there was another day of
national rejoicing as Americans celebrated George Washington's
sixty-third birthday. In Philadelphia, 150 ladies and gentlemen,
including most government officials and the diplomatic corps,
attended a ball and supper given in honor of Washington. One of the
toasts raised in tribute to the president neatly stated his position on
the captives. "Our fellow citizens in Algiers—May the exertions of
our government be soon rewarded by their liberation." These exertions were rewarded, and the government under Washington proved
itself equal to the task. Later in 1795, the United States and Algiers
agreed on a treaty, and two years after that, a few days before
Washington turned sixty-five in 1797, sixty of the surviving captives
returned to the United States. Their presence at various Washington's
birthday celebrations increased the "the joy of the day," one paper
said. In Gloucester, Massachusetts, former captive Samuel Calder
received throngs of his fellow townsmen and "expressed in the most
lively sense, his gratitude for their affectionate attention." His callers
returned to their homes "to reflect on the pleasing occurences of the
auspicious era."[29]

Joel Barlow, who had negotiated the Algerian treaty, recommended that charity be given the redeemed captives, some of whom were
now unable to support themselves. But Barlow acknowledged that it
would be "impertinent" of him to tell the government what to do,
and left it up to the government of the United States and the
American people to decide who should support the captives. The
Federalist *Gazette of the United States* praised Barlow, a Republican,
for his modesty and recommended that other Republicans follow his
example and let the government make up its own mind. The *Gazette*

was pleased to note that many of the captives were able to find jobs and quickly went back to work.[30]

The U.S. government and the Federalist administration felt it had already done enough for the captives by spending $800,000 to bring them home. The sixty captives who arrived in Philadelphia in February 1797 received nothing from their government. Their presence in the capital did not move President Washington to endorse public or private charity. But other individuals were touched by these sufferers. Throughout the winter of 1796 and 1797, an entrepreneur named St. Mary had been entertaining Philadelphia with his elephant. He was planning to leave for Baltimore, but when the captives arrived and he read Joel Barlow's plea for charity, St. Mary and his elephant stayed in Philadelphia. He announced a special benefit showing of his elephant for the captives, stating that he would donate all proceeds to them. He invited the redeemed men to honor his elephant with their presence at a special performance. Some of the ransomed captives came to see St. Mary and his elephant; other curious Philadelphians came to see both the elephant and the men who had suffered so much. The captives saw the elephant, St. Mary gave them the day's receipts, and the redeemed men left Philadelphia, taking with them all they would receive from their government.[31]

Captive John Foss, who had asked in 1794 what was taking his countrymen so long to redeem him, praised American generosity in his 1798 memoir:

> This generosity of the United States to us their enslaved countrymen was of inestimable value. It was more precious from being unexpected. No nation of christendom had ever done the like for their subjects in our situation. The Republican government of the United States have set an example of humanity to all the governments of the world.

This national generosity had taught the "merciless barbarians" to see "the character of the Americans...in the most exalted light," and the Algerians exclaimed that "the American people must be the best in the world to be so humane and generous to their countrymen in slavery."[32] In retrospect, American generosity, which had been the subject of so much controversy in 1795, became the decisive factor in freeing the captives, and indeed the decisive mark of the American people's special character.

Captivity in the Barbary states forced Americans both in captivity and at home to decide what kind of people they were. This task of defining character was somewhat easier for the men in captivity, who had only to survive to prove themselves. Most did survive. Some wrote of their experiences, and others took captivity as one of the consequences of their sea-faring lives. For their countrymen at home, captivity raised a number of troublesome issues. What kind of people are we, some asked, to leave our brothers in chains? Those asking this question were gravely concerned with their nation's moral character. Others were more vexed by the nation's political character. Some asked, why elect a government if we presume to do its job? Others asked, what kind of republican government does not want its citizens to participate in it? None of the answers posed to these political or moral questions of character seemed entirely satisfactory. The redemption and release of the captives resolved one issue, but the underlying problems their captivity had brought to the surface persisted: slavery, the government's power, and the American people's moral capacity to deal with both of them.

CHAPTER SEVEN

American Consuls in the Muslim World

The years between 1796, when the United States concluded a treaty with Algiers, and 1801, when Tripoli and the United States went to war, were quiet years when not much of significance seemed to happen. But to overlook these years is to misread history. If we ignore the years of peace between the United States and the Barbary states, we might infer that war was the natural state between the two worlds. We might mistake the hostilities between the United States and Tripoli for a continuation of the American–Algerian war; we might see it as an inevitable development and so fail to understand how wars start; and we might fail to grapple with the difficult problems of diplomacy and commercial relations between people, societies, and nations.

When John Adams became president in 1797, the United States was at peace with the Barbary states but on the verge of war with France. The war with France would preoccupy his administration, as French cruisers preyed on American merchant ships, and American and French war ships fought in the Caribbean and other places. A Boston insurance company reported in 1798 that France had captured nearly $200,000 worth of American shipping the previous year, Britain $40,000 worth. The Barbary states had only captured one ship, the Boston schooner *Eliza*, valued at $13,000. France was a much greater threat to American commerce than the Muslim states of North Africa. Though the Mediterranean seemed safe, Adams was not going to ignore it. He was determined to preserve the peace, and told Congress that though the United States could not hope to avoid friction with the Barbary states, or problems "arising from the misconduct or even the misfortunes of our commercial vessels" in the Mediterranean, the United States could minimize these problems by having a consul general in Algiers, who would have broad political as well as commercial responsibilities.[1]

Adams had already chosen Richard O'Brien to be consul general at Algiers. O'Brien, a prisoner in Algiers for ten years (1785–1795), had been de facto American consul in Algiers during his captivity, acting as spokesman for the other American captives and advising the string of actual agents and consuls the United States sent to negotiate with the dey. He corresponded with Adams, Jefferson, John Jay, and the U.S. Congress, and they all came to rely more on O'Brien for advice on Barbary affairs than they did on the formal agents they sent to negotiate. After his release in 1796, O'Brien opened negotiations with both Tripoli and Tunis. In the United States in 1797, he oversaw the construction of three cruisers commissioned by Dey Hassan. The State Department asked for O'Brien's views on Barbary affairs in the spring of 1797, and O'Brien wrote two long reports covering the whole range of American policy and interests in the Mediterranean.

O'Brien recommended that Joel Barlow, who was still in Algiers acting as consul after successfully negotiating the 1795 treaty, go to Istanbul, where he could "counteract the Christian nations influence" with the sublime porte. But Barlow was not interested in the mission or in staying in Algiers, though O'Brien thought Barlow was most qualified for the job. O'Brien knew the United States needed to send a good man to Algiers as consul general—and quickly. When no better-qualified individual came forward, O'Brien agreed to go.

O'Brien knew that the United States needed to act on its own; it could not trust Christian Europe for any favors. France was at war with the Americans, and O'Brien remembered that the British had instigated Algiers to go to war with the United States in 1785 and 1793. It was a grave mistake to look for friendship among the European powers or to expect any kind of Christian solidarity against the Muslim states of North Africa. O'Brien's years in captivity, and his experiences as a merchant sea captain negotiating on docks all over the world, had given him a clear, unsentimental opinion of human nature and international relations. He shared this view of power relationships with the dey of Algiers, who told him that in international politics the great nations "make laws to serve them," and "the large fish Eats the little ones." O'Brien recognized that the Barbary states operated outside the bounds of international law; they had "nothing to do with Blackston[e] or Vattel," whom the Barbary states, and O'Brien, saw as mere codifiers of European power relations. Despite their failure to follow a European interpretation of international law, O'Brien believed that the Barbary states were no worse than Britain or France, the large fish, which committed far worse depradations "then the people that is stiled pirates in Barbary."[2]

This conclusion was borne out when O'Brien arrived in Algiers in 1798. He found three American merchant ships in port, hiding from Spanish and French privateers. Peace with the Barbary states and with Turkey would give Americans more protection against the states of Europe and would help them guarantee commercial freedom in the Mediterranean. But if the United States did not act to preserve its peace with the Barbary states, O'Brien warned, "I have my fears that…it will fall through and all our hopes in being a sharer in the Valuable Branches of the mediterranian Commerce Blasted."[3]

In keeping with his view of power relations, O'Brien advised the United States to build a navy. He would greatly increase the six-frigate fleet then under construction, adding six battleships, six sloops of war, six brigs, six schooners, two smaller sloops, and a fleet of small cruisers. If this navy was too expensive, O'Brien proposed a scaled-down version—two battleships, two sloops, three brigs, three schooners, and twelve whaleboats, each carrying a six-pound cannon. The whaleboats could gather intelligence and carry messages, would be useful on lakes and rivers, and could engage in trade. The United States should set up schools to train sailors. O'Brien predicted that the next war, whether with France, Spain, or England, would be a privateering war, and a navy dispersed throughout the world, and American consuls in distant ports, would be a vital part of national defense. When the war came, O'Brien recommended that the Americans embargo their own ports, stopping American commerce and forcing "those fleets of Corsairs those sea robbers to return to Europe."[4]

Sending the marauding English and French back to Europe would be only one result of this embargo. By cutting the food supply to the West Indies, the United States could incite the slaves on those islands to rebel. The United States "has much of the fate of them Islands at present in its power," O'Brien said, and "the sooner the Negroes revolted the west india islands became independant Governed by the Blacks the better for this Country." Independence for the islands and freedom for their people would mean expanded trade for Americans. But O'Brien, having spent ten years in Algiers waiting for the United States to secure his own freedom, was not optimistic that the nation would seize its opportunities.[5]

In the Mediterranean, O'Brien wanted the United States to honor its treaties, promptly sending the military stores and other articles of tribute promised to Algiers, Tunis, and Tripoli. The treaty with Algiers stipulated that the United States would send the dey $20,000 worth of naval supplies every year. The United States had not promised annual supplies to Tunis and Tripoli but had promised large gifts. These gifts, and the gifts consuls were expected to give on arriving, on leaving, and on various state occasions, were the price of peace in the Mediterranean. O'Brien wanted the United States to secure this peace through prompt payment, and so achieve a neutral base in North Africa and the western Mediterranean against the depradations of Europe.

O'Brien reached Algiers in February 1798 on board the frigate *Crescent*, built in Portsmouth, New Hampshire, as a gift for Dey Hassan. When he and the *Crescent* reached Algiers, the *Muqueni*, an Algerian merchant ship, was unloading at Baltimore, the first commercial vessel from Algiers to cross the Atlantic. Despite these signs of improved relations, O'Brien found trouble in Algiers. The United States had so far failed to deliver the military stores promised by treaty, and of those that had arrived, the naval timbers and cannon-balls were too small (O'Brien learned that Algiers and the United States used different standards of measure) and the canvas was rotting. O'Brien had to borrow more money from David and Solomon Bacri, the leading Jewish bankers at Algiers, who had already loaned the United States $40,000 during the 1795 negotiations. In addition to this debt, the United States owed Algiers nearly $100,000 for two shipments of naval stores that had not arrived ($20,000 each), the gifts O'Brien as a new consul was expected to give on arrival, plus the customary biennial gifts, last paid in 1796. O'Brien borrowed another $40,000 from the Bacris, which he gave to the dey.[6]

O'Brien found American prestige very low in Algiers, the result of two episodes that show the problems of conducting honest trade in the Mediterranean. The misadventures of two ships—the *Fortune*, owned by the Bacris, and the Boston schooner *Eliza*—along with the American failure to send its tribute promptly, made many on the Barbary coast, merchants and rulers, Jews and Muslims, Algerians and Tunisians, distrust the Americans and consider them liars and thieves.

In January 1796 the *Eliza* was in Gibraltar, waiting for the United States to make peace with the "Mahometan powers." When the owner, Edward Rand of Boston, who was on the ship, heard rumors of peace, he decided to sail into the Mediterranean. The rumors were premature—Tunis and Tripoli had not yet signed treaties. Joel Barlow, still in Algiers, feared that Americans like Rand would foolishly sail into the Mediterranean on false rumors of peace. Barlow knew American captains would "sail into the mouth of hell" to sell their codfish if they heard rumors that the devil had turned Catholic.[7] Rand thought the Mediterranean was safe from the Barbary powers, and so perhaps let his guard down. In the French port of Adge, armed men robbed him of $8000, and the *Eliza* spent three months there waiting for the French government to catch the thieves or indemnify him. Neither happened, and Rand desperately needed to make up his losses. In June the *Eliza* sailed for Malaga, but was stopped by a Tunisian cruiser and claimed as a prize. Rand and the *Eliza* were captured the day before Tunis agreed to stop seizing American ships.

This run of bad luck for Rand made trouble for the United States. Joel Barlow, in Algiers overseeing the American negotiations with Tunis, agreed to pay the Tunisians $10,000 for the *Eliza* and its crew. He thought he could use the ship to carry the freed American prisoners from Algiers to Marseilles. The *Eliza* left Tunis carrying a load of wheat owned by the Bacris and by another Jewish merchant, Sampson, who sailed with it.

But the *Eliza's* misfortunes were not over. Captain Samuel Graves decided to punish Sampson "for what the Americans had suffered in Barbary," and had him flogged and dunked into the ocean. When the *Eliza* reached Sicily, Graves put Sampson ashore and sailed off with the wheat, which he sold in Cadiz. Graves had the *Eliza* repaired in Cadiz, charged the expenses to the U.S. consul there, and sailed home with the profits from Sampson's wheat.

Sampson made his way back to Algiers, where he protested the American's brutality to Dey Hassan. The dey, who was anxiously awaiting the late shipments of American tribute, demanded an explanation from Joel Barlow. "You are a liar & your goverment is a liar," Hassan told Barlow. Barlow knew the whole episode was a "most shameful & humiliating stroke, on the American character in Barbary." Jewish and Muslim merchants saw it as proof that the Americans could not be trusted, especially after they learned that Graves, not some unknown French thieves, had stolen Rand's $8000 in Adge. The Americans would not only steal from Jews and Muslims, they would steal from each other. Barlow knew that though his government could repay Sampson and the Bacris, the real "damages, in point of honour & character, will not be easy to calculate." But he managed to convince Dey Hassan that Graves and Sampson had had some sort of misunderstanding, that "probably...there was some blame on both sides," and that a storm had forced the ship to Sicily. He begged that Sampson not be punished for exaggerating, and he promised that the United States would repay him and the Bacris for their losses. O'Brien arrived in Algiers in 1798 with $6000 for them. Back in the United States, Edward Rand unsuccessfully petitioned his government for similar indemnification, arguing that the United States should have warned him about the Tunisians. The United States recognized, if Rand did not, that Tunisian pirates were the least of his problems.[8]

Barlow and the Bacris had another misunderstanding over the ship *Fortune*, which Barlow had leased from the Bacris in 1797 to carry the American prisoners out of Algiers. Since Algiers was at war with Genoa and Tuscany, Barlow did not want the crew of Americans, who had spent years in Algerian captivity, to be captured on their voyage to freedom and enslaved by the Italians. To prevent this, he allowed the ship to fly under the American flag. The Bacris saw that the American flag could protect Algerian ships from capture by Italians, so when the *Fortune* reached Marseilles, they asked the American consul there, Joseph Donaldson, who had helped negotiate the American—Algerian treaty, to issue a set of American papers for the *Fortune*. Donaldson obliged, and so the *Fortune*, owned by the Bacris but manned by Americans, former captives in Algiers, carried wheat from North Africa to Marseilles and even Genoa, protected by the American flag. But though the American flag protected the *Fortune* from Italy, England did not want anyone, under any flag, trading with France. A British frigate seized the *Fortune*, sent the crew to the United States, and took the Bacris' wheat as a war prize.

The Bacris were furious and demanded repayment from the U.S. Barlow was also furious and chastised Donaldson for giving the *Fortune* false American papers. He showed his diplomatic skill in getting out of this difficult situation. The United States was already heavily in debt to the Bacris, and he knew his country would need to borrow still more from them. "It is well known that the house of Bacri are the Kings of Algiers," he wrote to the secretary of state, "and that it is easier to oppose the Dey's interest than theirs." But Barlow threatened to expose the Bacris' role in this fraud to the dey, and he promised to repay the Bacris for some of their troubles. Relieved to escape these problems, Barlow left Algiers, leaving to O'Brien the problems of restoring American faith, credit, and character.[9]

O'Brien knew he did not have Barlow's diplomatic skill. The Americans could stall the Bacris, who were still willing to lend money as long as the United States promised to repay with interest. O'Brien could tell Dey Hassan that his tribute was being held up by hard winters and yellow fever epidemics. But O'Brien could not explain why yellow fever and frozen harbors and rivers were not preventing American merchant ships from coming to the Mediterranean. He came to realize that though his sound advice on Algerian affairs had earned him an appointment as consul general, it had not convinced the Adams administration to do as he said. Having sent him as consul, the United States ignored him, and neither honored its treaty commitments nor prepared for war which O'Brien knew was inevitable. If the United States chose not to honor its treaties, its only choices were war or withdrawal from the Mediterranean. "[D]epend Sir, we shall have war," he warned Secretary of State Pickering.[10]

O'Brien had already spent ten years in Algiers waiting for his country to secure peace. Now that it had peace, the United States did not seem interested in keeping it. The peace treaties with Algiers and the other regencies brought $1.5 million in annual profits to American merchants, O'Brien wrote; war would cost $1.5 million a year "and no profits." The United States had to "act with Punctuality or Energie" to secure these profits, avoiding "the Shoals that is under the Lee of the good Ship the CONGRESS." O'Brien would do all he could in Algiers for America's interests, but "I cannot be of service in this Country when I have neither money nor credit." He found himself "like unto a ship in a gale...trying...to keep within the latitudes prescribed." Until Dey Hassan received the promised tribute and the three cruisers he had commissioned the Americans to build, O'Brien could only stall, borrowing from the Bacris to pay off Algiers, Tripoli, and Tunis, "liveing in hopes of reliefe like unto a mariner on a wreck."[11]

When the *Lelah Eisha*, the first of the schooners Hassan had commissioned, finally reached Algiers in in January 1799, Hassan had been dead for nearly a year, and his successor, Mustafa Bobba, demanded it as a gift. After all, the United States had given Hassan the *Crescent*. Was he not also worthy? O'Brien, though he had no real options, tried to refuse. He could not give up the ship, he said; he had to rely on Mustafa to pay for it. Mustafa rejected the offer and ordered the red Algerian pennant flying from the *Lelah Eisha's* mainmast while in port, lowered as a sign that the ship was not welcome. If he could not have it as a gift, he did not want it. O'Brien responded with a bluff of his own. He ordered the American flag up in place of the Algerian pennant and a gun fired to signal war.

O'Brien had few options. Algiers, like the United States, was at war with France, and did not really want war with the United States, even though the Americans had given little proof that they would fight. He knew that the prime minister and the minister of marine wanted to keep peace with the Americans, but he also knew he could not prevent Mustafa from taking the *Lelah Eisha*. O'Brien might have stalled by asking for time to consult his government; perhaps that would give him another six months or a year. But he knew that his country would not respond quickly: The *Lelah Eisha* had brought O'Brien the first official news he had had from the United States in nearly a year. It was unlikely that the United States would respond quickly to any request for instructions and impossible that the instructions would give him the power to keep the ship.

Like Barlow, O'Brien found himself in a weak position. He decided to bargain with the appearance of strength. He knew the prime minister wanted peace, so he took a hard line, saying that his country had not sent him "to lavish away, their interests, & sacrifice my own character which I held in as high estimation as my life." If the dey took the *Lelah Eisha*, O'Brien warned, he would tell all American merchant ships to stay clear of the Mediterreanean, and the American frigates being built to fight France would instead come to Algiers. The United States did not want peace if the Algerians could not be trusted.

At this moment, the second of the ships Dey Hassan had commissioned reached Algiers. The *Hassan Bashaw*, O'Brien wrote, was "the most beautiful & compleat vessel" he had ever seen, and its "perfect order" and "regularity" impressed the Algerians, convincing them that "we have the abilities & resources in the United States to be a very active & stubborn enemy." The ship cooled the war fever in Algiers, and the dispatches it carried emboldened O'Brien even further. O'Brien read President Adams's message to Congress on the XYZ affair and was struck by the president's pledge never to send "another minister to France without assurances that he will be received, respected, and honored as the representative of a great, free, powerful, and independent nation." After reading this, O'Brien went to see Mustafa "as the representative of a great, free, powerful, & independant nation." O'Brien told the dey that he had "viewed the U.S. at war with Algiers & then at peace," and that he did not see much difference between the two. The Americans were prepared to fight, and the *Lelah Eisha* and *Hassan Bashaw* showed that the United States would now be a formidable enemy.[12]

But O'Brien still had little with which to negotiate. But when he learned that neither the prime minister nor the dey knew the exact terms of the American treaty, which required payment in naval supplies or in cash, he seized the opportunity to clear all American debts. He inflated the value of the American-built cruisers, which had cost $70,000 to build, telling the Algerians that they had cost over $100,000 and that Portugal had offered to buy all three for $120,000. Then he persuaded the dey to accept the two smaller ships, the *Lelah Eisha* and the *Skjoldebrand*, in full payment of American tribute and said that he would give the Dey the *Hassan Bashaw*. He said he consented to this only because the "United States found a pleasure...in encreasing the strength of Algiers in order to crush the French, who had turned robbers & persecutors of the Musselmen & of the Neutral Nations." O'Brien was giving up three ships but getting much more. He asked the dey for a written receipt and an acknowledgment that the United States was fully paid up. O'Brien was an experienced commercial seaman used to making bargains on the docks, and he did not want the dey to know that O'Brien had gotten the better deal. He told the dey he feared for his head when news of the bargain reached the United States. At this, perhaps, Mustafa realized O'Brien had outmaneuvered him. If

O'Brien lost his head, Mustafa said, "we should have a new consul here[;] one that did not so well know the place as you do."

As O'Brien was working his way out of the crisis, the other American consuls to the Barbary states arrived in Algiers. William Eaton was sent as consul to Tunis and James Leander Cathcart as consul to Tripoli. Eaton was a colonel in the American army whose friendship with Secretary of State Pickering had earned him his appointment. Eaton had never been out of the United States but had served on the Georgia frontier. His government considered his negotiations with the Creeks and Cherokees to be ample preparation for negotiating with Tunis. One American official told him before he sailed that the Barbary consuls were "a set of d–d savage agents—Indian agents—yes, a set of d–d Indian agents you Barbary consuls!" Eaton was inclined to agree. When the Algerian consul in Tunis professed friendship for the Americans, Eaton was not impressed. A Cherokee chief, he said, would do the same "for a bottle of rum and a rifle." In additional preparation for his mission, Eaton read Volney's *Travels through Egypt and Syria in the Years 1783, 1784, & 1785,* and he found Volney's descriptions of Turkish indolence and corruption even more apt in Tunis.[13]

O'Brien presented Eaton and Cathcart to Dey Mustafa just a few hours after the Americans on the *Sophia* fired a fifteen-gun salute in honor of George Washington's birthday. The dey asked what the Americans were celebrating, anticipating gifts for himself and his court in honor of the occasion. But O'Brien knew this and told the dey they had been drinking to his health. Eaton was impressed with O'Brien's diplomatic skill, particularly his "happy talent" of using *"secret arguments"* or bribes with his Algerian counterparts, "to which their *patriotism* does not forbid them to listen."[14]

O'Brien had been waiting for over a year to hear from the United States, and he told Eaton not to expect much support from his government. He advised Eaton to rely on his own wits, to "put your instructions in your pocket," or he would find himself "in a d'nd dilemma" with his government thousands of miles away. He must "concede to be governed by circumstances," stating that even if his country was inclined to direct his actions, it could not dictate his course "in variable winds on this treacherous coast." O'Brien compared the consuls to sea captains and the government to ship owners. During a storm at sea, he asked, would the captain have to write to the owners for permission to cut masts or throw guns overboard? Eaton agreed that in a crisis a captain would not wait for instructions, but that the owners could map out a general course to a destination. Eaton and O'Brien agreed on the destination, which was peace in the Mediterranean. They also agreed on the general course. The United States should fulfill its treaty obligations punctually and offer "*manly* resistance to *unjustifiable* demands." Eaton said simply, "Pay up and fight."[15] With their common outlook on American policy and blunt personalities, Eaton and O'Brien became friends, writing warm letters not only as fellow diplomats but as kindred souls in lonely outposts, corresponding in an idiom we would expect from a sea captain and a frontier soldier.

But despite their similarities and initial friendship, the relationship fell apart. Actually, the two were driven apart by the third member of the diplomatic contingent, James Leander Cathcart. Cathcart had been a prisoner in Algiers for ten years and had become Dey Hassan's chief Christian secretary. He accepted the post at Tripoli reluctantly, angry that O'Brien, and not he, had been made consul general. After all, Cathcart's experience gave him inside knowledge of Algerian affairs. He personally had given O'Brien his start in public life, on September 11, 1795, which Cathcart said was O'Brien's "political birthday," the day Cathcart had presented him to the dey of Algiers. Cathcart may have really believed that a man who corresponded with Washington, Jefferson, Adams, Jay, and the Congress of the United States was politically alive only when he met the dey of Algiers.[16]

Now Cathcart was miffed that O'Brien, not he, was made consul general and upset that another former captive, not he, had been made captain of the *Crescent*. He felt himself more than equal to either task. On the trip across the Atlantic on the *Sophia*, Cathcart had offended the captain by offering to run the ship. The captain declined the offer, becoming disgusted, as most people on the ship were, by Cathcart's "repulsive manners" and "sour, forbidding, self conceited" personality. The person most disgusted by Cathcart turned out to be Elizabeth Robeson, maid to Cathcart's pregnant fifteen-year-old wife. When the ship reached Algiers, Elizabeth Robeson demanded to be sent home immediately, refusing to go to Tripoli with Cathcart, whom she said had tried to seduce her. Instead of sending her home, O'Brien gave her refuge in the American consulate. Cathcart was offended by this, and then insulted when he and Mrs. Cathcart arrived for dinner and found Elizabeth Robeson sitting at the table. He would not make an equal of his servant, he said, stalking out with wife Jane in tow. That a representative of republican America would refuse to eat at the same table with a servant struck Cathcart as no more strange than the idea that political life came from the dey of Algiers. He refused to have any more to do with O'Brien.[17]

Eaton tried to conciliate Cathcart, telling him it was "useless to resent an injury which cannot be chastised—either knock the aggressor down, s[l]ap him, or pass the injury unnoticed—[.]"[18] Cathcart was not appeased. Two months later, Eaton, in Tunis, took a particular pleasure in sending word to the Cathcarts in Tripoli that O'Brien had married Elizabeth Robeson. "[A]las, poor devils, how they will be chafed on the occasion," Eaton wrote. "But be assured it gives great joy to—Eaton." Cathcart, offended at his servant's becoming his equal, was distraught when she became his social superior.[19]

In March, Eaton and Cathcart traveled on to Tunis, where three articles of the 1796 treaty needed to be renegotiated. The treaty had been negotiated by a French merchant, Joseph Etienne Famin, with a keen eye on his own welfare. He had inserted into the treaty an article setting a 3 percent tariff on Tunisian goods imported into the United States and on American goods brought to Tunis on American ships, but a 10 percent duty on European goods brought to Tunis on American ships. Since most Americans trading in Tunis dealt in

European goods, this article would in effect prevent Americans from doing business in Tunis, where they might compete with Famin. The United States had set a rate of 10 percent on most imports and had guaranteed to nations with "most favored" status that their merchants would not be charged rates higher than any other nation's. The 3 percent rate granted to Tunis gave Famin an advantage over all other merchants in the world but ultimately would destroy the American revenue system, since all "most favored" nations would enjoy the 3 percent tariff rate. Pickering told Eaton that this provision of the treaty "cannot be important to the Bey and Regency, tho' ruinous to us," and if Eaton managed to move carefully with Famin, he could renegotiate it.[20]

But Famin was a dangerous man. He was business agent for some important Tunisian merchants, including the sahibtapa, or seal keeper, Bey Hamouda Pacha's closest advisor. Famin also was offended that the United States had sent Eaton to look after American affairs, depriving him of a chance to profit from American trade. Secretary of State Pickering advised Eaton to *"anticipate"* Famin's claims and "prevent his *resentment.*" Eaton knew he had to act cautiously, but he was not surprised that the British and the Jewish merchants hated Famin. After all, Eaton knew, the British hated all Frenchmen, and the Jews saw Famin as a commercial rival. It was not criminal of Famin to secure his commercial position through political influence. He may have "secured to himself these friends to the mammon of unrighteousness," Eaton wrote, but neither international trade nor international politics were moved by righteousness. "[A]ccording to the world," Eaton wrote, "he has acted *wisely.*"[21]

Despite Famin's influence, it took the Americans only a few days to renegotiate the treaty. Eaton and Cathcart began by telling the bey that the 3 percent duties could not benefit him, since Tunisian merchants might never go to the United States. "True," Hamouda Pacha said, "my subjects have never yet been to America; but why do you hence conclude they never will?" The Americans patronizingly told him that Tunisians did not know the way to America. "Hitherto they have not known the way," the bey said, "but mankind are now becoming more enlightened and more enterprizing," and he hoped to send many vessels to America. Eaton did not appreciate the bey's appropriation of these two favorite American themes, enterprise and enlightenment. The bey and sahibtapa turned these themes to their advantage again when Eaton said the United States could not pay as much for their treaty as the Spanish, who got their gold and silver "in mass from the bosom of the earth: we get our cash in half pence, by laboring on its surface." The sahibtapa knew how to lead on the Americans. "You are however a strong and enterprizing people," he told them; they would soon take control of Spain's New World mines. Eaton and Cathcart responded that when they had the Spanish mines, they would give the bey a present.[22]

The Tunisians quickly consented to all the changes the Americans wanted, putting up only limited, playful resistance. The tone was set almost immediately when the Americans objected to a treaty provision requiring the U.S. to give the bey a barrel of gunpowder for every cannon fired in salute of an arriving American ship. Eaton and Cathcart said this degraded American honor. Hamouda replied, "You consult your honour; I my interest." It was in his interest to receive a barrel of gunpowder. If it would save American honor while benefiting his interest, he suggested that instead of a quid pro quo, the Americans simply give him fifty barrels of gunpowder every year. Eaton and Cathcart rejected this as "a proposition aimed at making us tributary," but they agreed to pay the Tunisians for any powder they used in saluting American ships. Feigning exasperation, Hamouda Pacha said he was not going to waste powder saluting strangers; he would only salute American ships that demanded recognition. The provision was dropped.[23]

After settling all points satisfactorily, Eaton distributed $6000 worth of gifts to the bey and members of his family and court. The prime minister complained that his gift was not as valuable as the sahibtapa's, and the admiral demanded a gold-headed cane, a gold watch, and twelve pieces of cloth. Eaton gave these men what they wanted, knowing he had to keep them on his side. But when the harbor master demanded a gift, Eaton said he would "as soon con-

tract to satisfy the grave, the barren womb, and the devouring fire" as
to try to satisfy this thirst for gifts, and he promised the harbor master a copy of the treaty. "Thus I have finished my first chapter of
accidents in this land of rapine and sodomy," Eaton wrote to
O'Brien. He was more convinced than ever that the United States
needed to show force in the Mediterranean. While negotiating and
distributing presents, he studied Algerian and Tunisian military
strength. These regencies, he said, "would hardly give a relish to a
british squadron—and would not furnish a breakfast to such force as
the United States could" send. While his government had sent Eaton
and Cathcart to cultivate peace and commerce, he was already imag-
ining military action. O'Brien agreed, but he knew that three regencies had "found by experience that when we are pushed we give
way." It became clear that his government either was not listening to
him or had no strength to show in the Mediterranean.[24]

Eaton and O'Brien kept the peace in Tunis and Algiers, but
Cathcart had not even stepped off the ship in Tripoli before he
brought on a crisis. Bryan McDonogh, Britain's agent in Tripoli,
came aboard to see Cathcart when the *Sophia* pulled into the harbor.
McDonogh may have sensed Cathcart's hatred for O'Brien and
played on it to his own advantage. O'Brien, he said, had wronged
him, too, and had failed to acknowledge McDonogh's valuable services in negotiating the 1796 American treaty with Tripoli. Despite
this, McDonogh said, he was still eager to help Cathcart and the
Americans. But Yusuf Qaramanli was in no mood to deal with the
Americans because O'Brien had also mistreated him. In 1796,
McDonogh said, O'Brien had promised to give Qaramanli a cruiser,
but he had never delivered it. The pacha would not receive Cathcart
until the Americans gave him either a ship (and McDonogh thought
the *Sophia* would do nicely) or $18,000.

Cathcart believed the worst about O'Brien, to whom he wrote to
protest the shabby way he had treated "our friend Doctr.
McDonogh." He borrowed the $18,000 from Leon Farfara, a Jewish
money lender, giving him notes payable by either Eaton or O'Brien,
gave McDonogh $800 for his help, and congratulated himself on

having corrected another case of O'Brien's perfidy. Cathcart did not know he had been taken. O'Brien had not promised a ship to Qaramanli, and McDonogh was a British agent.[25]

Minutes after Eaton learned of Cathcart's gift to the pacha, Farfara's agent was at his door in Tunis demanding the money. The United States had no credit in Tunis, and Eaton could not understand why Cathcart, who knew this, had written a bill payable there. Eaton had already made a personal loan of $2500 to Cathcart, but that was beside the point. Cathcart said that if he had not paid the pacha, he would have been beaten and thrown into a dungeon. "An *American*," Eaton wrote, "would have contemned the bragadocios menaces and despised his chains; he would have disdained to have sought this refuge." But unfortunately, Eaton wrote, Cathcart's ten years serving the dey of Algiers had made him unable to withstand these threats, had made him more terrified of "the nod of a turk" than of a " broadside of a man of war—such is the influence of habit, I may say education." As for McDonogh, Eaton saw him as "a renegade, and of course a rogue." Eaton did not like being put in the middle, having to either come up with cash for Farfara or risk war with Tripoli. If O'Brien had made this concession, giving Qaramanli or anyone else $18,000, he would have been censured for it. But despite Cathcart's error, Eaton did not think he should be fired. Though Cathcart had very little political savvy and no diplomatic skills, was a coward and had a knack for making people dislike him, Eaton believed he was honest, and he now had both a wife and an infant daughter. Eaton would not be responsible for taking the bread from a child's mouth, so he recommended that Cathcart be given more time to learn the ways of diplomacy.[26]

Eaton, having secured peace between the United States and Tunis, found it was more difficult to make peace between Cathcart and O'Brien. Cathcart answered Eaton's call for a truce with a catalogue of the wrongs he felt O'Brien had done him. O'Brien, he said, owed him money from the time when the two were captives, had campaigned against Cathcart's appointment to Tripoli after his release, and had added insult to all these injuries by marrying Cathcart's maid. Ater reading this diatribe, which filled seven printed pages, Eaton saw that Cathcart's "grievances with OB are not of a nature to be reconciled," apologized for mentioning the subject, and told Secretary of State Pickering that O'Brien and Cathcart "cannot allow each other any good qualities." He told Cathcart that Pickering looked on the feud "as the Chancellor of Heaven does the accusing spirit informing against the elect" and suggested to O'Brien that he simply leave Cathcart alone.[27]

O'Brien left Cathcart alone. Cathcart complained that O'Brien neglected him and did not respond in detail to Cathcart's long, rambling letters. Eaton summarized one Cathcart letter, which fills seven printed pages, in five lines: "Jews Distress Cathcart—Danger of Americans appearing at Tripoli—Danish Consul Arrives—Swedish Consul Departs—Corsairs go to sea with Swede passports." Cathcart's inability to condense his thoughts exasperated both Eaton, who felt compelled to read and respond to them, and O Brien, who did not. When Eaton passed along to O'Brien Cathcart's complaint that the consul general did not respond adequately to his dispatches from Tripoli, O'Brien wrote back, "The whole of Mr. Cathcart's communications amount to that in lieu of a printed Pass he has given a written one and 200 dollars—I forward you a letter in answr. to his sundry Volumes."[28]

Being long-winded is not necessarily a flaw in a diplomat, and even intense self-pity may be turned to advantage. But though Cathcart presented himself as an expert on Barbary affairs, he proved remarkably inept at understanding how his actions would be perceived by the people he was trying to influence. When the three consuls learned that George Washington was dead, O'Brien and Eaton both restrained themselves, knowing that the Algerians and Tunisians would consider any display of national emotion as an occasion for a gift. Gifts were given when a head of state came to power, took a wife, had a child, or died. O'Brien and Eaton knew that Tunis and Algeria would expect a suitable token of mourning when they heard that Washington was dead, even though he was no longer president. O'Brien confiscated all the American papers that carried news of Washington's death, and Eaton wore a simple black armband. When Hamouda Pacha asked the reason, Eaton simply said, "an aga of the camp...under whom I formerly served and whom I held in great veneration had died." This satisfied the Tunisian officials. Cathcart, though, ordered the flag at the U.S. consulate lowered, and had all the American ships in the harbor do the same and offer a twenty one-gun salute. He was pleased that all the European ships joined the salute. The noise caught Yusuf's attention. He seized this opportunity to ask again for the cruiser he had tried to get a year earlier. He told Cathcart that an additional $10,000 would appease his own grief at Washington's passing. This demand caught Cathcart by surprise, but O'Brien saw Cathcart's elaborate public mourning as the "source of the Nile," without which Tripoli would not have expected any gifts.[29]

Cathcart had not lobbied for the appointment to the Barbary coast to be a diplomat, so perhaps he did not think his diplomatic ineptitude important. Cathcart actually was anxious to involve himself in the Mediterranean trade, for which his service to the dey had given him a taste. Almost immediately on arriving in Tripoli, he had begun buying and selling goods to supplement his income. In July 1799, just a few weeks into his term at Tripoli, he sent a cargo of wine for Eaton to sell at Tunis, and in exchange asked Eaton to send him cloth to sell in Tripoli. "If the goods...arrives soon we will make a tolerable good spec," Cathcart wrote, and he told Eaton to make out two invoices for the cloth, one with the real price and the other inflated by 25 percent "for my government." Cathcart drew Eaton into a business partnership and looked for opportunities throughout the region. He wrote to Thomas Appleton, American consul at Leghorn (Livorno), anticipating a reopened commerce between Tripoli and Italy, "when I hope to have the pleasure of hearing often from you." He asked for a trade gazette, and told Appleton what goods he could sell in Tripoli and what goods Tripoli could produce.[30]

But Cathcart's initial venture into Tripolitan trade was disappointing. Leon Farfara, acting as his business agent, took some of

Cathcart's cloth to Yusuf Qaramanli, who kept it but did not pay for it. Cathcart raged against Farfara and against all Jewish merchants: "It is neither in the power or nature of a Barbary Jew to render a christian service," he wrote to Eaton, "'tho it often is to do them an injury." But mostly Cathcart raged against O'Brien. O'Brien, he believed, was deeply involved with the Bacris, the Jewish bankers who had already loaned the United States so much money. The Bacris had been Cathcart's competitors during his days in Algiers; now, he believed, they feared his commercial power. O'Brien needed the Bacris as a source of credit for the United States, and just as Barlow had said, O'Brien was reluctant to defy the Bacri interest. Cathcart ignored the crucial difference between his own private dealings with Farfara and O'Brien's public dealings with the Bacris. He lashed out at O'Brien for letting American interests suffer due to his involvement with Jewish bankers. Cathcart spent most of the winter of 1799–1800 trying in vain to get the pacha to pay him. Finally, he lied and told the pacha that an American fleet was on its way to Tripoli; the lie induced Yusuf Qaramanli to pay Cathcart.[31]

Eaton watched all of this, both O'Brien being compromised by his public reliance on the Bacris and Cathcart becoming embroiled in commercial misdeeds. In it he saw a lesson: that consuls should not engage in trade. It was impossible for a consul to be both a diplomat, representing the United States, and a private merchant, advancing his own interests. He could not serve two masters. But Eaton gradually became more deeply involved in Cathcart's schemes and justified his own commercial activity on the grounds of its compatibility with American interests. By becoming a merchant, Eaton argued, he could divert Tunisian trade into American vessels, which would benefit Americans, and he could teach the warlike Tunisians the benefits of peaceful commerce.[32] "Nothing was more distant from my ideas" than speculation, he told the secretary of state. He could cooperate with the sahibtapa's business ventures, and since the sahibtapa was both a leading merchant and the bey's advisor and lover, this commercial connection would would stabilize American relations with Tunis. Secretary of State Pickering agreed, telling

Eaton that the bey would be "under strong and lasting obligations to the Consul and nation who shall place him" in an advantageous commercial position. Blinded by this prospective benefit, Pickering and Eaton apparently forgot the real dangers if American consuls became traders. Eaton, too, forgot his earlier reservations, as he found trade had great short-term rewards. He wrote to Cathcart, "I am getting rich against my own inclination."[33]

Commerce, instead of making the world more peaceful, widened the war in the Mediterranean. The Bacris of Algiers, with strong commercial ties to France, pressed Dey Mustafa Bobba to break his allegiance to Turkey, which was at war with France, and instead go to war against England. Under the Bacris' influence, the dey turned Algeria's cruisers against Britain's allies, the Italian states, Portugal, and Russia. France and England and their allies needed Algeria's wheat, and both used their influence to get it. This experience of having England and France trying to woo him convinced the dey in O'Brien's words "that the world was like unto a Dutch cheese— under his feet & he kicking it. Every nation bows to the potent Dey," and this veneration made him believe that "he is Patroon Grandi of all the world." Algiers began attacking European ships but left the neutral Americans alone, as France in late 1799 was anxious to secure peace with the United States. In Tunis, the sahibtapa recognized the value of American neutrality to his own commerce and warmed up to Eaton. The sahibtapa hoped to use American ships, which alone were free from attack by France, Algiers, or England, to carry his own wheat to Spanish markets.[34]

Though Tunis was warming up to the United States and Eaton was getting rich against his inclination, he was soon reminded that the Mediterranean trade was dangerous. In 1800 Julius Cesar Alberganty, agent for the Livorno firm of Suame and Shwartz, came to Tunis to buy wheat. Suame and Shwartz wanted to buy up all the wheat in Tunis, driving up the staple's price in Italy. Tunisian merchants and agents of Algerian merchant houses invested heavily in the scheme, which would have yielded immense profits in North Africa had it succeeded. But it did not. In the summer of 1800

Suame and Shwartz collapsed, taking with them over $120,000 invested by Tunisian and Algerian merchants. This failure had potentially disastrous implications for the United States. Alberganty claimed to be an American citizen, and had also offered Eaton his services in exchanging bills of credit between Tunis and Algiers and Livorno. Eaton had declined the offer. Had he accepted, Alberganty would have been a recognized agent of the United States, whose government then would have been liable for Suame and Shwartz's debts. A delegation of Jewish merchants in Algiers, whose Tunisian agents had lost money to Alberganty, called on O'Brien to demand indemnification. Alberganty was an American merchant, they said, so the United States had to make good their loss.[35]

Though Eaton managed to get clear of Alberganty, he saw this episode as more than just a simple attempt by a merchant to go into debt at someone else's expense. Eaton's isolation in Tunis, far from home and caught between O'Brien, whom he liked but did not trust, and Cathcart, whom he trusted but did not like, preyed on a natural paranoia and pushed him over the edge. Eaton finally came to believe Cathcart's wild stories about O'Brien, and saw in Alberganty's schemes a conspiracy involving Algerian Jews and Italian Catholics to destroy him. Suame and Shwartz's collapse had caused "much commotion among *God's ancient covenant people*," and the Alberganty case convinced Eaton that Jews were a "treacherous, lying, hypocritical, dangerous race of men" who were now his commercial rivals, as well as his nation's chief creditors in North Africa. Eaton began to see O'Brien's indebtedness to the Bacris as treasonous. Was O'Brien so heavily in debt to the Bacris that he would subvert his country's interests to those of the Jewish bankers? He and O'Brien continued to agree on American policy in North Africa, but Eaton came to see O'Brien as his enemy in a vast conspiracy against him. When O'Brien cautioned that the U.S. government would not act, Eaton began to suspect that O'Brien did not want the government to act. If the Jews had tried to destroy Eaton, why did O'Brien continue to do business with them? Eaton would have nothing more to do with the Jewish bankers and strongly advised O'Brien to do the same.[36]

But O'Brien saw things differently. "As to the Algerine Jews at Tunis or at Algiers," O'Brien wrote to Eaton, "…you can act by them as you think proper." O'Brien knew that the Bacris could find better uses for their money than lending it to the Americans, who were not doing the Bacris a favor by borrowing it. The European war had cut off Dutch and Swiss credit, and O'Brien needed to borrow money since his government was chronically late in sending tribute. "If you Can borrow money at Tunis or in Europe to an advantage to the *U.S.* it should be preferred to the terms borrowed at Algiers for I would sooner do anything then beg & pray & afterwards *pay*." Eaton mistook this for an apology for being connected with the Bacris. On the reverse of O'Brien's letter, Eaton wrote, "A Jew Advocate!"[37]

In September 1800 the American frigate *George Washington* arrived in Algiers with the long overdue tribute to the dey. At the moment of its arrival, Mustafa was in trouble with the Ottoman sultan, and needed to send his own ambassador and tribute to Istanbul. The previous year, when an American mission to Istanbul had been planned, O'Brien had warned that if an American frigate stopped in Algiers on its way to Turkey, the dey might insist on its carrying his own ambassador along. Spain had allowed the dey to use one of its frigates for such a mission, but O'Brien thought the United States should not.[38] As O'Brien had feared, when the *George Washington* reached Algiers, Mustafa demanded that it carry his tribute to Turkey. O'Brien and Captain William Bainbridge, the frigate's commander, had no bargaining strength. Though the *George Washington* had brought the tribute, it had arrived late, and O'Brien had no money or credit. The United States was heavily in debt to the dey and to the Bacris. O'Brien and Bainbridge negotiated as best they could, and did get an American merchant ship excused from the mission. It would be easier for the Americans to keep their frigate if it carried the tribute than it would be to keep the smaller, unarmed merchant ship, and though O'Brien continued to believe war against Algiers would be necessary to prevent this kind of humiliation, he knew that the United States was not prepared for war. He and Bainbridge relented, and the *George Washington* made the first official American visit to Turkey.

O'Brien found the episode deeply demoralizing. He was in precisely the same position he had been in when he arrived in Algiers as consul general, and practically the same position he had been in when he had arrived as a prisoner in 1785. He took some solace in the fact that the *George Washington* had come at all: It brought word from the new secretary of state, John Marshall, that the Adams administration was now going to pay more attention to Barbary affairs. With the elevation of Marshall, John Adams took command of his administration, replacing the cabinet officers more loyal to Hamilton than to the nation. Marshall replaced Timothy Pickering, who had tried to undermine Adams's peace negotiations with France. But now O'Brien took solace in the administration's new direction. Marshall had pledged that "barbary affairs will be attended to," O'Brien wrote, and with the administration's new commitment to peace with France, the American fleet could now turn to Algiers. "All is right," O'Brien wrote, "That the People wills."[39]

But though the *George Washington* episode brought some solace to O'Brien, he could not help but be demoralized. He was deeply disappointed that his successor had not arrived on the frigate. "I am heartily tired of Barbary," he wrote to Eaton, noting that he had asked to be relieved in June. "—I think any employment in the US should be preferred to our despised rank in Barbary." On the day the *George Washington* sailed for Turkey, O'Brien wrote to Cathcart, who still blamed the consul general for maneuvering him out of the plum assignment to Algiers: "I...shall return to the *U.S.* I am sick of Barbary."[40] He blamed the United States for sending consuls to the Barbary states and then ignoring them, and he now urged not only an increased military presence in the Mediterranean—six frigates like the *George Washington*—but also military action. "[N]othing can make the U.S. respected or any other nation at Algiers but war," he wrote to Cathcart, and he asked, "Can we be a nation of Independant freemen and Suffer Those indignities[?]" War, he thought, was now preferable "to degradation and a state of Vassalage to The Scruff. of *Asia* & *affrica.*"[41]

O'Brien was weary as the *George Washington* sailed for Turkey, but William Eaton was furious. "Genius of my country!" Eaton exclaimed. "How art thou prostrate!" Was there not one American, he asked, "whose soul revolts; whose nerves convulse, blood vessels burst, and heart indignant swells" at this disgrace? His own soul, nerves, blood vessels, and heart did all of these things, and he never completely recovered. Eaton's real fury was directed at O'Brien, whom he now believed was a tool of the Bacris, who, Eaton thought, had arranged the *George Washington's* hijacking to fulfill some dark scheme of their own. Otherwise, Eaton asked, if the Bacris were as influential as O'Brien kept saying they were, why did they not prevent the "national degradation" of "an *American ship of war* pressed into the *service of the pirate of Algiers?*" This was "an *original sin*" that the "blood of all the Jews of Barbary cannot wash away," and it would "stamp original shame on our character."[42] Eaton charged that O'Brien had not resisted the dey's demand for the ship because he was part of the Bacris' plot, and further, that O'Brien was conspiring with the Bacris, the Jews of Tunis, the Catholics of Livorno, and the American enemies of Pickering to bring down Eaton. O'Brien had been relieved at Pickering's dismissal, but Eaton was irate. It was more than the loss of his patron. Eaton saw Pickering as an honest man, like himself, beset by conspirators. "[I]n G-'s name," he asked, "what has been the cause of Mr. Pickering's removal? If he be not an honest man I begin to suspect there is no such thing." All of these separate episodes—the Alberganty case, the *George Washington* seizure, Pickering's dismissal—Eaton saw as part of a dark conspiracy, and O'Brien was either the unwitting tool of the Bacris or the evil genius behind it all. The disagreement became a death struggle. "In short," Eaton wrote, "either OBrien or Eaton must fall!" He added, "If there is justice in Heaven or penetration in Govt I shall rise."[43]

Unfortunately for the United States, the bitter struggle among its consuls came to a head just as American relations with Tripoli reached a crisis. Yusuf Pacha Qaramanli was negotiating a treaty with Sweden, and once it was concluded, he promised to turn on the United States. Turkey's orders for the Barbary states to resume the war against France delayed Tripoli's declaring war on the United States, but the consuls knew that the Grand Signior could not prevent Yusuf Qaramanli from ultimately doing what he wanted. O'Brien wrote that "The Levant Snarling has only saved us so far." Eaton wrote Cathcart that he "hoped the event [the Grand Signior's orders for Tripoli to declare war on France] will offer an occasion to you to restore tranquility to our affairs with him." Turkey's insistence on a united front, the consuls knew, was only an opportunity: it was up to the United States to use it. As they expected, the United States did nothing. War was delayed further because Tripoli's government was divided: Foreign Minister Muhammad D'Ghies did not want war, but Admiral Murad Reis, a Scottish renegade formerly named Peter Lisle, did and wanted to teach the Americans a lesson for rebelling against England. These divisions might delay war, but neither O'Brien nor Eaton expected that their government, the Ottoman empire, Muhammad D'Ghies, or Cathcart could save the peace.[44]

In February 1801, O'Brien tried to stall the threatened war by circulating reports that eight American warships and two brigs were on their way to the Mediterranean, expected to arrive around March 10. In cypher, O'Brien told Cathcart and Eaton that he had made up this rumor to stall Yusuf Qaramanli's war plans. Cathcart had launched a similar report in 1799 when he wanted Pacha Yusuf to pay him for a load of cloth. Now, when O'Brien spread the rumor to preserve peace, Cathcart and Eaton refused to go along. "I shall not be the organ of Mr. OBrien's vision!" Eaton wrote on his copy of the letter.[45]

The consuls had little hope of help from the United States, and the prospect of a new president seemed to promise more delay, not a change in policy. "Whilst the U.S. is busy chuseing the main mast and foremast for the good ship," O'Brien wrote, "those states is laying schemes to Capture americans and Enslave the Citizens of the U.S." Eaton's metaphor was perhaps more apt. "Miss Liberty spends so much time about her *head dress,* that she risques to expose parts equally precious to the *open elements.*" Cathcart suggested amending the Constitution so that no man could be president who had not spent six months as a consul in North Africa. None of the candidates—John Adams, Thomas Jefferson, or Charles Cotesworth Pinckney—had this experience. O'Brien predicted "a great contest between Adams Jefferson & Pinckney" and preferred Pinckney, whom the Federalists had endorsed for vice president, but now Alexander Hamilton was promoting Pinckney for president. O'Brien thought Pinckney had "more of the real American then—The other two." Eaton liked John Adams, not because he distrusted Jefferson but "because Mr. Adams...has conducted us through a tempestuous night—Let him enjoy the calm of our tranquil day." But Eaton saw little real difference between the two. He "never supposed the fate of our country depended on this election," he wrote, and between Adams and Jefferson the choice was "Six of one and half a dozen of the other." As to Jefferson's unorthodox religious beliefs, Eaton asked, "what relation there is between the *negociation of a treaty* and the *Lords Supper*"? In April 1801, O'Brien heard that Jefferson and Burr were elected, but in a British paper Eaton read that Adams was reelected and Pinckney was vice president. O'Brien's news was right, and Eaton hoped Jefferson would pursue a new policy toward "the African Regencies...a worse than the present would be difficult to frame."[46]

By this time, April 1801, war seemed inevitable. O'Brien rejected the dey's suggestion that the United States give Tripoli $100,000. O'Brien had heard nothing from the United States since the *George Washington* arrived, and the Bacris, to whom the United States owed over $100,000, would not lend any more. He tried to persuade the dey to use the little influence he had with Yusuf Qaramanli to prevent war, but the dey had no influence with Yusuf, who had driven the Ottomans out of Tripoli and considered himself subordinate to no man or regency. Part of Yusuf's hostility to the U.S., in fact, came from the Americans' insistence that he was somehow subordinate to

Algiers. O'Brien knew war with Tripoli was almost certain and advised Cathcart, "Be cautious. Enter into no new treaties. Mind the honour and dignity of your Country and your own responsibility."[47]

Cathcart minded his responsibilities, advising all American consuls in the Mediterranean that war was inevitable. But he also attended to his own business. He wrote to a British merchant in Malta, advising him that the United States and Tripoli were likely to be at war within three weeks, but if war was averted, he asked if the merchant could find him a young clerk who wrote legible English and, if possible, French and Italian. Cathcart wondered if the merchant could act as Cathcart's business agent in Malta, buying "any little matters" Cathcart might want there.[48]

On May 9, Yusuf Qaramanli, still wavering between war and peace, met with Cathcart five times but could not come to terms.[49] Yusuf said time alone was the object; he would allow Cathcart eight months to give him the presents and annuities he thought Tripoli deserved. Cathcart tried to get the grace period extended for a year, reminding Yusuf that he had not heard from the United States in fifteen months and that his country was notoriously slow in acknowledging its Barbary consuls. Yusuf lost his patience. There would be war, he said, unless Cathcart negotiated a new treaty that would pay Tripoli an annuity—a small one if the nations were at peace, a larger one if they went to war. Cathcart said he could accept the eight-month grace period but could not promise any more money. When Qaramanli and Cathcart broke off negotiations, D'Ghies suggested, through Danish consul Nicolas C. Nissen, that Cathcart offer Yusuf $40,000. Cathcart refused. D'Ghies told Cathcart to send his wife, again pregnant, and their two-year-old daughter to another consulate so that they would not be alarmed when the American flag was cut down in front of their house the next morning.

The next day, Monday, Cathcart waited at the consulate, but no one came. By eleven, when there was still no sign of the crew sent to cut down the flag, he called on D'Ghies. He tried to get the foreign minister to promise that Tripoli would not to attack American shipping for forty days, but they could not agree. Yusuf sent word that evening that he would have the flag cut down on Thursday. On Wednesday, Cathcart asked for another ten or twelve days, reminding Yusuf that he had not heard from America in fifteen months, and perhaps, he said, word was on its way. D'Ghies urged Yusuf to give the Americans time, but he told Cathcart that Yusuf expected to get much more from an American war than he would from a Swedish or Danish war, and if he had set his mind on war with the United States, a $50,000 or $60,000 gift would not stop it. Cathcart wrote Eaton that he would be coming to Tunis, to expect him in forty days. O'Brien wrote Cathcart that he hoped the dey's letter to Yusuf would buy enough time to warn American commerce, but he knew that was all the dey's letter might buy, " & war will be the Result of detention & neglect."[50]

On Thursday, May 14, Yusuf notified Cathcart that men were on their way to cut down the American flag. Cathcart made one last offer of $10,000, which Yusuf rejected. The men arrived at the consulate, first trying to snap the flag pole in two, but found it would not break easily. They spent the next hour chopping at the pole; finally "they effected the grand achievement" and the flag pole lay on the consulate terrace, a sign that Tripoli had declared war on the United States. Cathcart and his family spent ten days packing up, and Yusuf's movements were no more hurried. Tripoli launched a few warships on May 26 and 27 but made no more preparations. Cathcart left American affairs in the hands of Nissen, the Danish consul, and left Tripoli.[51]

Every day Eaton expected the Cathcarts to arrive in Tunis, where they could coordinate American strategy. But instead of Tunis, Cathcart and his family had sailed for Livorno, where he assiduously pursued his own business interests. He finally wrote to Eaton on June 13, three weeks after he had left Tripoli, asking him to pay a bill of $200 and to advance $1000 in credit, "as I must eat." Britain's blockade of Italy had raised wheat prices, and if Eaton could ship a cargo of wheat before the Italian harvest, Cathcart wrote, it would fetch a good price. Cathcart had one of his own ships sent to Tunis to be loaded with wheat but asked that his ownership be kept secret.

The ship sailed under the Holy Roman Empire's flag, the only flag safe from the British. Cathcart promised to let Eaton know "whether a cargo of wheat is worth the trouble of sending here or not," and the next week he urged speed. The price of wheat was going up fast, and Eaton would "make a grand speculation" if he could get a cargo or two in before other grain vessels arrived. Cathcart wanted to invest a few thousand dollars, but only if Eaton could guarantee no risk, "as I am poor as JOB." To tide him over until these ships came in, Cathcart asked Eaton for a $1000 loan. Eaton authorized credit for him in Livorno and Marseilles.[52]

In September, Cathcart finally came to Tunis, where he and Eaton discussed the idea of using Ahmed Qaramanli, the older, deposed brother of Yusuf, as an American agent in Tripoli. Ahmed was then living in Tunis. It would be up to Eaton to convince both Ahmed and the United States that their interests were the same. This became Eaton's obsession, his way of righting the wrongs done by the conspirators around him. Cathcart, having set the plan in motion, went back to Livorno to await the American fleet. He expected to be sent to Algiers to replace O'Brien, but the dey would not have him. So as the United States fought Tripoli, Cathcart wandered around the Mediterranean before being made consul at Cadiz. Before leaving Livorno, Cathcart quarreled with the firm that handled Eaton's interests there. Eaton, he said, could do as he wished, but Cathcart would have no more to do with the firm. The firm might not be dishonest, but they knew how to manipulate bills of sale. The firm's partners were as bewildered as Eaton. "[T]here are indeed moments," one of them wrote, "when Mr. C. is really not to be dealt with or understood." Cathcart was miffed that Eaton continued to do business with the firm and finally sent his former associate all their mutual books, closed all his accounts with Eaton, and said he hoped this would show Eaton "the difference between real & interested friends." This was the last Eaton heard from Cathcart until long after he had retired to his farm in Massachusetts. Cathcart, now appointed consul to Madeira, wrote to encourage Eaton to invest in a new business venture.[53]

Cathcart and Eaton had nothing but bad words for O'Brien. But O'Brien praised Cathcart's handling of the final month before Tripoli declared war. Though he did not think Cathcart suited for diplomacy, O'Brien now said "he went further to try to save the peace of the US—Then I should have done or that I am convinced the Govt would have ordered." O'Brien still had criticism for his government and for the American consuls in Spain, who refused to publish Cathcart's warnings that Tripoli was at war with the United States. The U.S. consuls in the Barbary states were the only ones paid for their services; others were local merchants who would earn money through fees charged to American ships. It was in the interest of these consuls to keep American ships coming in: To tell Americans to stop trading would hurt these consuls' income, even if it would help the United States. The selfishness of these consuls meant that "our countrymen will stupidly run into difficulties," O'Brien wrote. These difficulties would come, O'Brien knew, but he hoped that once the United States was at war, it would not show the same indifference and neglect that had brought the war on. "I want a General Squall," he wrote, and since Pacha Yusuf was determined to have war, "in the name of God let him have Enough of it."[54]

When war came, the three consuls followed different paths. They had arrived in North Africa four years earlier, sent to carry out an American policy that was not clearly defined. Americans at home could not agree on the nation's role in the world and saw the North African regencies either as tools of European powers or as symbols of corruption and lawlessness. Eaton, O'Brien, and Cathcart had disagreed before; war brought their differences into clearer focus. Eaton's military solution will be discussed in more detail in the next chapter; it is perhaps the best known aspect of American policy in North Africa. Cathcart believed himself central to American policy. He applied for O'Brien's post as consul general in Algiers, but the dey refused to receive him. He stayed in the Mediterranean on private business until the war ended, then returned to the United States. When Tunis sent Sidi Soliman Mellimelli as ambassador to the United States in 1805, Cathcart was charged with conducting the

Tunisian from Washington to Boston. But Mellimelli accused Carthcart of being drunk, dishonest, and disrespectful. Cathcart was dispatched to Madeira and other minor consulates, then President Monroe sent him to Florida and Louisiana to inspect timber.

Cathcart's best years, it turns out, had been the ones he spent as a captive in Algiers. He had been young and successful. The bold dreams fired in that moment of success he could never bring to fruition. The great prize he sought—the consul generalship in Algiers—continued to elude him, though mounting debt brought on by extravagant dreams and a growing family did not. For the last twenty years of his life he was a minor clerk in the Treasury Department, spending his spare moments filing futile claims against the United States for debts owed him, he believed, for his service in the Mediterranean. If his government paid his claims, Cathcart planned to build an estate in Indiana. Unlike farmers who first plant crops and build barns before raising their shelter, Cathcart planned to begin with the mansion house, modeled on "the country seats near Boston." He predicted his house would endure for fifty years at least at Cathcart's Seat, near LaPointe, Indiana. He never grew tired of dreaming, though reality had an unpleasant way of intruding into his reveries. Below the sketch of the house of his dreams he wrote: "NO CLAIMS, NO HOUSE!" In his last surviving letter, written shortly before his death in 1843, Cathcart was still bitter about "faithfully serving an ungrateful country."[55]

O'Brien, relieved as consul general to Algiers, stayed in the Mediterranean to advise the American fleet. After the war he moved to Pennsylvania, was elected to one term as a state representative, and then with his wife Elizabeth retired to a farm near Carlisle. He had spent nearly twenty years in Algiers and had come to know a city that existed for most Americans only as a symbol. Algiers stood for lawlessness, for piracy, for plunder. It was the most vivid example of Muslim tyranny. O'Brien learned, and tried to convince his government of the fact, that this world was more complicated than they imagined. The United States believed, when it sent O'Brien as consul general, that Americans could teach the Algerians the benefits of honest commerce and wean them from war and piracy. O'Brien arrived in Algiers, though, to find that the indigenous merchant communities, Jewish and Muslim, distrusted the Americans, who were unable or unwilling to change this perception. Cathcart and Eaton, sent to cultivate peace and honest trade in the Mediterranean, instead pursued their own commercial interests, which they confused with American interests. The U.S. government, preoccupied with European politics, neglected the Barbary coast and the consuls they had sent there. The Muslim world was always more complicated than Americans believed. The model of honest trade the Americans provided, the lesson in commerce given by men like Captain Graves and consul Cathcart, did not entice the commercial people of North Africa to change their own ways. Unsuccessful in keeping the peace on their own terms, the Americans decided on war.

CHAPTER EIGHT

Remembering
the Tripolitan War

Americans had hardly begun to fight Tripoli before they turned the war into a moral fable. Andrew Sterrett's August 1801 victory at sea became the basis for a play, *The Tripolitan Prize, or, American Tars on an English Shore*, performed in New York in November 1802. No copies of this play survive, though our literature can bear the loss. What we know of the play comes from a scathing review Washington Irving wrote. We can still enjoy Irving's harsh, satirical judgment on this forgotten play. It is more troubling to understand Irving's harsh judgment on the audience. Irving was nearly alone in condemning the play, and he was perplexed by the audience's response—he sneered, but the rest of the audience cheered, stomped, and huzzaed.[1]

The Tripolitan Prize had a fairly simple story: An American ship captured a Tripolitan ship, and a storm blew both ships from the Mediterranean into the English Channel. The American captain's son falls in love with an English girl and wants to abandon the navy to stay with his sweetheart, setting up a conflict between duty and love. Meanwhile, another Tripolitan ship has chased the Americans to England, and after a prolonged sea battle (which an English crowd on stage watches) the Americans win, the Tripolitan surrenders, and the captain's son realizes that duty to his country comes first.

A simple, if implausible, plot. We and Irving might not suspend our disbelief, but the New York audience did. Most of the play was "taken up with hallooing and huzzaing between the captain, his crew, and the gallery." The captain, whom Irving described as a great swearing oaf, berated his son for betraying his sailor's honor for love bellowed: "What! an American Tar desert his duty!" The audience answered: "Impossible! American tars forever! true blue will never stain! !"

If there were a printed text of this play, it would not have this dialogue between the cast and the audience. Irving's review gives us the plot and, more important, the audience's reaction. Irving hated the play; the crowd loved it. Irving was disgusted, the crowd thrilled. The audience was loudly and enthusiastically on the side of duty and the American sailors. Real excitement came in the play's climax, the battle between the Americans and the Tripolitans. It was inconceivable that such a battle would take place off the English coast, a fact Irving used to ridicule the play. But this geographical impossibility had a real dramatic, patriotic function. On stage, a crowd gathered on the English shore to watch the American victory. Thus, the audience was treated to a play within a play, and had the pleasure of watching both the triumph of American tars and England's reaction to the triumph. "The battle was conducted with proper decency and decorum," Irving wrote, "and the Tripolitan very politely gave in—as it would be indecent to conquer in the face of an American audience." Or, for that matter, in the face of an English audience.

This play, though it did not survive, did in fact become the way Americans remembered the war against Tripoli. It has all the themes that run through the surviving poetry, songs, paintings, books, and plays. Americans and Tripolitans fought and the Americans won, but not because of superior military force or even courage. The Americans beat the Tripolitans because the Americans were true blue; the American sailors were enterprising (the name of the first victorious American ship was the *Enterprise*) as well as courageous, intelligent as well as strong. While the Tripolitan soldiers were made to fight out of fear, the Americans had volunteered, and fought out of love for their country and its republican ideals. The gallery mob watching a play was doing more than cheering for the home team; it was in fact feeling a connection with the men fighting halfway around the world.

Joseph Hanson's 1806 poem, "The Musselmen Humbled, or a

Heroic Poem in Celebration of the Bravery Displayed by the American Tars, in the Contest with Tripoli," asked "what can be effected by the slaves of tyrants? who fight for plunder and despotic masters: who defend no laws, but such as are oppressive; and protect no pow'r, but that which disrespects 'em." The Americans, on the other hand, were inspired by those inestimable treasures, "their own rights and Columbia's," and "the formidable powers of justice and freedom" gave the Americans "that invincible courage, which terrified and overcame the plundering vassals of the tyrannical bashaw."[2]

An 1804 song, "National Prosperity," cast this difference between Americans and Tripolitans in blatantly political form. It was not enough that Americans were different, this song said: Americans owed their blessings to the leadership of Jefferson, the "well chosen chief of the nation," who was oblivious to faction and "vile defamation," concerned only with wisdom, order, and law. This song celebrates America's escape from European entanglements, from the military buildup of the Adams years, and from religious bigotry. The "blest happy nation" under Jefferson enjoys "peace and plenty," able to do so because people who work hard do not have to pay oppressive taxes. The nation's " highest ambition" is not conquest or power but "freedom and trade." Louisiana, "a new link in the Union," improved American chances to realize that ambition at home; abroad, the song promised, soon "the pirates of Tripoli" would either "Render us justice, or encounter our blows."[3]

Federalists disputed how much of this was Jefferson's doing, and argued that he had bungled the war. But Jefferson had pursued a policy different from that of his predecessors, and the outcome was significantly different. We can contrast here two captivity poems: "The American Captive in Algiers," written in 1795, and William Ray's "Ode to Liberty," written while Ray was a captive in Tripoli in 1805. In the anonymous "American Captive in Algiers," the galley slave finds freedom only in death. Ray finds freedom, too, and blesses "the power that brings release." But this power is not God, but the American navy. Blasphemous perhaps, but it suggests a change in perceptions. Liberty was no longer the gift of God but something men and women must protect for themselves. The American captives who had come home from Algiers did not uniformly praise their government for speedy action. Those in Tripoli may have chafed at every day of captivity, but they also saw spectacular naval bombardments and even witnessed what the era's greatest naval hero, Horatio, Lord Nelson, called "the most bold and daring act of the age," Decatur's February 1804 raid into Tripoli harbor to burn the *Philadelphia*.[4]

Decatur's raid, as suggested in a previous chapter, transformed the embarrassing loss of the *Philadelphia* into a display of American prowess. Federalist critics of Jefferson's handling of the war tried to turn Decatur to their advantage, arguing that Decatur destroyed the ship, he did not recapture it; his heroism failed to release a single prisoner; and anyway, if Jefferson had sent an adequate force to the Mediterranean, the whole thing would not have been necessary. Then the Federalist critics argued with lineage: Decatur was the son of a good Federalist, and the whole navy was a Federalist idea. The New York *Evening Post* prefaced the first reports on Decatur's raid, "'*We will rejoice*' because we have found it best to burn one of our own frigates, which cost us four hundred thousand dollars."[5] This kind of argument would not work, any more than Washington Irving's disdain would quiet the gallery mob watching *The Tripolitan Prize*. The pro-administration *Aurora* gleefully reprinted the *Post*'s "sneer," calling it too detestable for comment. Jefferson, recognizing the changes Decatur had wrought, immediately promoted him to captain, and the Republican Congress voted to give him a sword.

Barely a week after news of Decatur's raid reached the United States, it was the subject of a pantomime, a silent play, *Preparations for the Recapture of the Frigate Philadelphia*. The spectacle featured a procession honoring Decatur's victory "over the Tripolitan corsairs," and it concluded with the gallant crew singing a new patriotic song and "bearing the American Flag Triumphant." Within two weeks of the news reaching America, a New York composer wrote an overture describing the *Philadelphia*'s loss and Decatur's attack. Perhaps he could not finish the work before its premiere on June 7, so the overture ended with the song "Hail Columbia." Another contemporary song writer promised that if any other despot dared insult the American flag, "We'll send them Decatur to teach them 'Good Manners.'"[6]

Decatur had created for the American people a real-life version of *The Tripolitan Prize*. But he was not through. During the bombardment of Tripoli in August, Stephen Decatur and his brother James had commanded ships at opposite ends of the battle line. At the end of the day, Stephen Decatur and his victorious men were sailing from the harbor when he learned that James Decatur had been killed by a Tripolitan captain whom he had captured. Stephen immediately ordered his ship back into the harbor, where they tracked down his brother's killer. Decatur and his men boarded the ship, engaging the enemy hand to hand, killing the captain, and making a prize of the ship. This is valor enough, with one brother returning to the battle scene to avenge his brother. But as the story was retold, a sailor named Daniel Frazier became the hero, though his name was subsequently changed to Reuben James. In this embellishment, as the American and Tripolitan captains square off on the deck, a Tripolitan sailor raises his sword over Decatur's captain. Frazier, or Reuben James, places himself between the sword and his captain, taking the blow and saving Decatur's life. It was thus in the power of every individual to display courage and self-sacrifice, and Daniel Frazier, or Reuben James, endures as a naval hero as great as the captain whose life he saved. Frazier/James showed that true blue would never stain, and with his captain won the admiration not only of the English public, but of the greatest English naval hero of all time.

Decatur had shown what Americans could do, and to Federalist consternation the proof redounded to Jefferson's benefit. The Philadelphia *Aurora* hoped Decatur's heroism would bring on that "proud day" when the nation would unite with one sentiment, "unclouded by the spirit of faction, unseduced by the influence of a foreign nation, which has incessantly annoyed her peace, corrupted her citizens, or plundered her property," to see "with an undivided spirit, the virtues and the valor of her heroes and statesmen, exerted in the maintenance of her rights, and the assertion of her independence and her honor." The *Aurora* hoped to see "national joy" and "civic congratulation" replace party spirit and "common love of country" replace factionalism.[7]

The Republicans seized on Decatur and would not let him go. His heroism became the focus of their July 4 celebrations, as Republicans who had been harsh critics of the navy under Adams now became its warmest admirers. The Democratic-Republican Society of Chester County, Pennsylvania, toasted Decatur and his "intrepid companions," hoping their bravery and valor would "be a terror to their enemies, an example to their countrymen, and finally procure them the esteem of every true American." Philadelphia's Democratic-Republicans toasted "The navy and army of the United States—May they always, like young Decatur, be gallant in a good cause." A Morristown, New Jersey toast hoped that the navy would "ever be adequate to the protection of our commerce against depredation, and to procure the freedom of our citizens, whether by European or African barbarians." A Philadelphia militia company toast echoed Jefferson's First Inaugural Address, praising "commerce, the handmaid of agriculture," and looked forward to the release of the American hostages "through the interposition of a wise administration," concluding with praise for Decatur, the militia, and the navy, "May they be employed only as the scourge of tyrants and the basis of western freedom." Another company of Philadelphia militia used Decatur to vindicate Jefferson: "It has been said our executive lacking strong nerve would disgrace his country's proud call, ask the Barbary powers and hear what they say,'have those pirates e'er forced him a tribute to pay?'—'Yes, with powder and ball!'"[8]

Philadelphia's Southwark Theater presented a full Republican bill on July 4, celebrating both the acquisition of Louisiana and Decatur's triumph over Tripoli. A new five-act "national comedy," *Liberty in Louisiana*, celebrated Jefferson's acquisition of the territory and was followed by "The Temple of Fame," a transparent painting of Liberty, Justice, and Columbia with naval columns "in honor of Capt. DECATUR and his brave associates." The Republicans, who had opposed building the navy, now became its firmest friends. Images of liberty, citizen soldiers, and republican virtue became entwined with the heroic image of Decatur. Jefferson and Decatur had made the navy safe for the republic. The Federalists lost Decatur as a hero. As Americans left the East Coast and settled on the frontier, they carried with them the name of this aristocratic Philadelphia navy officer. Towns in Georgia, Alabama, Mississippi, Tennessee, Indiana, and Illinois were named for Decatur, and as the next generation of Americans crossed the Mississippi they named towns for Decatur in Texas, Arkansas, Iowa, Kansas, and Nebraska.[9]

All Americans saw evidence of their own courage in the valorous acts of Decatur and his comrades. This happened well before the war was over: Though Decatur was celebrated in the summer of 1804, the war would not end for another year. There would be more opportunities for valor and heroism, but with the outpourings of patriotic devotion in 1804, it is almost surprising that the war did not end immediately. The Federalist critics were right: Decatur's brave exploit had not brought an end to the war, any more than Jefferson's administration had brought an end to the need for war. But Decatur's heroism changed the way Americans perceived the war and themselves. As Joseph Hanson asserted in *The Musselmen Humbled,* "on this side the Atlantic, dwells a race of beings! of equal spirit to the first of nations." Decatur had proved Americans were the equal of anyone else. Not only Americans said this: From the Vatican, Pope Pius VII declared that *"The American Commander, with a small force, and in a short space of time, has done more for the cause of Christianity than the most powerful nations of Christendom have done for ages!"* Having this acknowledged by the Catholic church, as well as by Lord Nelson, was especially gratifying.[10]

Decatur had taken defeat and turned it into victory, both with the destruction of the *Philadelphia* and in avenging his brother's death. Americans were prepared to do the same with any misfortune. In September 1804, the Americans tried to do to Yusuf Qaramanli's castle what Decatur had done to the *Philadelphia.* They loaded the gunboat *Intrepid* with explosives, making it into a floating bomb, and fifteen sailors volunteered to pilot it into the harbor late at night, anchor it below the castle, and blow it up. But something went wrong. Before the *Intrepid* reached the castle it exploded, killing instantly all aboard. No one knew what had happened. Perhaps it was an accidental spark or an enemy sniper that set off the blast. But the official explanation ignored these possibilities. The brave sailors, according to the official report, realized they had been discovered by the Tripolitans, and rather than be captured, they themselves set off the explosion. In an 1806 panoramic painting, "The Blowing up of a Gunboat," the crew swim from the flaming wreckage while they "contrive to join in huzzaing acclamation of defiance to the enemy."[11] The Philadelphia *Aurora* noted that history was full of examples of bravery and self-sacrifice, but these were all by men "trained from their childhood in the field of warfare, and inured to danger," and it was "peculiarly honorable" to Americans to see themselves showing the same bravery when they were "for the first time engaged in hostilities." The Americans had proved themselves better sailors and warriors than the Tripolitans and better people than the English.[12]

England's victory over France in Egypt was still fresh in the American public's memory. In 1804 a huge panoramic painting of the battle of the Nile toured American cities. In this depiction, the British and French navies contested their dominance of the world off Alexandria. By March 1805, an American artist had produced an American replacement for this historical piece, "Tars in Tripoli," which showed the American navy bombarding Tripoli. The American fleet is in the foreground, and in the background is Pacha Yusuf's castle and a mosque, one spire of which had been shot away by the *U.S.S. Constitution*. The despot's political power and Islam's religious power were both shattered by the well-aimed cannons of the American frigate. This seemed to fulfill another promise of William Ray's captivity poems, "The American Captive in Tripoli," which speaks of the "lurid Domes" and "tott'ring columns" that stand as monuments to the "despot's desolating hand" but that would be destroyed by a just heaven, Columbia's sons, and the "immortal Washington," who would make the "Devoted Tyrants," the "Beys and

Bashaws," kneel in submission, while restoring equal rights and "sweet liberty." The *Constitution* destroyed these tottering columns, and the enterprising sailors, at least in their poetic and painted forms, triumphed over the forces of darkness.[13]

The American sailors had a remarkable capacity to do what had never been done before. Yet there were historical antecedents for their valor and enterprise. John Scudder, a painter of historical scenes, had a show in Philadelphia in 1808. The promotional material for his exhibit shows an eagle clutching a banner emblazoned with the words "Bunker's Hill/Tripoli." The two paintings highlighting this show depicted these two critical American battles. Bunker Hill in 1775, though it had been a loss for the Americans, had proved that they could fight back against the British. The naval bombardment of Tripoli proved to England not only that Americans would fight, but that they would not stoop to the bribery and corruption with which European states had curried the favor of the Barbary states. Thus these two battles, in 1775 and 1804–1805, demonstrated to the world the exceptional nature of the American people's character, resolve, and independence. Scudder was not alone in connecting Bunker Hill and Tripoli. A New York theater presented a double bill in February 1806. The *Historical Tragedy of Bunker Hill, or, the Death of General Warren*, was part one. Part two was a new two-act musical, *Tars from Tripoli*, which concluded with a "TRIUMPHANT NAVAL PILLAR" in tribute to the sailors, whose costumed representatives danced on the stage, and for the grand finale "Columbia descends supported by Liberty and Justice." Columbia made a speech, then ascended back to the heavens, leaving below the "Tripolitans bending to her decree."[14]

The Federalists could not recapture Decatur from the Republicans, but they could try to advance another hero. While Decatur and the naval heroes had captured the public imagination, William Eaton, former consul to Tunis, had engaged in a dramatic military exploit of his own. Eaton had tracked down Yusuf Qaramanli's hapless brother Ahmed, whom Yusuf had deposed in the 1790s and had alternatively exiled and restored to official favor.

Ahmed had been made governor of Derne, an eastern province, but had proved as incompetent there as he had been as pacha of Tripoli. Eaton first met Ahmed during the latter's exile in Tunis and thought the wandering prince might be a useful tool in American diplomacy. Eaton believed that if he marched Ahmed back into Tripoli with sufficient military support, the people would rise up against Yusuf and restore Ahmed to power, and Ahmed would reward the Americans with peace and friendship. Eaton won the indirect support of the Jefferson administration. Secretary of State Madison instructed naval officers to cooperate with Eaton, but told Eaton to promise Ahmed only that the United States would not leave him in a worse position than it had found him. Eaton was not to promise Ahmed that the United States would commit military force to restore him to power.

Eaton tracked Ahmed down in Egypt, signed a convention with him, and raised a force of Greek, Albanian, and Arab mercenaries, together with a handful of American marines. By this convention, Eaton became a general; his highest rank in the American army had been colonel, but henceforward he was General Eaton. He and Ahmed and their troops marched across northern Libya and captured the city of Derne in June 1805. But to Eaton's consternation, nothing else went right. The people of Tripoli refused to rise up, and the American warship that appeared off Derne after Eaton's victory did not bring reinforcements. It brought news that the United States had made peace with Yusuf. Eaton had orders to evacuate the Americans, and after some work he convinced the American captain to bring Ahmed out as well.

Eaton felt betrayed by Jefferson and Madison. He returned home as Americans were celebrating the valor of Decatur and the navy; his own contribution was slighted. The Federalists had denounced Eaton. In 1804 "An American" had attacked him in the New York *Evening Post* for outrageous interference in Tripoli's domestic politics, and in August 1805 the Federalist *Political Register* had dismissed him as the leader of "an expedition of banditti." But when Federalists perceived that Eaton might be useful in discrediting Jefferson, they embraced him.[15]

The Federalists proposed presenting a ceremonial sword to Eaton, just as one had already been presented to Stephen Decatur. This proposal raised questions, since Decatur commanded sailors in the U.S. navy, Eaton a band of Arab and Greek mercenaries. Proposing a sword to honor Eaton raised problems for the administration: If it admitted that Eaton had acted under its authority, was it also admitting to having betrayed Eaton and his ally? The real issue behind the Federalist desire to honor Eaton, the *Aurora* said, was "hostility to the executive." While the Federalists used Eaton to charge Jefferson with inconsistency, the Republican press could point to the Federalists' own inconsistency. In their "great zeal" to honor Eaton, the *Aurora* asked, why did they forget "the compliment" the *Political Register* had paid, that he and his band were "an expedition of banditti?" The only explanation the *Aurora* could think of was that "their professed admiration" was "the result of system, of *grimace*, and *insincerity*."[16]

To counteract any damage Eaton might do, the Republican press reversed the perceptions of Yusuf and Ahmed Qaramanli. While the administration had supported Ahmed Qaramanli, he had been called the "rightful Bashaw," and Yusuf was the "usurper." Now the roles had changed. "The character of the two brothers is represented by our countrymen in very different colours," the *Enquirer* wrote in the fall of 1805. It turned out that Ahmed acutally had very "little capacity" and was "addicted to sordid propensities," while Yusuf had "elevated sentiments," "aspiring ambition," and a "strong understanding." Tripoli's foreign minister, Muhammad D'Ghies, "would adorn any of the cabinets of Europe." The pro-Jefferson press now insisted that he was not only wise but popular. His legitimacy was confirmed by the fact that when Eaton had offered the Tripolitan people a chance to throw out Yusuf and restore Ahmed, they had rejected it. Far from being the cause of the people, Ahmed's was the cause of the usurper.[17]

Captain William Bainbridge could not imagine how "such an impolitic & extraordinary measure" as Eaton's plan to use Ahmed had "intruded itself on our Govt." Bainbridge called Ahmed a "poor effeminate fugitive" who could not help the United States or hurt Yusuf. He had already spent ten years wandering in "exile from

Country, wife & children,...without giving the present ruler of Tripoli the least inquietude." When he had power he "had not the courage" to maintain it, and he did not have "influence enough among his own religious sect to reinstate him."[18]

But the Federalists, looking for any way to embarrass Jefferson, clung to Ahmed Qaramanli and any promises the administration may have made to him. "O! shame! shame!" the New York *Evening Post* wrote. "Who but blushes for the honour of his country as he reads the history of this dishonourable, the mean, base, and treacherous transaction?" The *Post* reprinted a report on the administration's conduct prepared by Eaton's ally, Vermont Federalist Stephen Bradley, and wondered how the "Richmond Enquirer, the Aurora, the Citizen, the Boston Chronicle" or any other Republican paper could justify Jefferson's conduct. Jefferson had led Ahmed Qaramanli to believe he would help restore him to power. Then, when Ahmed was on the verge of marching to Tripoli, Jefferson had made a separate peace with the treacherous Yusuf.[19] Most naval officers, who were determined to uphold the honor of their own branch, disputed Eaton and the Federalist claims. Richard O'Brien said Eaton's scheme was irrelevant, and most informed navy men agreed. John Quincy Adams, a wavering Federalist, took the occasion of Bradley's report to denounce the Federalist attempt to smear Jefferson. The report, Adams said, was "founded upon a supposed state of facts altogether erroneous, and a view of the whole subject altogether incorrect." Adams repeated what Bainbridge, Commodore Barron, and Yusuf Qaramanli had all known: that Ahmed Qaramanli had no power or popular support. Despite Eaton's belief that Ahmed's mere presence in Derne would inspire a popular revolt, the exile had been forced to flee when American support was withdrawn. Adams asked "what were the means, what were the resources, of this sovereign prince" who had to flee his own country, a province he had once governed, on an American warship? Adams asked, "Does this look like marching to the throne of Tripoli?"[20]

William Eaton was outraged. "That man has sold the honor of his country," Eaton said when Adams was finished demolishing Ahmed's case. Nonetheless, Federalist leaders could not do enough for the contentious Eaton. William Plumer, who was coming to regard Eaton as a vain braggart, thought other Federalists "extravagant in their encomiums," as the people "huzzaed" Eaton and mistook his "rashness" for "*bravery*."

Eaton, like the American people, was apt to confuse the two. Jefferson believed Eaton was merely trying to raise his own importance by destroying the reputations of Lear and Barron. The president did not go so far as to say that the Federalists were using Eaton to destroy the administration and raise their own importance, but the Federalists saw that Eaton was a useful tool. Eaton may have been unaware that he was being used, but he was prepared to enjoy the fleeting adulation. Eaton saw Bradley's report as proof that "the character of the nation is not wholly absorbed in the pusilanimity of the Executive"; that "honor, justice, & indignation against baseness" still lived, at least in the Senate.[21]

Federalists were not the only ones anxious to use William Eaton. Aaron Burr, former vice president, also believed Eaton could be useful for his own ends. Even now historians cannot agree on what exactly Aaron Burr's intentions were. Was he trying to separate the Ohio and Mississippi river valleys from the United States, join them to Mexico, and create his own empire? Or was he planning to do what the United States itself would do forty years later, invade Mexico and add its northern provinces to the United States? Whatever Burr's plans, he thought William Eaton could be part of them. Eaton was flattered at Burr's attention and briefly believed the former vice president intended to restore American dignity and honor by wresting Mexico from Spain. But Eaton grew wary of Burr and threatened to destroy him with "one solitary word...Usurper!" He had called Yusuf Qaramanli the same name; it did not destroy either Qaramanli or Burr.

Eaton was the government's main witness at Burr's trial for treason. Though his Federalist neighbors back in Brimfield had elected Eaton to the Massachusetts legislature, he spent most of his term testifying in Richmond. Chief Justice John Marshall, presiding at the trial, wearied of Eaton's long rambles though his adventures in Libya and turned his sarcastic wit on the hero of Derne. Was it not true that Eaton had given his deposition against Burr at about the same time, in January 1807, that the U.S. government agreed to pay him $10,000 for his services in Tripoli? Marshall and the jury found Burr's story more credible than Eaton's. Burr was acquitted, Eaton returned to Massachusetts, took his seat in the legislature in time to deliver a rambling attack on Marshall, alienating whatever Federalists in his district might have supported him. He was not re-elected, and he returned home to lose his lifelong battles with paranoia and alcohol.[22]

William Eaton died a broken and bitter man. His glory ended in partisan squabbling, his life in an alcoholic fog. But the Federalists had managed to raise him above both. The Massachusetts Federalists, building a new state capital that they hoped would endure the rising tide of Jeffersonian Republicanism, placed it above Beacon Street, naming the street immediately behind it Mount Vernon, in honor of Washington. Parallel to Mount Vernon is Derne Street, named not only to honor Eaton but, more important, as a permanent rebuke to the president who raised him up and then abandoned him.

Eighty years after Eaton tracked down Ahmed Qaramanli in Egypt, Henry Adams wrote that for "at least half a century every boy in America listened to the story with the same delight with which he read the Arabian Nights." Though Eaton had in fact not accomplished anything he had set out to do, he had failed heroically. Boston's General Eaton Fire Society celebrated Eaton in 1808 with an ode by Federalist poet Robert Treat Paine. To the tune of "God Save the King," Paine made Eaton the sole hero of the Tripolitan war:

> ...Eaton, a glorious name!
> Struck from the flint of fame,
> A spark whose chymick flame
> Dissolved their chains.
>
> O'er Lybia's desert sands,
> He led his venturous bands,

Hovering to save;
Where fame her wings ne'er spread
O'er Alexander's head,
Where Cato bowed and bled
On glory's grave.

Though earth no fountain yield,
Arabs their poignards wield,
—Famine appeal;
Eaton all danger braves,
Fierce while the battle raves,
Columbia's standard waves
On Derne's proud wall....[23]

Eaton did not merely take his place beside the heroes of antiquity, he replaced them. He succeeded where Cato and Alexander failed. The siege of Derne, instead of being a side show to the naval bombardment of Tripoli, became the key to American victory. An anonymous poet wrote that "Eaton trod in triumph o'er his foe/Where once fought Hannibal and Scipio." Eaton differed from the heroes of antiquity not only in his success, but also in the nature of his mission. The classical heroes had "traversed deserts to enslave nations," while Eaton, "the American chief," braved the desert "to liberate his brave countrymen." Eaton, in these poetic memorials, had actually accomplished what he set out to do. He had broken the captives' chains, and the victory became decisive in retrospect.[24]

Six months after Eaton's death in 1811, a play based partly on his exploits premiered in Boston. James Ellison's *The American Captive, or Siege of Tripoli*, has two questions at its center: What constitutes legitimate power? and What is an American? In the play, Abdel Mahadi has seized power in Tripoli, declaring his older brother, Ali ben Mahadi, too weak to rule. This follows the Tripolitan situation, in which Yusuf had replaced Ahmed. Abdel holds Ali ben's daughter hostage, telling her that her father was "too mild to reign," that his "weakness turned the public will against him"; Ali ben had "courted peace, and peace attain'd created heavy taxes!" Instead of peace, Ali ben should have "courted the crimson hand of war." Immorina, faithful to her father, tells this "base usurper" of an uncle that her father was mild but just. He "sought not blood" but was brave and enjoyed the people's support "till thou, thou fiend, with deadly shafts assail'dst him" and deceived the people.[25]

Abdel revels in his power, vowing that "the darling passion of my soul" will be glutted, that "PLUNDER" will save his throne and his subjects from "that damn'd abyss, to which my brother's mild and milky reign had doom'd them." Peace brings only "misery and want"; plunder alone "can prop our sinking realm." Immorina's fiancé Suleiman, laments this triumph of "AMBITION" over "VIRTUE," taking solace that while "CRIME may for a season triumph," only "VIRTUE" can secure "a monarch's bliss, his count[r]y's welfare, and his subject's love."[26]

While the Tripolitans ponder virtue and ambition, one of their cruisers captures an American ship and cargo. This provokes a second question. "And do you know what *Americans* are?" Suphelia, an old gossip, asks Immorina. The enlightened princess answers, "*Men*, are they not, like other men?" "Pshaw," Suphelia says, the Americans are not men, but are "*Indians!* Yes indeed, *Indians!* That they are," and these "Americans, that is Indians" would scalp any man or woman they caught, "and I'm sure this proves them not to be *men*." Rather than press her argument for equality to include even the Indians, Immorina corrects Suphelia's misimpression of Americans. The Indians, she says, are the natives of America, but only "inhabit the western regions of that vast country, and are savage, and barbarous, like our wild Arabs." On the other hand, "those whom we denominate Americans" are like the Europeans in "customs and manners"— civilized, polished, enterprising, brave, and hospitable.[27]

These characteristics describe the title character, Anderson, the master of the captured American ship. The contrast between Anderson, the American captain, and Abdel, the Tripolitan ruler, is borne out in their first meeting. Abdel, arrayed in a "sumptuous Turkish habit," his turban decorated with a large diamond crescent, his jeweled sash barely hiding the dagger on his hip, asks if Anderson's father is a nobleman. The American answers, "If to be the son of him who served his country, in the time of peril, be that which you call noble, I am of the most noble extraction, but if, from pamper'd lords and vicious princes, alone descend the gift, then I am not." His father, Anderson says, bore "the proudest title man can have": He was "An honest man."[28]

Anderson, as the son of an honest man, contrasts with the corrupt Abdel, but even more significant are the contrasts between Anderson and the play's other American and European characters. The play opens with a slave driver complaining about an insolent Irish slave who has refused to work. The Irishman's violent but ineffective rebellion is crushed by the overwhelming power of the state. Jack Binnacle, a sailor taken captive with Anderson, wonders why the United States does not simply "blow Algiers, Tunis, and Tripoli up, and put an end to these nests of pirates?" This would effect on a grand scale the Irishman's small-scale rebellion, but Anderson tells him that would be pointless: Destroy the coastal towns, and the "marauders" would move into their country's interior. Though Anderson applauds Binnacle's spirit and is himself ready to "fight till my heart-strings snap" rather than "be tributary to any nation," he wants a permanent solution. Instead of either impulsive rebelliousness or overwhelming military force, Anderson plans to escape, enlisting the help of Princess Immorina and Ishmael, a Jew. Once Anderson is out of Tripoli, he will secure the American navy's support for Ali ben, who will return to power and end the scourge of Barbary slavery once and for all. The rash Binnacle agrees to keep silent and let Anderson perfect his scheme, and when he learns that Anderson has escaped, he sings a song about a virtuous farm lad.[29]

Anderson's plan works, and he returns in glory to Tripoli with Ali ben. In the play's climax, Immorina and Ali ben both try to kill Abdel but cannot, and as Abdel prepares to kill Ali ben, Anderson announces that "A SLAVE has power to strike a TYRANT dead" and kills the evil tyrant. This power to kill the tyrant has been gained by careful planning, not rash attempts to overpower superior forces.

Anderson has deftly allied himself with those who share his goal—Ali ben, Immorina, and Ishmael. Though Immorina tells Anderson that he now ranks "among the Prophets," the American is more interested in being placed alongside Washington. To the strains of "Washington's March," Anderson and Ali ben enter Tripoli, and Anderson prays to be infused with "that heroic courage, that energy of soul, which so distinguish'd the father of my country, the matchless hero of the western world."[30] The heroes of Tripoli had taken their place alongside Washington and the heroes of the Revolution, who ranked far above prophets in the pantheon of honor.

Eaton himself remained at best an ambiguous hero and would not be transformed into a fabled character until after his death. Others returned home to take their places immediately beside Washington, that matchless hero of the Western world. In Albany, New York, Lt. Jonathan Thorn was honored by a song written to the tune of "Anacreon in Heaven," a difficult tune made more so by the lyricist's working in the names of other heroes of Tripoli: Barry, Preble, Truxton, and Decatur. "[T]he name of a Thorn, / On Fame's list long borne, / Shall proudly the page of fair Hist'ry adorn" the song proclaimed, and the refrain promised that American commerce would "long spread her sails o'er the Main," while "Freedom protected at home shall remain." Every American heart was stirred by the brave Americans at Tripoli, "And our children hereafter astonish'd shall read, / How freemen have humbled a barbarous Nation." The ode to Thorn celebrated the navy that protected foreign trade and domestic freedom. The navy had triumphed because of its commitment to commerce and freedom, and its spirit in defense of liberty and trade would inspire all Americans.[31]

Testimonials to the heroes of Tripoli ranked them beside the Revolutionary fathers and placed the post-Revolutionary generation in a new, heroic light. The Revolutionaries had beaten the British; this generation had bested the scourge of Christendom. The ode to Thorn had future generations marveling at the Tripolitan heroes' deeds; another contemporary song, to the same tune, reversed this order—the Revolutionary fathers would read with amazement of their sons' heroic deeds. This song, written by Maryland lawyer Francis Scott Key in honor of Decatur in 1805, so successfully conveyed this idea that Key rewrote it nine years later, and it became the national anthem.

> When the warrior returns from the battle afar
> To the home and the country he has nobly defended,
> Oh! warm be the welcome to gladden his ear,
> And loud be the joys that his perils are ended!
>> In the full tide of song, let his fame roll along.
>> To the feast flowing board let us gratefully throng.
> Where mixt with the olive the laurel shall wave,
> And form a bright wreath for the brow of the brave.

This verse could apply to any warrior, any battle. The second becomes more specific:

> Columbians! A band of thy brothers behold!
> Who claim their reward in thy heart's warm emotion:
> When thy cause, when thy honour urg'd onward the bold,
> In vain frown'd the desert—in vain roared the ocean,
>> To a far distant shore—to the battle's wild roar,
>> They rush'd thy fair fame, and thy right to secure.
> Then mixt with the olive the laurel shall wave,
> And form a bright wreath for the brow of the brave.

The third verse brings in the imagery of the conflict between the Muslim world and the United States:

> In conflict resistless each toil they endur'd,
> Till their foes shrunk dismay'd from the war's desolation:
> And pale beam'd the Crescent, its splendor obscur'd
> By the light of the star-spangled flag of our nation,
>> Where each flaming star gleam'd a meteor of war,
>> And the turban'd head bowed to the terrible glare.

Then mixt with the olive the laurel shall wave,
And form a bright wreath for the brow of the brave.

Finally, unlike the ode to Thorn, which had the heroes' children listen
with awe to tales of their fathers' deeds, in Key's final verse the
fathers hear with pride of their sons' valor:

Our fathers who stand on the summit of fame,
Shall exultingly hear, of their sons, the proud story,
How their young bosoms glow'd with the patriot flame,
How they fought, how they fell, in the midst of their glory,
    How triumphant they rode, oe'r the wandering flood,
    And stain'd the blue waters with infidel blood;
How mixt with the olive, the laurel did wave,
And form a bright wreath for the brow of the brave.[32]

Key so vividly imagined the horrors of a naval battle that when he
actually saw one nine years later, he already knew what to look for.
The parallels between this song and the one he wrote after watching
the British bombard Fort McHenry in September 1814 are striking.
The tune is the same, as is the rhyme scheme of the chorus. In the
more famous later version, the fate of the "star-spangled flag of our
nation" is in doubt throughout the perilous fight. In this song, however, it obscures the Muslim crescent, whose hollow splendor is cast
in shadow by the true glory of the American flag and the republic it
symbolizes. Key's two songs, his ode to the heroes of Tripoli and his
ode to the flag, reaffirm the Americans' commitment to their fathers'
legacy. In this Tripolitan ode, the Revolutionary fathers will remember the deeds of their children, who must not forget the principles of
the fathers. In the ode to the Tripolitan heroes, their fathers will hear
"exultingly" of their sons' triumphs, as Decatur and his comrades had
carried on the Revolutionary work begun by Washington, proving
their own commitment to the republic their fathers had created.

CHAPTER NINE

James Riley, the Return of the Captive

The United States had won peace in the Mediterranean and was determined to keep it. To prevent any more of the misunderstandings or appearances of weakness that had led to the war with Tripoli, Jefferson thought it would be prudent to keep American ships in the Mediterranean. Two ships were there in the early months of 1807: the schooner *Enterprise*, hero of the first engagement of 1801, was on cruise, and the frigate *Constitution* was in Naples picking up the monument of Italian marble commemorating the sailors who died in the assaults on Tripoli. In June 1807, Jefferson sent the frigate *Chesapeake* to relieve the *Enterprise*, committing the nation's peace, safety, and honor to the "vigilance, patriotism, and skill" of its commander, James Barron.[1]

But Barron never reached the Mediterranean. Within hours of leaving port, the *Chesapeake* was stopped by the British ship *Leopard*. The British captain believed there were British deserters among the *Chesapeake's* crew, and he demanded their return. Barron refused, the *Leopard* opened fire, and the American navy, which had proved its valor against Tripoli, learned it was no match for Britain. Commodore Barron had not expected a fight so close to the American coast and had failed to provide matches for his gunners. The British fired three broadsides that the *Chesapeake* could not return, leaving three Americans dead, eighteen badly hurt, the *Chesapeake* crippled, and Barron with no options but surrender.

This was a disaster greater than the loss of the *Philadelphia*. The administration knew the country was not prepared for war with

England, yet without war there seemed no way to stop this kind of harrassment by the British navy. With limited options, the administration turned once again to Stephen Decatur. Barron was court-martialed, and Decatur was given command of the *Chesapeake,* with orders to get the crippled frigate in shape to defend Washington, D.C., from British attack. A heroic poem from the Tripolitan war had promised that if any despot dared insult the American flag, Decatur would be sent to teach them good manners. No one knew better than Decatur and Jefferson that the British would be much less amenable to this lesson than the Tripolitans had been. In November, the *Constitution* returned to Boston with the marble monument to the heroes of Tripoli. While the monument was being shipped to Washington, Jefferson and his administration weighed their response to continued British attacks. The war against Tripoli, Jefferson believed, had shown that the United States was not bound by European precedent. If all Europe believed in bribing the Barbary states, the Americans did not. Now, threatened with being drawn into a war between Britain and France, Jefferson decided to teach the Europeans another lesson about the American spirit. Believing that both Britain and France depended on American produce to support their constant war with each other, Jefferson thought that if the United States refused to sell, Britain and France would both be crippled and would realize the folly of their ways. As the monument to the fallen heroes of Tripoli rose in the Washington Navy Yard, Jefferson and the Republicans closed all American ports, putting an embargo on American international trade, using American commerce as the ultimate weapon against belligerent Europe.[2]

The embargo lasted a year, ending on the day Thomas Jefferson left office. His successor, James Madison, tried other strategies to preserve American neutrality but in 1812 gave up. The United States and England went to war. The war was a disaster on land for the Americans. The British captured Detroit, burned Washington, D.C., and narrowly missed capturing James Madison. New Englanders, their economy crippled first by the embargo and then by the war, tired of being subject to government by the Virginia Republicans and talked openly of seceding from the Union. But at sea and at the bargaining table, the Americans were successful. The navy had already proved itself against Tripoli; now, on the Great Lakes and in the open ocean, American sailors once again triumphed over England. The British diplomatic corps was preoccupied with delicate European negotiations, trying to maintain an international alliance against Napoleon. Britain did not send its best bargainers to the peace conference at Ghent; the Americans did. John Quincy Adams, Speaker of the House Henry Clay, and Treasury Secretary Albert Gallatin led the American negotiators, and the two sides simply agreed to stop fighting. The Americans did not lose any of the territory, in Maine or the Northwest, that the British had captured. The diplomats signed the treaty late in 1814. News of it reached Washington, D.C., on the same day the rejoicing capital learned of Andrew Jackson's brilliant victory at New Orleans, where Jackson, with a force of Kentucky and Tennessee militia, free black creoles, and Caribbean pirates, massacred a far superior British force. Jackson secured the Mississippi River for the United States and, more important, ended this unpleasant war on a triumphant note.

The British war was over, but the United States once again had problems in the Mediterranean. Hajj 'Ali Pacha, the dey of Algiers, had declared war on the United States in 1814, anticipating a British victory over the Americans. His expectations were proved wrong, and President Madison followed the policy he had helped lay out as secretary of state under Jefferson; to negotiate from strength. Within weeks of receiving news of the American victories at New Orleans and Ghent, Madison sent a team of negotiators to settle differences with Algiers and to reaffirm the treaties with Tunis and Tripoli. Jefferson, who had wanted to send John Paul Jones to Algiers twenty years earlier, must have been pleased at Madison's chosen emissaries. Stephen Decatur and William Bainbridge were the chief negotiators, one sent back to the scene of his greatest victory, the other to the scene of his most profound humiliation, to form a peace treaty.

Along with them Madison sent William Shaler, a diplomat and businessman, who would remain after the navy had gone as consul general in Algiers.

While Madison was thus moving to protect American trade throughout the world, American businessmen themselves hurried to resume the enterprises that eight years of war and embargo had ruined. A group of investors in Hartford, Connecticut, built a new merchant brig, which they named *Commerce*, in anticipation of its part in the newly reopened international market. One of the investors, James Riley, who would be captain of the *Commerce*, desperately needed a turn of good fortune. Riley had nearly been ruined by eight years of embargo and war. In 1807 he was a captain, thirty years old, having worked himself up from a cabin boy on a ship out of New London to a successful merchant captain out of the more lucrative and competitive port of New York. But in 1807 Riley's luck changed, though his capacity for hard work did not. A British man-of-war chased his ship into a Spanish port, where he was safe from Britain but not from the French, who seized the boat and cargo. Riley spent two years in France, the years of the embargo, unable to get home to his wife and four children or to his career. When he did come home, he learned that American captains found it almost impossible to get cargoes in Europe, and no amount of patriotism could convince Americans to ship on American vessels that were likely to be seized. Riley worked at odd jobs and at farming, desperately trying to support his family through honest hard work. When war came in 1812, he applied for a navy commission, which he did not get. Another opportunity arose: smugglers and dealers in contraband, who would even trade with the enemy in Canada and the West Indies, were anxious to have experienced captains in a risky though extremely profitable trade. Riley was not afraid of risk and was tempted by the profits, but he refused this offer. Though his country had not asked him to serve, he would not serve the enemy. Riley remained loyal, though many in New England did not. While others in Connecticut talked openly of secession, Riley organized unemployed sailors into a militia unit to defend the coast.

Riley emulated the moral example given him by his parents. He had been born in 1777, the fourth of thirteen children eventually born to Asher and Rebecca Sage Riley. Asher was a farmer, and a successful one. But in the years after James Riley's birth, the family fortunes suffered. Asher became sick, and the Revolution ruined the economy. But Asher and Rebecca persisted, worked hard, and made sure the children worked hard. James went to school for four years, until he was eight and the Riley's had to hire him out to more prosperous farm families. His own parents protested when the families to whom he was hired failed to send him to school. But his masters satisfied Asher and Rebecca that James had had enough schooling. He could read, and he already knew more of the Bible, the Presbyterian catechism, and sang hymns better than other boys his age. Asher and Rebecca agreed. They had already taught James the most important lessons to supplement his brief formal education: "to be honest, industrious, and prudent; to govern my passions (which were violent,) to feel for and relieve the distresses of others when in my power," and, above all, that mild, pleasant manners and virtuous actions were the true measure of happiness. Asher and Rebecca had prepared James, as they prepared all of their children, for a life of adversity, which he could overcome through honest hard work and perserverance.[3]

Riley sailed the *Commerce,* with a crew of ten, on its maiden voyage to New Orleans in May 1815, the same month Decatur, Bainbridge, and Shaler sailed for Algiers. Riley picked up a cargo for Europe. The American negotiators captured two Algerian ships on their way to the negotiations. Riley and the *Commerce* sailed for Gibraltar as Decatur and his fleet sailed into Algiers. The Americans learned in Algiers that Hajj 'Ali Pacha had been strangled by the janizzaries who had elected him, who then strangled his immediate successor. The new dey, Umar Agha, anxious for peace and a bit awed by the size of the American force, agreed to all of the Americans' terms within forty-eight hours. Riley sailed to Europe under an American flag that for the first time in its history was at peace with all the world.

But while the *Commerce* sailed into a peaceful world, it was not safe from the chastising hand of Providence or the mercies of people who recognized no flag or nation. In August 1815, the *Commerce* hit a rock off Cape Bojador, in what is now the Spanish Sahara. Riley and his men managed to escape while the ship foundered, loading the long boat with anything that might be useful on the barren shore. Riley also brought off the ship's gold. It would be useless against hunger, thirst, or the blazing sun, but Riley was thinking ahead, knowing that if his men survived the extremes of nature and encountered any desert nomads, the gold could buy their way to freedom, to a port city like Mogadore, Tangier, or even Algiers or Tripoli. Riley divided the gold among the men, explaining to them that in case they were separated, they must use every opportunity to contact the American consul at Tangier, James Simpson, or any European consul in Mogadore.

Their first encounter with a native did not bode well. Riley saw a man, his complexion between that of a Negro and an Indian, naked except for a cloth that hung from his chest to his knees, with bushy hair and beard, red eyes, a wide mouth, and full set of sharp white teeth. Riley spotted this man, who looked more like an orangutan than a man, investigating bits of the *Commerce* and its cargo that had washed ashore. Riley made the friendliest gestures he could, but the man was not interested in friendship. Instead he came back with his family: two women whose front teeth stuck out like a boar's tusks; a girl, eighteen to twenty years old, whom Riley said was "not ugly"; and five or six children. They all went to work opening the crates and taking whatever they wanted. The women tore apart Riley's feather mattress; they only wanted the outer lining, but they thoroughly enjoyed making the feathers fly and flutter in a cloud around them. Riley knew he and his men could easily have driven off these scavengers. But Riley also knew his men had nowhere to go, while the marauders could perhaps find reinforcements and come back to do worse than tear up mattresses.

These nomads were not the only ones pillaging the *Commerce*'s wreckage. Some of the crew opened the casks of wine, and by afternoon were too drunk to do one another any good. In a situation as hopeless as theirs, perhaps it made little difference whether they faced it drunk or sober. But Riley and three of the men put themselves to work and managed to repair the long boat. Certain of death, Riley thought of his five children at home, who would grow up without a father. He would not allow himself to despair. The next morning the nomads attacked. Riley's clearheadedness paid off as he led his crew through the surf back to the wreck of the *Commerce*. The ship's lone passenger, Antonio Michel, did not make it in time. Riley and the survivors watched in horror as the nomads drove a spear through Michel's chest and dragged his corpse, along with the rest of their loot, over the sandhills. Riley came to the grim realization that though Michel was dead, eleven other men were alive, and perhaps Michel's death was a necessary sacrifice. He realized he was completely in God's hands, and he would not question God's intent, but only keep himself and his men moving.

Riley and his men packed what provisions they could in the long boat and gathered for a last time on the *Commerce's* deck, this time to pray. Riley led the men in prayer, casting them on God's mercy, asking protection for their wives and children at home. Riley knew—all the men knew—that it was almost impossible that they would ever see their families again. But at that moment, as if in answer to their prayers for deliverance, the winds stopped and the men were able to get the long boat away from their ship. They left the *Commerce* to its fate, going with varying degrees of faith and despair to their own. With no rudder, Riley steered with a broken piece of wood. Blinded by fogs and smashed by waves, they spent nine days and nights in the boat, which began to leak like a basket. After nine days at sea, they beached at Cape Blanc, 350 miles south of their shipwreck. Now they were desperate. Their boat was destroyed, they did not know where they were, and they were alone on this strange shore. Above their heads loomed huge black cliffs, which seemed to offer no way up. Even if they did reach the top, there was no assurance, or even a hint, that what they found there would be better than what they had on the shore, which was merely the chance to drown or starve or die of thirst. Like Sinbad, Riley and his men managed to escape one disaster only to face another: They had been shipwrecked and managed to reach the shore, only to be attacked by a marauding desert family; they had escaped to their wrecked ship, only to face certain death in the pounding surf; they had spent nine days at sea in the long boat, only to reach this even more desolate place. Whatever lay ahead, Riley could only trust once more that Providence had some purpose beyond his understanding.

The men moved north. Rocks cut their feet; the sun burned their flesh. Their water gave out; they had nothing to drink but their urine. Riley thought of throwing himself into the waves to end this misery, but ten men depended on his leadership. Only because he seemed to know where to go, only because he seemed to have no fear, the men followed him. Riley knew as well as they did, perhaps better, that their situation was hopeless. They would certainly die of thirst if they did not soon find water, and wherever there was water there would be people. Any people they met would be just as vicious, maybe more so, than the marauding family who had pillaged the *Commerce* and killed Michel. But Riley had to maintain an appearance of hope and confidence to keep his men moving.

On the night of September 9, one of the men spotted a light. All but Riley were overjoyed. The light meant a camp, where surely they could get water, for which they were desperate. They would prostrate themselves before the camp and beg for water. The men slept soundly that night, with the promise of deliverance in the morning. Riley could not sleep. Though he knew he could not survive another day without water, he also knew that once the men reached the camp, they would likely be sold as slaves by the Arabs. He knew he could not endure long in slavery, but again, he thought of the other men. Perhaps they could. Perhaps one of them might escape and reach Mogadore, or be able to contact Consul James Simpson at Tangier, or an American consul in Algiers, Tunis, Tripoli, or even Gibraltar. Slavery, Riley realized at the end of a sleepless night, was the means Providence had given his men for their survival. They could not refuse it.

Before he led his men to the Arab camp, Riley instructed them as to their probable fate. They would be slaves, but must use every opportunity to remember their fellow captives and take any chance to escape. If any of them reached Mogadore, he should contact any European consul there. He reminded them again that James Simpson was the American consul at Tangier. They must remember his name, and if they had the chance, they must tell him where they had last seen the other survivors. If by chance they were near Algiers, Tripoli, or Tunis, they should write to the American consul there, or at Gibraltar, if they had a chance. Riley and his men would have to accept slavery as a temporary expedient; survival was the immediate goal. If any survived, Riley had faith that they would once again be free. He reminded them of Providence's interposition for them during their struggles of the past two weeks. He warned them that mildness and submission now would save their lives; stubbornness would only make them more miserable and less likely to live.

The men advanced to the camp, coming first to a herd of camels. When the Arabs spotted the eleven emaciated, burned men, they rushed to them, tearing off their remaining clothing, claiming one or the other for their own, fighting for over an hour with other Arabs who tried to claim the men as slaves. Riley and Richard Delisle, the black cook, were taken together. They were led naked back to the camp and spat upon by curious women who had come to see these strange creatures. Riley and Delisle were led to a well and given a bucket of water. After the Americans had drunk from the bucket, like camels, the women mixed in some milk, and again Riley and Delisle drank. Their thirst was gone, but they had violent stomach cramps and diarrhea.

After the Arabs settled the rights of ownership, their leader, an old, dignified man quizzed Riley in Arabic and Spanish about where he and his men were from, what they were doing, and how they had gotten there. He asked if Riley knew where Morocco was. Riley nodded and pointed north. He told the Arab that the sultan was a friend of Riley and his nation and would redeem Riley and the crew. Riley asked to be taken to Mogadore, the nearest port city. No, the Arab said, it was too far; there was not enough to feed the camels along the way. It would not pay them to take these eleven men to Mogadore to collect the promised ransom.

That night was another restless one for Riley. But finally his misery and worries could keep him awake no longer, and he fell asleep and dreamed. He was "naked and a slave," the Arabs driving him with red-hot spears through a fire a mile long. Riley begged the Almighty to deliver him from suffering. In answer, Riley saw an eye overhead, and below it an arrow pointing north. Riley understood that if he turned north he would be saved, and so changed course from south to north. The flames subsided, though the Arabs continued to prod him with their iron spears. Soon Riley found himself in a green valley, where cattle, sheep, and oxen ate grass and drank from a cool, clear stream. He threw himself to the ground and drank, thanking God for such mercies. Riley's captors continued to drive him north, toward the eye overhead. Through mountains and thorny paths they went, until they were met by a young man in European clothes. This man set a feast before Riley, who fainted at the sight. "Take courage, my dear friend," the stranger said. "God has decreed that you shall again embrace your beloved wife and children."

Riley awoke. A dream was precious little to go on, but it was all he had throughout the days that followed, as he and his men suffered through days of exposure to the sun, hard work, thirst, and nights of hunger and ridicule from their captors. Though Riley's master seemed to be the group's religious leader, conducting each evening's prayers, he showed the captives no pity, and his women showed even less. Riley had to watch, powerless, as some of his men were beaten, others sold away. Riley's faith in Providence and deliverance weakened but did not disappear.

At the end of September, two strangers came to the Arab camp. The women told Riley that these men, Sidi Hamet and his brother Said, were traders who might be able to buy the Americans and take them to Morocco. Riley was astonished at the women's concern. Their conduct toward him had not made him expect any pity. He did not entirely believe that these Arabs would deliver him, but he still believed he would be delivered. The Arabs did show an interest. Sidi Hamet, who spoke only Arabic, took Riley aside and as best he could asked about Riley's home, his family, and the Prophet Muhammad. Sidi Hamet wept when Riley said he had five children at home; the Arab himself had young children at home in Morocco. In answer to Sidi Hamet's questions about Islam, Riley had observed enough of his master's worship services to know that Muhammad had lived in Mecca but now was in heaven. This was enough for Sidi Hamet, who began calling Riley "Rais," or captain, out of respect. He took Riley out of earshot of his captors and promised to buy him, and as many of the crew as he could, and take them to Mogadore. Riley again promised a handsome reward for his troubles.

Over his brother's objections, Sidi Hamet bought Riley and four of the remaining crew. Said wanted to sell the captives at a profit or kill the ones who did not move quickly enough. It was a long and treacherous journey to Mogadore; the Arabs had only Riley's promise of a reward. Said could not understand his brother's zeal to help these Christians. But Sidi Hamet would not let his brother hurt the captives or sell them. When they neared Mogadore, Riley wrote a letter to the English consul, praying that the consul would be there, and Sidi Hamet went off with it.

William Willshire was England's consul at Mogadore. He was at home when Sidi Hamet arrived, and when he read Riley's letter, he immediately went to work for the captive Americans. Willshire paid Sidi Hamet for bringing the men out of the desert, and sent him ahead with mules to carry Riley and his men the rest of the way to the city. He himself set out to direct their way. He caught up with Sidi Hamet and Riley's party at a village outside the city. Riley was amazed—William Willshire was the same man who had set the feast before him in the dream promising deliverance. Willshire now repeated the pledge and carried Riley and the survivors to Mogadore. He promised to try to find the other survivors of the *Commerce*, now scattered among the tribes of the Sahara.

Only when he reached the consul's house did Riley realize the ordeal he had survived. Willshire had Riley and all the men shaved, and their tangled, vermin-infested hair clipped off. A Jewish doctor, born and educated in Moscow, administered medicine, and for the first time in three months, the men had solid food and rest. Riley had weighed 240 pounds; he now weighed 90. The strain of surviving and of keeping his men alive and focused on their own survival, suddenly broke through. Safe in Willshire's house, Riley's mind and emotions collapsed. He cried uncontrollably for three days; the sight of another human being made him shudder with fear. Riley wrestled in a dark corner of his room with the overpowering memories and visions tormenting him. For three days, Willshire and the other men feared for Riley's survival, all but giving up on his sanity. But just as Maria Martin emerged from her own sufferings with a renewed sense of purpose, Riley awoke from his delirium with a new sense of the wisdom of Providence. On the fourth day, he looked in a mirror. The drawn, burned face did not shock him. He remembered all he and his men had suffered, but now, instead of despairing, Riley "could contemplate with pleasure and gratitude the power, wisdom, and foreknowledge of the Supreme Being, as well as his mercy and unbounded goodness." His life, he now realized, was not what he thought it had been. Events he had thought of as misfortunes in fact had been meant to prepare him for this great ordeal. "I clearly saw that I had only been tutored in the school of adversity, in order that I might be prepared for fulfilling the purpose for which I had been created."[4] Riley had been created to save his men, and everything in his life had prepared him to do this.

James Riley returned to the United States in 1817. Having survived his captivity and led some of his men to safety, Riley was something of a hero in a nation looking for heroes. President Monroe met with Riley in Washington, D.C., and the captain called on Henry Clay, John C. Calhoun, and John Quincy Adams. Governor De Witt Clinton of New York took great interest in Riley and eagerly read the manuscript Riley had written about his adventures. Riley himself thought he was through with life at sea; his joints still ached from his travels in the Sahara. To relax, and perhaps put to rest his memories, he decided to travel through the American interior. Eager to put the ocean behind him, Riley lobbied for a government job as a surveyor or Indian agent, thinking the government could use an honest, sober man; however, he did not get an appointment.

Riley traveled through Kentucky, Indiana, and Ohio, going back to New York by way of the Great Lakes and the Erie Canal. The president of Transylvania University and other distinguished westerners toasted Riley, and the hero of the Sahara noted with real pride the sites of American naval victories on the Great Lakes. The War of 1812 had secured to the United States the commerce of this "Mediterranean of the interior of America," and Riley forecast a great future for towns like Buffalo and Cleveland. The interior was flourishing, and ambitious men like Riley no longer needed to go to sea. America could turn its attention inward. Riley decided to move his family to Ohio, and in January 1821 they began their lives as pioneers on the St. Mary's River, clearing trees and building cabins and a mill in a settlement they named Willshire, after the benevolent British consul.

But pioneer life proved just as hazardous as life at sea. Riley and his family worked hard, and his neighbors rewarded his hard work by sending him to the state legislature. But each year the whole family was sick with fevers from late spring through early winter. Spring rains carried away the mill dams; destitute neighbors relied on Riley to help them through hard times; and he was again rejected for a government job (as Indian agent at nearby Fort Wayne, Indiana: he was not a resident of Indiana). He spent one term in Ohio's legislature, trying to get that state to adopt a public school system like Connecticut's. Life on the frontier proved frustrating, impoverishing, and finally almost fatal. In 1826, ten years after he had survived the horror of the Sahara, Riley's health collapsed completely in Ohio. His family carried him by boat to the healthier climate of New York City. When he recovered, he went back to sea. Riley sailed for Morocco, once again seeing his benefactor Willshire, as well as the emperor, and then sailed to Algiers. Riley spent the rest of his life at sea, dying on a trading voyage to the West Indies on March 13, 1840. His body was committed to the waves two days later.

But this was not the end of Captain James Riley. He had failed as an American pioneer, and embargos, wars, and shipwrecks had prevented him from becoming a wealthy merchant captain. But he had done two remarkable things in his life. First, he had survived the rigors of the Sahara and experienced that intangible satisfaction his parents had taught him about. Second, he had written a book which brought fame and influence, if not wealth. Riley's *Authentic Narrative of the Loss of the American Brig Commerce* was one of the most popular books of the nineteenth century. First published in 1817, in Hartford, New York, and London, the following year it was translated into French and German for European audiences. Riley took his manuscript with him to the West. It was published in Lexington, Kentucky, and Ohio, and editions appeared regularly in Hartford until the Civil War. More than a million copies of this book appeared, and eleven years after Riley died, his son, William Willshire Riley, issued a sequel. After the Civil War, portions of the original *Narrative* were published as *What he Saw and Did in Africa*. Thirty-three years after he died and sixty years after his adventure, Riley's *Narrative* retained its power as a story.

Riley's *Narrative* was the most successful of the American captivity tales. Though other captives suffered as Riley had and wrote about their experiences, none of their books enjoyed the remarkable success of Riley's. Daniel Saunders, whose ship, also named the *Commerce*, wrecked off Arabia in the summer of 1792 published an account of his ordeal similar to Riley's. But Saunders disappeared after one printing. John Foss, captured by the Algerians in 1793, returned home in 1797. His story went through two editions in 1798, none afterward. Royall Tyler's novel based on these captivity stories, *The Algerine Captive*, had two American editions: one in 1797 and the second in 1816, but then it disappeared. Maria Martin's novel had its last printing in the same year Riley's *Narrative* had its first. Riley himself encouraged Judah Paddock, shipwrecked off the Moroccan coast in 1800, and Archibald Robbins, a fellow survivor of the *Commerce*, to write their own stories, and Riley subsidized their publication. But these books did not survive as Riley's did.[5]

Jared Sparks, editor of the *North American Review* and future president of Harvard, admired Riley's "good faith and sailor-like frankness" and praised the book's simplicity.[6] Indeed, Riley's book is still a compelling story, and his simplicity of style is a big part of its attraction. But the other captives wrote of their ordeals with similar frankness and simplicity. Style alone does not explain why Riley's book sold so many more copies, nor does it explain the phenomenal response of readers. Riley's story is similar to that told by Saunders, Foss, Tyler, Martin, Robbins, and Paddock. Why was his book so much more successful? Riley captured the imaginations and engaged the sympathies of his readers in a way that would make any writer wonderous or envious. Elijah Browne of South Carolina named his son Sidi Hamet after the benevolent Arab. A reader in Flat Rock, North Carolina, said that after reading the *Narrative* he was ready "to shoulder my gun, to go and seek redress of them Arabs." When Riley wrote to this reader, C. Barnett, the whole town of Flat Rock gathered round to hear his letter; some of them had doubted that Riley really existed. But Riley did exist, though they had so identified with his character—strong, persevering, with an abiding sense of Providence's power—that they did not think he could be real. A Massachusetts reader, Henry David Thoreau, thought of Riley as he walked along the outer beach of Cape Cod, contemplating shipwrecks and the eternal struggle between men's intentions and the overwhelming power of nature. Though Barnett and Thoreau found different messages in Riley's book, each found it compelling and memorable.[7]

Jared Sparks praised Riley for merely describing his travels, leaving to more qualified writers "the more weighty and less obvious concerns of governments, national character, and historical disquisitions." Sparks did not consider Riley competent to discuss these weighty matters, and thought it wise of him to acknowledge his own limitations. He thought that Riley's book was interesting and entertaining, and concluded that Riley had shown good sense in merely telling the story without forcing a moral. But Sparks was wrong. Riley's *Narrative* was popular precisely because it did engage the reader in moral and political questions. Riley's *Narrative*, more than any other account that came out of the American experience with the Muslim world, was a commentary on American character and a sermon on American sinfulness. It is a powerful book, not because Riley relates the tale of his own suffering in a compelling way, but because he uses his own suffering to achieve a more important goal.

Riley realized in Mogadore, as he recovered his sanity, that his task was not complete. He would go home to a country "whose political and moral institutions are in themselves the very best of any that prevail in the civilized portions of the globe," where his fellow citizens enjoyed "the greatest share of personal liberty, protection, and happiness." But, strange as it might be, "my proud-spirited and free countrymen still hold a million and a half, nearly, of the human species, in the most cruel bonds of slavery, many of whom are kept at hard labour and smarting under the savage lash of inhuman mercenary drivers, and in many instances enduring besides the miseries of hunger, thirst, imprisonment, cold, nakedness, and even tortures." All of these miseries Riley and his men had endured; his *Narrative* made the reader feel them as acutely as he had. Now Riley issued the same moral challenge Franklin and the author of *Azem* had done in the 1790s. "This is no picture of the imagination," Riley lamented; he himself had seen these scenes. But his own suffering had taught him a lesson. "I will exert all my remaining faculties in endeavours to redeem the enslaved," and he endorsed the American Colonization Society's efforts to abolish slavery through gradual emancipation.[8]

Jared Sparks criticized Riley for including a long twenty-fifth chapter that tells Sidi Hamet's story. Sparks discounted the Arab's story of his trading journey to Timbuctu and a Negro kingdom somewhere southeast of that fabled city. Sparks was interested in descriptions of Timbuctu but did not trust Sidi Hamet as a source. Sparks missed the moral and literary congruence between Riley's story and Sidi Hamet's. Like Riley, Sidi Hamet was a merchant trader. Instead of sailing across the ocean, Sidi Hamet conducted caravans across the Sahara. He had set out from Morocco on a trading mission to Timbuctu with a huge caravan: 1000 men and 4000 camels. But the caravan met with disaster after disaster, reducing Sidi Hamet to a slaving mission to Wassanah, a Negro kingdom southeast of Timbuctu. Like Riley, Sidi Hamet realized, under the tremendous strain of trying to survive in this vicious world of men and commerce, that his only hope was in Providence. Of the vast caravan that had set out, only four men returned. Sidi Hamet was a lucky survivor, but his two years of trading for gold, gum, and slaves along the Niger had left him destitute. His father-in-law underwrote an expedition to buy ostrich feathers, and Sidi Hamet and his brother set out on this mission, a step down from being the captain of a vast Sahara caravan. But on this mission Sidi Hamet found his own salvation. Commercially, it failed: Sidi Hamet was no more successful at buying ostrich feathers than he had been in trading at Timbuctu. But Sidi Hamet told Riley, "the great God directed our steps to your master's tent, and I saw you." The sight of Riley awakened Sidi Hamet to a sense of his own sinfulness and to the possibility of redemption. Each man, the Muslim from Morocco and the Christian from Connecticut, saw that God had directed him to this place, and that God had a very important reason for doing so.

Sidi Hamet confessed to having been a bad man, a slave trader. The sight of Riley and the emaciated, sunburned Americans changed him. "I had been in distress and in a strange land, and had found friends to keep me and restore me to my family; and when I saw you naked and a slave, with your skin and flesh burnt from your bones by the sun and heard you say you had a wife and children, I thought of my own former distresses, and God softened my heart, and I became your friend." After seeing Riley safely in the British consul's house, Sidi Hamet had "the high pleasure of knowing I have done some good in the world" and pledged "in the future [to] do what is in my power to redeem Christians from slavery." He went back to the desert to find the rest of the *Commerce*'s crew. Sidi Hamet died trying to rescue Riley's shipmates.[9]

Providence brought these two ordinary traders, James Riley and Sidi Hamet, together. Providence made two ordinary men do extraordinary things. Sidi Hamet left Riley with a mission: to redeem the enslaved. Riley closed his *Narrative* with the same mission. He prayed that the Almighty who had rescued him would induce his country-men to destroy the "accursed tree of slavery, that has been suffered to take such deep root in our otherwise highly-favoured soil." Riley, like Sidi Hamet, had learned some "noble lessons" in his adversity. He recalled the American slaves he had seen in New Orleans; the memory "chill[ed] my blood with horror." Riley pledged "to redeem the enslaved, and to shiver in pieces the rod of oppression," hoping that every "good and pious, free, and high-minded citizen" and all "friends of mankind throughout the civilized world" would join the noble work.[10]

Riley, like the humanitarian proponents of charity in the 1790s, wanted Americans to join together in smashing the rod of oppres-sion. In his own suffering at the hands of Muslims, Riley saw a reflection of the sufferings inflicted by Americans. Riley's antislavery message could not have been more clear. Almost alone of the Americans who wrote of their sufferings at the hands of Muslims, Riley saw this connection and would not let his countrymen off the hook. Slavery was wrong, and as wrong for a Connecticut sea cap-tain as it was for a black African.[11]

Sparks missed this point, but other readers did not. In 1860, when he was a candidate for president of the United States, Abraham Lincoln was asked what books had most influenced him. He named six: the Bible, and *Pilgrim's Progress*, Aesop's *Fables*, Weems's *Life of Washington*, Franklin's *Autobiography*, and Riley's *Narrative*. All of these books reinforced ideas of self-reliance and hard work justified by divine Providence, which might at any moment call on an ordinary man to do extraordinary things. All of a man's life would be prepara-tion for that moment when Providence would call on him. Each of these books delivered this message; only in Riley's did Providence call on men to end slavery, the issue on which Sidi Hamet, James Riley, and Abraham Lincoln were called to action.[12]

James Riley drew a powerful lesson from his captivity. Though the United States had triumphed over Tripoli and Algiers, it had not tri-umphed over its own sins. Any loss of liberty was slavery, and

Americans could accept neither the "slavery" of their citizens in Algiers or Morocco nor the slavery of Africans or African-Americans in their own land. Americans could not be complacent in the face of injustice, either at home or abroad. Riley persevered, refusing to submit, relying on Providence and his own indomitable spirit to deliver him. To endure was not enough. Riley and the others had to prevail. Riley's challenge to his readers was to look into their own and their nation's heart for proof that they could prevail in a way that made the effort worthwhile. Riley delivered from Morocco a lesson on self-reliance, endurance, and a Providence that delivered neither the oppressor nor those who submit to oppression.

Notes

CHAPTER ONE
American Policy Toward the Muslim World

1. TJ to James Currie, Paris, 27 Sept. 1785, Julian P. Boyd et al., eds., *The Papers of Thomas Jefferson* (24 vols., Princeton, 1950–) 8: 559 (hereafter *PTJ*); TJ to Benjamin Franklin, Paris, 5 Oct. 1785, *PTJ* 8: 585–586.

2. *New York Journal and Patriotic Register*, 20 Oct 1785, quoted in Syed Zainul Abedin, "In Defense of Freedom: America's First Foreign War. A New Look at United States–Barbary Relations, 1776–1816," 81 (Ph.D. diss., University of Pennsylvania, 1974); John Bannister to Thomas Jefferson, 2 Dec. 1785, *PTJ* 9: 75–76.

3. Samuel House to TJ, 28 May 1785, *PTJ* 8: 169.

4. James le Maire to Patrick Henry, Richmond, 3 Dec. 1785, *Calendar of Virginia State Papers and Other Manuscripts*, William P. Palmer, editor and compiler (Richmond, Va.: 1884) (hereafter *CVSP*), 4: 70.

5. Ray Watkins Irwin, *The Diplomatic Relations of the United States with the Barbary Powers 1776–1816* (Chapel Hill, 1931), 25–28; Gary Edward Wilson, "American Prisoners in the Barbary Nations, 1784-1816," 29–32 (Ph.D. diss., North Texas State University, 1979). At Spain's request, Morocco released the *Betsey* in the early summer of 1785. (William Carmichael to TJ, Madrid, 28 July 1785, *PTJ* 8: 321–322.)

6. John Page to TJ, Rosewell, VA 28 Apr. 1785, *PTJ* 8: 119; Richard Henry Lee to TJ, New York, 16 May 1785, *PTJ* 8: 154. Lee also reported that one of the first American vessels to trade with China had returned from Canton after a fourteen-month voyage.

7. John Adams to Benjamin Franklin and TJ, Auteuil, 20 Mar. 1785, *PTJ* 8: 46–47.

8. William Carmichael to TJ, 29 Mar. 1785, *PTJ* 8: 64–66; see also Carmichael to Franklin, 15 Apr. 1785, *PTJ* 8: 83–84.

9. John Jay to American Commissioners, [11] Mar. 1785, *PTJ* 8: 20.

10. William Foushee to Patrick Henry, Richmond, 6 Dec. 1785, *CVSP* 4: 71.

11. James Madison to TJ, Richmond, 22 Jan. 1786, *PTJ* 9: 196.

12. William Carmichael to TJ, 19 Apr. 1785, *PTJ* 8: 95; Francis Hopkinson to TJ, New York, 20 Apr. 1785, *PTJ* 8: 99; Eliza House Trist to TJ, 24 July 1786, *PTJ* 10: 169.

13. TJ to John Adams, 11 July 1786, Lester J. Cappon, ed., *The Adams— Jefferson Letters* (Chapel Hill and London, 1988), 142 (hereafter Cappon); TJ to John Page, 20 Aug. 1785, *PTJ* 8: 418–419; TJ to Monroe, 11 May 1785, *PTJ* 8: 150.

14. William Carmichael to TJ, 29 Mar. 1785, *PTJ* 8: 64–66; TJ to Carmichael, 17 Apr. 1785, *PTJ* 8: 95; TJ to Carmichael, 18 Aug. 1785, *PTJ* 8: 401.

15. Carmichael to TJ, 5 [May] 1785, *PTJ* 8: 138; TJ to Philip Mazzei, 12 May 1785, *PTJ* 8: 152; TJ to De Pio, 21 July 1785, *PTJ* 8: 309.

16. John Bondfield to TJ, after 14 July 1785, *PTJ* 8: 294; TJ to John Adams, 28 July, 1785, *PTJ* 8: 317; TJ to John Jay, 14 Aug. 1785, *PTJ* 8: 376; TJ to Nathaniel Tracy, 17 Aug. 1785, *PTJ* 8: 399.

17. John Paul Jones to TJ, 31 July 1785, *PTJ* 8: 334.

18. John Adams to John Jay, 16 Feb. 1786, *The Diplomatic Correspondence of the United States of America, from the Treaty of Peace to the Adoption of the Present Constitution* (7 vols., Washington, D.C.: Francis Preston Blair, 1833–1834; hereafter *Diplomatic Correspondence*), 4: 486–487; TJ to David Howell, 27 Jan. 1786, *PTJ* 9: 233; TJ to Nathanael Greene, 12 Jan. 1786, *PTJ* 9: 168; John Jay to TJ, 19 Jan. 1786, *PTJ* 9: 186; Louis Guillaume Otto to TJ, 15 Jan. 1786, *PTJ* 9: 176; Ezra Stiles to TJ, 14 Sept. 1786, *PTJ* 10: 386.

19. John Adams to TJ, 3 July 1786, Cappon, 138–139. On the Navy debate, see Marshall Smelser, *The Congress Founds the Navy, 1787–1798* (Notre Dame, Indiana, 1959); Craig Lee Symonds, *Navalists and Anti-Navalists: The Naval Policy Debate in the United States, 1784–1827* (Newark, 1980); Joseph George Henrich, "The Triumph of Ideology: The Jeffersonians and the Navy" (Ph.D. diss., Duke University, 1970–1971); and Julia H. MacLeod, "Jefferson and the Navy: A Defense," *Huntington Library Quarterly* 8 (February 1945).

20. Richard O'Brien to TJ, 24 Aug. 1785, *PTJ* 8: 440–441; TJ to Richard O'Brien, 29 Sept. 1785, *PTJ* 8: 567–568; Carmichael to TJ, 29 Sept. 1785, *PTJ* 8: 566–567; Carmichael to TJ, 2 Sept. 1785, *PTJ* 8: 465.

21. TJ to Monroe, 10 May 1786, *PTJ* 9: 500; Burrill Carnes to TJ, Nantes, 10 June 1786, *PTJ* 9: 628; TJ to Thomas Pleasants, 8 May 1786, *PTJ* 9: 472–473.

22. Lafayette to Henry Knox, 6 Mar. 1786, *PTJ* 9: 319n; Lafayette to TJ, 6 Mar. 1786, *PTJ* 9: 318–319.

23. John Adams to John Jay, 20 Feb. 1786, *Diplomatic Correspondence* 4: 494.

24. John Adams to TJ, 21 Feb. 1786, Cappon, 123.

25. George Washington to Henry Lee, 5 Apr. 1786, *The Writings of George Washington*, John C. Fitzpatrick, ed. (39 vols., Washington, D.C., 1931–1944) 28: 402–403.

26. Irwin, *United States and Barbary Powers,* 32–34; TJ to Patrick Henry, 13 Aug. 1786, *PTJ* 10: 206–207. Lafayette quoted in Irwin, 34.

27. John Adams to TJ, 29 June 1786, *PTJ* 10: 79 and note; Del Pio to TJ, 4 July 1786, *PTJ* 10: 88 and note.

28. Washington to Lafayette, 18 June 1788, Fitzpatrick, *Writings of Washington*, 29: 523–524; Gilbert Chinard, *Volney et l'Amerique d'apres des Documents Inedits et sa Correspondance avec Jefferson* (Baltimore and Paris, 1923), 14.

29. William Carmichael to TJ, 18 July 1786, *PTJ* 10: 150; TJ to Monroe, 11 Aug. 1786, *PTJ* 10: 224–225. In December, Jefferson wrote to the ambassadors of Russia and Portugal proposing an alliance. Neither these letters or the answers have been found (*PTJ* 10: 559).

30. Lafayette to TJ, [23 Oct. 1786], *PTJ* 10: 486. Lafayette wrote to Washington and McHenry 26 Oct. 1786 and to Jay 28 Oct. 1786 (*PTJ* 10: 562–563n).

31. Jared Sparks, MS 32, Miscellaneous Particulars and Copies from Manuscripts Examined in London and Paris, 1828–1829, Vol. 1, 105–106, Sparks Papers, Houghton Library, Harvard University.

32. Robert Montgomery to TJ, Alicante, 25 Aug. 1787, *PTJ* 12: 57–58.

33. See TJ to Richard Henry Lee, 12 July 1785, *PTJ* 8: 287; TJ to Ezra Stiles, 17 July 1785, *PTJ* 8: 300.

34. Chinard, *Volney et l'Amerique,* 14; TJ to John Jay, 22 Sept. 1787, *PTJ* 12: 166–167; John Paul Jones to TJ, St. Petersburg, 31 Jan. 1789, *Diplomatic Correspondence* (1834), 7: 395; see also John Paul Jones to Minister at St. Petersburg, secret note, 6 June 1789, ibid., 395–396.

35. TJ to Edward Carrington, 21 Dec. 1787, *PTJ* 12: 446–447.

36. David Humphreys to TJ, Hartford, 5 June 1786, *PTJ* 9: 609; W. S. Smith to TJ, Bordeaux, 19 May 1787, *PTJ* 11: 366.

37. TJ to John Jay, 3 Nov. 1787, *PTJ* 12: 313.

38. Report of Secretary of State on American Prisoners at Algiers, 28 Dec. 1790, *Naval Documents Related to the United States Wars with the Barbary Powers* (7 vols., Washington, D.C.,1939–1946), I: 18–22 (hereafter *BW*); Report of Secretary of State on Mediterranean Trade, 28 Dec. 1790, *BW* I: 22–26.

39. Washington to Senate, 22 Feb. 1791, *BW* 1: 26–27; Senate Resolution to Ransom Prisoners, 22 Feb. 1791, *BW* I: 34–35; Act Pertaining to U.S. Navy, 3 Mar. 1791, *BW* I: 27; Secretary of State to Thomas Barclay, 13 May 1791, *BW* I: 30–32; Report of Committee on Mediterranean Trade, 6 Jan. 1791, *BW* I: 26.

40. Secretary of State to John Paul Jones, 1 June 1792, *BW* I: 36–41.

41. On Humphreys, see Chapter 6, this volume, pp. 131–133, 143–144.

42. George Washington to Senate and House, 16 Dec. 1793, Fitzpatrick, *Writings of Washington*, 33: 185–186.

43. 27 Dec. 1793, *History of Congress*, 3d Congress, 1st Session, 149–150.

44. 10 Feb. 1794, *History of Congress*, 3d Congress, 1st Session, 447.

45. Lyman, 10 Feb. 1794, *History of Congress*, 3d Congress, 1st Session, 445; Clark, 6 Feb. 1794, 433–434.

46. "Algerine Treaty" from the Charleston *Gazette*, reprinted in Boston, *The Mercury,* 6 Sept. 1796; Boston *Federal Orrery,* 8 Sept. 1796; Newburyport (Massachusetts) *Impartial Herald,* 10 Sept. 1796.

47. "Domestic Intelligence," Philadelphia, 22 June 1796, Portsmouth (New Hampshire) *Oracle of the Day,* 7 July 1796.

48. Thomas Jefferson, First Inaugural Address, 4 Mar. 1801, James D. Richardson, ed., *A Compilation of the Messages and Papers of the Presidents* (11 vols., Washington, D.C.,1908), 1: 322–323 (hereafter Richardson); Jefferson, First Annual Message, 8 Dec. 1801, Richardson 1: 326–237.

49. Kola Folayan argues that the war was not undertaken to suppress Tripolitan piracy; Tripoli seized only one American ship between 1797 and 1801. Folayan attributes the war to America's failure to recognize Tripoli's sovereignty and the United States's continuing reliance on the dey of Algiers to coerce the Pacha of Tripoli. Folayan's explanation is much more convincing than the explanations most American historians have offered. The United States did not go to war to suppress piracy or to stop outrageous demands from an avaricious pacha. Syed Zainul Abedin, a reliable student of the relationship between the United States and North Africa, is on less firm ground when he argues that Jefferson's decision to send the fleet

was not called for by the situation, but was a strategic move to silence domestic opponents of the navy and to precipitate a foreign crisis. Abedin has overlooked both Jefferson's long commitment to military force and Pacha Yusuf's threats of action if the United States did not treat him as a sovereign equal to the dey of Algiers. Abedin's analysis says more about the Gulf of Tonkin than of Sidra.

Two decisions for war were actually made, in Tripoli and in Washington. Neither group was aware of what the other was doing. Jefferson was predisposed to go to war and arrived in office to read Cathcart's reports of deteriorating relations with Tripoli, reports dating up to very early 1801. Without knowing that Jefferson had decided to send the fleet, Pacha Yusuf in May ordered the American flag staff cut down. Seven days later the American fleet sailed, with orders to cruise and prevent hostilities. This was the war Jefferson had wanted since 1785. (See Kola Folayan, *Tripoli During the Reign of Yusuf Pasha Qaramanli* [Ile-Ife, Nigeria, 1979], 31–35; Syed Zainul Abedin, "In Defence of Freedom: American's First Foreign War," xxxvi.)

50. Gallatin to Jefferson, Notes on President's Message, Nov. 1801, *The Writings of Albert Gallatin*, Henry Adams, ed. (3 vols., New York, 1960 [1879]), 1: 63; Jefferson, First Annual Message, 8 Dec. 1801, Richardson, 1: 326–327.

51. 15 Dec. 1801, Thomas Hart Benton, ed., *Abridgement of the Debates in Congress from 1789 to 1856* (New York, 1863), 2: 571 (hereafter Benton, *Debates in Congress*); New York *Evening Post* 29 Nov. 1804.

52. Jefferson, Second Annual Message, 15 Dec. 1802, Richardson 1: 343.

53. *National Intelligencer*, 7 Dec. 1803; Jefferson to Senate and House, 5 Dec. 1803, Richardson, 1: 365.

54. Quoted in Henry Adams, *History of the United States During the Administrations of Thomas Jefferson and James Madison* (4 vols., New York, 1917), 2: 431.

55. New York *Evening Post*, 13 Apr. 1804.

56. Gallatin to Jefferson, recd. 16 Nov. 1801, *Writings of Gallatin*, 1: 71.

57. *Charleston Courier*, 7 Apr. 1804, quoted in Wilson, "American Prisoners in the Barbary Nations, 1784–1816," 250, n. 24; New York *Evening Post*, 28 Mar. 1804; William Plumer, 26 Mar. 1804, *Memorandum of Proceedings in the United States Senate, 1803–1807*, Everett Somerville Brown, ed. (New York, 1923), 180.

58. New York *Evening Post*, 29 Sept. and 26 Oct. 1804. See the *Aurora*, 29 Sept. 1804.

59. 17 Oct. 1804, Boston tribute to Rufus King, New York *Evening Post*, 26 Oct. 1804.

60. New York *Evening Post*, 12 Apr. 1804, from the Frederick Town *Herald*; New York *Evening Post*, 29 Nov. 1804; Plumer, 31 Dec. 1804, *Memorandum*, 234–235.

61. William Bentley, 16 May 1804, *Diary*, 3: 86.

62. Kola Folayan's point that the American victory was not as decisive, or even as clear, as American historians have claimed is borne out by the bitter recriminations that followed the treaty in the American press and in Congress. The Federalists charged Jefferson with selling out Ahmed Qaramanli and allowing Lear to negotiate a bad treaty. But the Federalists had to mute their criticism, since Tobias Lear, who negotiated the treaty, had been one of Washington's closest aides, and the navy officers almost unanimously objected to the Ahmed Qaramanli scheme. Folayan also notes that Tripoli's navy and army had been able to withstand the American forces, gallant as Decatur and his colleagues might have been. The peace treaty, in short, was the best the Americans could get and was not a decisive victory.

63. New York *Evening Post*, 15 and 22 Nov. 1805.

64. Philadelphia *Aurora*, 4 and 19 Oct. 1805.

65. Philadelphia *Aurora,* 17 Oct. 1805, from the Richmond *Enquirer.*

66. Plumer, 2 Apr. 1806, *Memorandum*, 470. For a perceptive account of Jefferson and Tripoli, see David A. Carson, "Jefferson, Congress, and Leadership in the Tripolitan War," *Virginia Magazine of History and Biography* 94 (1986).

67. New York *Evening Post*, 4, 5, 9, 11 Mar., 4 Apr. 1805; New York *Chronicle,* 5 Mar. 1805. See also George C. Odell, *Annals of the New York Stage* (New York, 1927), 2: 229–230.

68. Philadelphia *Aurora*, 19 Oct. 1805.

CHAPTER TWO
The United States and the Specter of Islam

1. Royall Tyler, *The Algerine Captive* (New Haven, 1970 [orig. pub. 1797]), 216. On European perceptions of Islam, see especially Norman Daniel, *Islam and the West: The Making of an Image* (Edinburgh, 1960) and

Islam Europe and Empire (Edinburgh, 1966); Maxine Rodinson, *Europe and the Mystique of Islam*, Roger Veinus, trans. (Seattle and London, 1987).

2. *The Life of Mahomet; or, the History of that Imposture which was Begun, Carried on, and Finally Established by Him in Arabia; and Which has Subjugated a Larger Portion of the Globe, than the Religion of Jesus has Yet Set at Liberty. To Which is Added, an Account of Egypt.* (Worcester, Mass., 1802), 85, 83–84.

3. "Account of Egypt," *Life of Mahomet*, 153–154.

4. Humphrey Prideaux, *The True Nature of Imposture, Fully Displayed in the Life of Mahomet* (Philadelphia, 1796), introduction, 3, 117. On Prideaux (1648–1724), see Rev. Alexander Gordon in *Dictionary of National Biography*, 46: 352–354. On Moyle (1672–1721), see William Prideaux Courtney, DNB, 13: 1143–1145.

5. Prideaux, *Imposture*, 13, 17.

6. Prideaux, *Imposture*, 20–21.

7. John Adams, "Discourses on Davila" (1790), in *The Works of John Adams*, Charles Francis Adams, ed. (Boston, 1851), 6: 275; John Quincy Adams quoted in Merrill D. Peterson, *Thomas Jefferson and the New Nation: A Biography* (London, Oxford, and New York, 1970), 440.

8. Humphrey Prideaux, *The True Nature of Imposture, Fully Displayed in the Life of Mahomet* (Fairhaven, Vermont, 1798). Aside from the preface, which the Fairhaven edition omits, the Philadelphia and Fairhaven texts are identical.

9. 22 Feb. 1799, Benton, *Debates in Congress*, 2: 367. On Lyon and the Sedition Act, see James Morton Smith, *Freedom's Fetters: The Alien and Sedition Laws and American Civil Liberties* (Ithaca, N.Y., 1956), ch. 11, 221–246.

10. Prideaux, *Imposture*, 76–77.

11. Benton, *Debates in Congress*, 2: 367; Prideaux, *Imposture*, 17.

12. *A Republican Magazine*, Fairhaven, Vermont, 4 issues (1798), title page.

13. François Marie Arout de Voltaire, *Le fanatisme ou Mahomet le Prophete* (Paris, 1742), adapted by James Miller, *Mahomet, the Imposter* (London, 1744). In this discussion, which follows the Miller adaptation, I have maintained Voltaire's spelling of "Mahomet," which was the standard eighteenth-century European spelling of Muhammad, to differentiate this fictional creation (Mahomet) from the historical Muhammad. David Reynolds argues that Voltaire used the Muslim metaphor to undercut Christian orthodoxy. Though Reynolds does not cite *Mahomet*, he could very well have done so.

In Voltaire's play, the pagan leaders of Mecca could be secular humanists and Mahomet the religious fanatic. However, while Voltaire may have had a purely religious intention, it is more likely that his audiences responded to the broader implications of the story, political and social as well as religious. (David S. Reynolds, *Faith in Fiction: The Emergence of Religious Literature in America* [Cambridge, Mass., and London, 1981], 13–14 and passim.)

14. *Mahomet,* Act V, 75–76. The final act was written by libertarian pamphleteer John Hoadly.

15. George C. Odell, *Annals of the New York Stage* (New York, 1927), 1: 215. On the theme of patricide in American literature, see Jay Fliegelman, *Prodigals and Pilgrims: The American Revolution Against Patriarchal Authority, 1750–1800* (Cambridge and New York, 1982).

16. [John Trenchard and Thomas Gordon], *Cato's Letters* (4 vols., London, 1723), 2: 194–195; Cotton Mather, *The Christian Philosopher* [1721] in *Selections from Cotton Mather,* Kenneth B. Murdock, ed., (New York, 1926), 301–302; John Foss, *A Journal of the Captivity and Sufferings of John Foss, Several Years a Prisoner at Algiers: Together with some account of the Treatment of Christian Slaves when Sick:—and Observations on the Manners and Customs of the Algerines* (Newburyport, Mass., 1798), 75–76.

17. Abbe Constantin François de Chasseboeuf Volney, *Travels through Egypt and Syria in the Years 1783, 1784, & 1785* (2 vols., New York, 1798), 1: 7; Volney, "Manners and Character of the Inhabitants of Syria," *Massachusetts Magazine,* Vol. 2 (May 1790), 267. Other extracts from Volney appeared in the *Ladies Magazine* (London), 1787, and in America in the *Weekly Magazine,* 1799, and the *Philadelphia Repertory,* 1811.

18. Volney, "Manners and Character," 266–267.

19. Philadelphia *Aurora,* 17 Dec. 1806. On Fulton, see George Dangerfield, *Chancellor Robert R. Livingston of New York 1746–1813* (New York, 1960), 403–407.

20. Volney, *The Ruins, or a Survey of the Revolutions of Empires* (London, 1792; first American edition New York, 1796; new translation, Philadelphia and Richmond, 1799; Barlow translation, Paris 1802). See also Gilbert Chinard, *Volney et l'Amerique.* I am indebted to Mr. Robert Rabil for insight into Volney and the ruins of Baalbec.

21. Jean Charles Léonard Simonde de Sismondi, "Arabian Literature," John S. Smith, trans., *American Register* (1817), 235–249.

22. Edward Stanley, *Observations on the City of Tunis, and the Adjacent Country: With a view of Cape Carthage, Tunis Bay, and the Goletta, Taken on the*

Spot (London, 1786), 36; [Mathew Carey?], *Short Account of Algiers, and of its several wars, etc.* (Philadelphia, 1794), 3; See Foss, 2d ed., p. 45. The *Short Account* had two editions in 1794 and was republished in 1805 by Evart Duyckinck in New York. A version of this *Short Account* was bound together in 1806 with Maria Martin's *History of the Captivity and Sufferings* (Boston, 1807). As Maria Martin's book was republished, the separation between her narrative and the history blurred, so that in 1815 *An Historical Account of the Kingdom of Algiers*, by Maria Martin, was published in Rutland, Vermont. This 1815 *Historical Account* is merely a reprint of the *Short Account*. (On Maria Martin, see Chapter 3, this volume pp. 79–83.) Henry Adams, *History of the United States During the Administration of Thomas Jefferson*, 1: 13–14.

23. [Penelope Aubin], *The Noble Slaves. Being an Entertaining History of Surprizing Adventures and Remarkable Deliverances from Algerine Slavery of Several Spanish Noblemen and Ladies of Quality* (Boston, 1797), preface. Evart Duyckink brought out two New York editions, in 1806 and 1814. See also Aubin's *Strange Adventures of the Count De Uinevil and his Family...whilst they Resided at Constantinople* (2d ed., London, 1728).

24. *Cato*, 2: 194–195; 2: 47–48; 1: 192.

25. John Foss, *A Journal of the Captivity and Suffereings of John Foss, Several Years a Prisoner at Algiers* (2d ed., Newburyport, Mass., 1798), 66. Compare *Cato* 1: 193.

26. William Eaton, Letterbook, 13 Feb. 1799, 28–29; Eaton Papers, HEH; Eaton to Pickering, 24 June 1800; [Charles Prentiss], *The Life of the late General William Eaton* (Brookfield, Mass., 1813), 140; Eaton to Pickering, 15 June 1799, Prentiss, *Life*, 95–96; Eaton Journal, 5 Aug. 1799, Prentiss, *Life*, 123; Eaton to Eliza Danielson Eaton, 6 Apr. 1799, Prentiss, *Life*, 153.

27. Mordecai Manuel Noah, *Travels in England, France, Spain, and the Barbary States in the Years 1813–14 and 15* (New York, 1819), 133–134. On the European Enlightenment view of the Barbary coast, see Ann Thomson, *Barbary and Enlightenment: European Attitudes towards the Maghreb in the 18th Century* (Leiden and New York, 1987).

28. [Carey], *Short Account*, 12–13; "A Concise History of the Algerines," *Massachusetts Magazine*, Vol. 1, 1–4 (Jan.–Apr. 1789), 198. At least the first part of this "Concise History" was reprinted in the *Impartial Herald*, Newburyport, Massachusetts, 3 Jan. 1794. Royall Tyler may have borrowed this description; see *Algerine Captive*, 171.

29. *Cato* 2: 260–261; Gibbon, referring to Montesquieu's *On the Grandeur of the Romans*, is quoted in Ann Thomson, *Barbary and Enlightenment*, 55; *A*

Republican Magazine, Vol. I (Oct. 1798), 37; *The Papers of James Madison*, vol. 17: *31 March 1797–3 March 1801*, David B. Mattern et al., eds. (Charlottesville, Va., and London, 1991), 165, n. 7

30. Isaac Bickerstaffe, "The Sultan, or a Peep into the Seraglio" (London, 1787); Watkins, "An Interesting Description of Constantinople," *New York Magazine, or Literary Repository* (July 1795), 6: 418–419; Lady Mary Wortley Montagu to Elizabeth Hervey, Countess of Bristol, 1 Apr. 1717, *The Letters and Works of Lady Mary Montagu*, Lord Wharncliffe, ed. (2 vols., Philadelphia, 1837), 1: 254.

31. Dollard, South Carolina Convention, 22 May 1788, in *The Debate on the Constitution*, Bernard Bailyn, ed. (2 vols., New York, 1993), 2: 593–594; Webster, "A Citizen of America," *Debate on the Constitution*, 1: 150–151; Patrick Henry, Virginia Convention, 16 June 1788, *Debate on the Constitution*, 2: 696.

32. Alexander Hamilton, Federalist 30, in *The Federalist*, Jacob E. Cooke, ed. (Middletown, Conn., 1961), 188.

CHAPTER THREE
A Peek Into the Seraglio

1. [Penelope Aubin], *The Noble Slaves* (1797), preface.

2. *Claypoole's American Daily Advertiser*, Philadelphia, 20 Mar. 1798, reprint from Bombay *Courier* 1 Apr. 1797, quoting what was "professing to be an extract from the Bagdad *Gazette*," 17 Dec. 1796.

3. Susanna Rowson, *Slaves in Algiers, or A Struggle for Freedom* (Philadelphia, 1794), 60.

4. Major George Henry Rooke, "Description of the City of Mocha," *The Boston Magazine* (August 1786), 3: 333; Saint-Sauveur quoted in Lucette Valensi, *On the Eve of Colonialism: North Africa before the French Conquest, 1790–1830*, Kenneth J. Perkins, trans. (New York and London, 1977), xx.

5. John Foss, *Journal of the Captivity and Sufferings*, 2d ed., (1798), 65; Volney, "Manners and Character of the Syrians," *Massachusetts Magazine* (May 1790), 265–266.

6. Charles Secondat, Baron de Montesquieu, *The Spirit of the Laws*, Thomas Nugent, trans. (New York, 1949), 255–257.

7. Volney, "Manners and Character of the Syrians," 265–266.

8. Volney, "Manners and Character of the Syrians," 265–266; Montesquieu, *Spirit of the Laws*, 254; [O'Brien] to Eaton, 10 [Jan. 1800], EA 434;
Eaton to Secretary of State, 15 June 1799, Prentiss, *Life,* 97–98.

9. Lady Mary Wortley Montagu to Lady Elizabeth Rich, Belgrade
Village, 17 June [1717], *The Letters and Works of Lady Mary Montagu*, Lord
Wharncliffe, ed. (2 vols., Philadelphia, 1837), 1: 291. See also *Embassy to
Constantinople: The Travels of Lady Mary Wortley Montagu*, Christopher Pick,
ed., (London, 1988), which has useful annotation and an excellent introduc-
tory essay on Lady Montagu by Dervla Murphy.

10. Lady Mary Wortley Montagu to Frances Erskine, Countess of Mar, 1
Apr. 1717, *Letters and Works,* 1: 258–259; Lady Mary Wortley Montagu to
Alexander Pope, 12 Feb. 1717, *Letters and Works*, 1: 244.

11. Lady Mary Wortley Montagu to Lady Elizabeth Rich, 1 Apr. 1717,
Letters and Works, 1: 247–248. In his 18th-century introduction, Rev. James
Dallaway wrote that Lady Mary could not have been invited to the bath in
1717, since the wife of a later British ambassador to Istanbul was refused
admittance in 1799, and "the customs of the East are known to be
unchangeable, and more respected by the oriental nations than our laws by
us." It is a peculiarly Western idea that other people are bound by tradition,
and that something true for one British ambassador's wife would have been
true for another eighty years earlier. (*Letters and Works*, 1: 71).

12. Lady Mary Wortley Montague, "Specimen of Turkish Manners," *The
New York Magazine* (March 1795), 6: 148–150. This is an excerpt from Lady
Mary Wortley Montagu to Elizabeth Hervey, Countess of Bristol, May 1718,
in *Letters and Works*, 1: 308–314, and *Embassy to Constantinople*, 188–194.

13. Susanna Rowson, *Slaves in Algiers, or, A Struggle for Freedom*
(Philadelphia, 1794), 13.

14. *The Portfolio*, Series 2, 21 Mar. 1807, 3: 179–181. In [Washington
Irving, James Kirke Paulding, et al.], *Salmagundi, or the Whim-Whams and
Opinions of Launcelot Langstaff* (New York, 1857), 30–33.

15. Eaton Journal, 5 Aug. 1799, Prentiss, *Life*, 123.

16. Montesquieu, *Spirit of the Laws*, 255. Bickerstaff had based *The Sultan*
on both, or either, J. F. Marmontel's *Solyman le Second*, or Charles Simon
Favart's 1761 *Soliman II*. As *The American Captive*, a reworking by John
Hodgkinson, the play premiered in New York 3 May 1794 and had least
twenty two more productions by 1840. Hodgkinson and Bickerstaff may
have had the most popular adaptation of Favart's play, but the most enduring

adaptation was Wolfgang Amadeus Mozart's 1782 opera *Die enteuhrung aus dem serail* (*Abduction from the Seraglio*). On Bickerstaff, see Peter A. Tasch, *The Dramatic Cobbler, The Life and Works of Isaac Bickerstaff* (Lewisburg, Pa., 1971).

17. Bickerstaff, *The Sultan,* 575, 574.

18. Bickerstaff, *The Sultan,* 579. On marriage in America at this time, see Jan Lewis, "The Republican Wife: Virtue and Seduction in the Early Republic," *William and Mary Quarterly,* 3rd series (1987), and Linda K. Kerber, *Women of the Republic: Intellect and Ideology in Revolutionary America* (Chapel Hill, N.C., 1980).

19. Volney, *The Ruins* (Albany, N.Y., 1822), 278, note M. Note from p. 63.

20. "The Story of Solyman and Almena," *Rural Magazine, or Vermont Repository* (September 1796), 2: 435–442.

21. Lady Montagu to Alexander Pope, Belgrade, 12 Feb. 1717, *Embassy to Constantinople,* 83; *The Portable Arabian Nights,* Joseph Campbell, ed., John Payne, trans. (New York, 1952).

22. Rowson, *Slaves in Algiers,* 65–68, 71.

23. Rowson, *Slaves in Algiers,* 5.

24. Rowson, *Slaves in Algiers,* 9–10.

25. Rowson, *Slaves in Algiers,* 71, 72.

26. Rowson, *Slaves in Algiers,* 73.

27. "Concise History of the Algerines," *Massachusetts Magazine,* Vol. 1 (1789), 23–24, 110–112, 170–171, 196–198; see also Newburyport (Massachusetts) *Impartial Herald,* 3 Jan. 1794. For a concise study of Algerian history in this period, which puts it in the context of European and Turkish Mediterranean politics, see Jamil M. Abun-Nasr, *A History of the Maghrib* (Cambridge and New York, 1971), 159–177. The letters published in the "Concise History" may or may not be authentic. They appeared in Laugier de Tassy's 1727 *Historie du Royaume d'Alger* , which was translated into English in 1750 as *Compleat History of the Piratical States of Barbary.* Laugier de Tassy wrote that few in Algiers knew the story of Queen Zaphira's virtuous resistance. The Englishman Joseph Morgan, who wrote his own *Complete History of Algiers* in 1731, said that de Tassy, "is certainly right in saying, that very few people" knew the story of Zaphira and Barbarossa; however, the reason was not their ignorance of history but their unfamiliarity with this French novelist's invention. Morgan insisted that de Tassy had made this story up. John Brown, a playwright, was more interested in dramatic effect than in historical accuracy, and certainly Barbarossa's desire for

the beautiful queen Zaphira is a more interesting focus for a play than is his desire for naval superiority. Brown drew his story from de Tassy, and for those whose historical appetite had been whetted by the play, Brown wrote a pamphlet also drawn from de Tassy. It is nearly impossible for us to determine the historical truth of this episode. For instance, Ferdinand Braudel, the Mediterranean's most thorough modern student, recommends for those interested in Barbarossa's life a biography which Braudel calls "highly-coloured, fictionalized, but often very accurate" biography for those interested in Barbarossa's life (Laugier de Tassy, *Historie du Royaume d'Alger* [Paris, 1727]; Joseph Morgan, *A Complete History of Algiers. To which is Prefixed, an Epitome of the General History of Barbary, from the Earliest Times: Interspersed with many Curious Passages and Remarks not Touched on by any Writer Whatever* [London, 1731], 239; *A Compleat history of the Piratical States of Barbary* [London, 1750]; John Brown, *An Account of Barbarossa, the Usurper of Algiers, Being the story on which the new Tragedy is founded* [London, 1755]; Donald D. Eddy, *A Bibliography of John Brown* [New York, 1971]; Ferdinand Braudel, *The Mediterranean and the Mediterranean World in the Age of Philip II*, Sian Reynolds, trans. [London, 1973], 905n).

28. "Concise History of the Algerines," *Massachusetts Magazine* (1789), 24, 110–111.

29. [John Brown], *Barbarossa, A Tragedy* (Boston, 1794), 12.

30. [Brown], *Barbarossa*, 46–47.

31. Maria Martin, *History of the Captivity and Sufferings of Mrs. Maria Martin, who was Six Years a Slave in Algiers* (Boston, 1807), 44. There is no extant copy of the first American edition, listed in Evans as Boston, 1804. An 1804 edition seems incredible, since Maria Martin claims to have been shipwrecked in 1800, before spending six years, according to the title, in Algerine slavery. This work was reprinted in Boston, 1806, 1807, 1810; Philadelphia, 1809, 1811; Trenton, N.J., 1811; New Haven, Conn., 1812; New York, 1812, 1813; St. Clairsville, Ohio, 1815; and Brookfield, Mass., 1818. The 1813 New York edition is bound together with *The Life of Mahomet*, and the Brookfield edition is bound with Mathew Carey's *Short Account of Algiers*. This confused a Vermont publisher, who published both Martin's book and the *Short Account of Algiers*, attributing both to Martin. The 1810 Boston edition changes her name to Lucinda Martin, and the Algerian city of Tenes becomes Tunis. The Brookfield edition is considerably simplified, keeping only the outlines of the plot. Though Mrs. Martin said

she was born in England, and though her history, as published in America, claimed to be a reprint from the English edition, I have found no record of her book being published in England. Henry Martin, Maria's husband in the book, was a captain for the East India Company. It may be coincidental that a Henry Martin who died in 1721 wrote a pamphlet, *Considerations on the East India Trade* (1701), defending that trade against charges that it led to a loss of English bullion and unemployment for English workers.

32. On Puritan captivity narratives, see Roy Harvey Pearce, "The Significances of the Captivity Narrative," *American Literature* 19 (March 1947); Alden T. Vaughan and Edward W. Clark, "Cups of Common Calamity," *Puritans among the Indians: Accounts of Captivity and Redemption, 1676–1724* (Cambridge, Mass., 1981); Laurel Thatcher Ulrich, *Good Wives: Image and Reality in the Lives of Women in Northern New England 1650–1750* (New York, 1982), esp. chs. 9–12. Capt. Greg T. Siemenski, "The Puritan Captivity Narrative and the Politics of the American Revolution," *American Quarterly* 42 (March 1990), shows the persistent political relevance of some seventeenth-century narratives at the time of the American Revolution.

33. Martin, *History* (Boston, 1807), 45–46.

34. Martin, *History* (Philadelphia, 1809), 58.

35. Martin, *History* (Philadelphia, 1809), 44.

36. Martin, *History* (Boston, 1807) 69–70.

37. Martin, *History* (Boston, 1807), 69–70.

38. "The Story of Irene," *Rural Magazine, or Vermont Repository* (May 1796), 2: 211–214. This story is in René Aubert, Abbe de Vertot (1655–1735), *The History of the Knights Hospitallers of St. John of Jerusalem, Styled Afterwards, The Knights of Rhodes, And at Present, The Knights of Malta* (5 vols., Edinburgh, 1757), 2: 262–265.

CHAPTER FOUR
American Slavery and the Muslim World

1. Jefferson, *Notes on the State of Virginia* [1787] in Merrill D. Peterson, ed., *The Portable Thomas Jefferson* (New York, 1975), 214–215; John Adams to Jefferson, 22 May 1785, Lester J. Cappon, ed., *The Adams–Jefferson Letters* (Chapel Hill, N.C., 1959), 21; Charles Thomson to Thomas Jefferson, New York, 2 Nov. 1785. *PTJ* 9: 9.

2. Martha Jefferson to Thomas Jefferson, Paris, 3 May 1787, *PTJ* 11: 334.

3. *The American in Algiers, or the Patriot of Seventy-Six in Captivity* (New York, 1797).

4. Curses of Slavery," *Rural Magazine, or Vermont Repository* (March 1795), 118–124. Cato Mungo's story was reprinted in the Salem, Massachusetts, *Gazette* 13 Jan. 1795; (Boston) *Federal Orrery*, 29 Jan. 1795; Portsmouth *Oracle of the Day*, 31 Jan. 1795.

5. [Mathew Carey], *Short Account of Algiers* (Philadelphia, 1794), 16; William Eaton, Letterbook, 24 Feb. 1799, EA 199, 38, Eaton Papers, HEH; Eaton to Eliza Danielson Eaton, Tunis, 6 Apr. 1799, Prentiss, *Life,* 154.

6. Tyler, *Algerine Captive*, 118, 224.

7. Tyler, *Algerine Captive*, 139; "Retrospective Review," *The Monthly Anthology* 9 (November 1810), 346.

8. Tyler, *Algerine Captive*, 142. For a reading of *the Algerine Captive* that places this debate with the mullah in the context of changing American ideas about religion, see David S. Reynolds, *Faith in Fiction: The Emergence of Religious Literature in America* (Cambridge, Mass., 1981), 16.

9. *Humanity in Algiers or, the Story of Azem. By an American, Late a Slave in Algiers* (Troy, N.Y., 1801), preface.

10. *Humanity in Algiers*, 3–4, 98–99.

11. *Humanity in Algiers*, 5–10; Robert Middlekauf, *The Glorious Cause: The American Revolution 1763–1789* (New York, 1982), 323–324; Jay Fliegelman, *Prodigals and Pilgrims: The American Revolution Against Patriarchal Authority, 1750–1800* (Cambridge, Mass., 1982), 140–141.

12. "Copy of a Letter from an English slave driver at Algiers to his Friend in England,"
New York Magazine (October 1791), 584; Salem *Gazette,* 10 Feb. 1795.

13. "Profession vs. Practice," Boston *Federal Orrery*, 24 Nov. 1794; Boston *Mercury,* 25 Nov. 1794; Newburyport, Massachusetts, *Morning Star,* 26 Nov. 1794.

14. James Ellison, *The American Captive, or Siege of Tripoli* (Boston, 1812), 37–38.

15. "Slaves in Barbary," *The Columbian Orator* (Boston, 1797), 112, 115.

16. "Slaves in Barbary," 112, 115; William S. McFeely, *Frederick Douglass* (New York, 1990), 18–19.

17. 11 Feb. 1790, Benton, *Debates in Congress*, 1: 208.

18. Benjamin Franklin, "On the Slave Trade," *The Works of Benjamin Franklin*, Jared Sparks, ed. (London, 1882), 2: 517–521.

CHAPTER FIVE
American Captives in the Muslim World

1. David Brion Davis, *Slavery and Human Progress* (New York and Oxford, 1984), esp. Part One, ch. 4. See also Paul E. Lovejoy, "Slavery in the Context of Ideology," in *The Ideology of Slavery in Africa*, Lovejoy, ed. (Beverly Hills, Calif., and London, 1981), and Norman Robert Bennett, "Christian and Negro Slavery in Eighteenth-Century North Africa," *Journal of African History* 1 (1960).

2. Daniel Saunders, *A Journal of the Travels and Sufferings of Daniel Saunders, jun.* (Salem, Mass., 1794); "A Reader," Salem *Gazette*, 10 Feb. 1795, reprinted Newburyport, Massachusetts, *Impartial Herald*, 24 Feb. 1795.

3. "A Reader," Salem *Gazette*,10 Feb. 1795.

4. Gary Edward Wilson, "American Prisoners in the Barbary Nations, 1784–1816," 320–322 (Ph.D. diss., North Texas State University, 1979).

5. On the *Betsey*, see Irwin, *Diplomatic Relations of the United States with the Barbary Powers,* 28; on Mercier, see Jefferson to Patrick Henry, 9 Aug. 1786, *PTJ* 10: 206–207; Edmund Randolph to Jefferson, 28 Jan. 1787, *PTJ* 11: 83; Jefferson to Thomas Barclay, 5 May 1787, *PTJ* 11: 347.

6. See also Saunders, *Travels and Sufferings*; James Riley, *An Authentic Narrative of the Loss of the American Brig Commerce, wrecked on the western coast of Africa in the Month of August, 1815* (Hartford, Conn., 1817). Riley's *Narrative* is discussed in Chapter 9 of this volume.

7. Boston, *Federal Orrery*, 26 Jan. 1795, repr *Salem Gazette*, 27 Jan. 1795; "American Captive in Algiers," New York *Weekly Museum* 8: 378 (8 Aug. 1795).

8. William Knight to Thomas L. Bristoll, 1 Nov. 1803, *BW* 3: 180; John Foss to his mother, Algiers, 12 Apr. 1795, Salem *Gazette*, 11 Aug. 1795; James Taylor to his owners in United States, 3 Nov. 1793, Newburyport, Massachusetts, *Morning Star*, 22 Apr. 1794; William Ray, *Horrors of Slavery, or the American Tars in Tripoli* (Troy, N.Y., 1808).

9. Laurence Sterne, *A Sentimental Journey Through France and Italy by Mr. Yorick* [1768], Gardner D. Stout, Jr., ed. (Berkeley, Calif., 1967), 195–202.

10. James Leander Cathcart, *The Captives*, J. B. Newkirk, compiler (LaPorte, Ind., [1902]), 12, 18, 24.

11. Eaton to William L. Smith, Tunis, 18 July 1799, EA 199, 189–190, Eaton Papers, HEH; Eaton to Secretary of State, 23 June 1800, *BW* 1: 358.

12. Preble to Warrant and Petty Officers, etc. [4 Jan. 1804], *BW* 3: 312; Bainbridge to Preble, 8 July 1804, *BW* 4: 258; on slavery in American thought, see Bernard Bailyn, *Ideological Origins of the American Revolution* (Cambridge, Mass., 1967), 232–246; Duncan MacLeod, *Slavery, Race, and the American Revolution* (Cambridge, Mass., 1974); David Brion Davis, *The Problem of Slavery in the Age of Revolution 1770–1823* (Ithaca, N.Y.,1975); and Gary Nash, *Race and Revolution* (Madison,Wisc., 1990).

13. Richard O'Brien to Cathcart, n.d. [1793], Cathcart Papers, Box 1, File 1, quoted courtesy of Astor, Lenox, and Tilden Foundations, New York Public Library.

14. Portsmouth, New Hampshire, *Oracle of the Day*, 1 Sept. 1796, 15 Mar. 1797.

15. Bainbridge to Preble, 8 July 1804, *BW* 4: 258; William Wass Langford to Preble, 7 July 1804, *BW* 4: 255; Midshipman James Renshaw to Captain John Rodgers, 6 Nov. 1804, *BW* 5: 125–125; officer quoted in New York *Evening Post*, 2 Oct. 1804.

16. Jonathan Cowdery, *American Captives in Tripoli, or, Dr. Cowdery's Journal* (Boston, 1806), 12; William Ray, preface to "Elegy on the Death of Hilliard," in *Poems on Various Subjects, Religious, Moral, Sentimental, Humorous* (Auburn, N.Y., 1821), 73–74. The "Elegy on Hilliard" also appeared in New York *Evening Post*, 9 Oct. 1804.

17. Richmond,Virginia, *Enquirer*, 16 May 1804. See Cowdery's less gothic description of the prison, *American Captives in Tripoli*, 9.

18. Bainbridge to Preble, 25 Nov. 1803, *BW* 3: 176; William Ray, "Sketch of Author's Life," in *Poems*, 233.

19. Wilson, "American Prisoners in the Barbary Nations," 189, 178, n. 14.

20. O'Brien to Congress, 28 Apr. 1791, *BW* 1: 29; Cathcart to [?], n.d., [1794?], Cathcart Papers, Box 1, File 1, New York Public Library.

21. John Foss, *Captivity and Sufferings*, 2d ed., 40–41. This anecdote is not in the first edition.

22. Mordecai Manuel Noah to James Monroe, Cadiz, 31 May 1814, in Noah, *Correspondence and Documents Relative to the Attempt to Negotiate for the release of the American Captives in Algiers, 1813–1814* (Washington, D.C., 1816) 66–67.

23. Ray quoted in Wilson, "American Prisoners in the Barbary Nations," 274.

24. Cathcart, *The Captives*, 144.

25. Saunders, *Travels and Sufferings*, 22–23.

26. Saunders, *Travels and Sufferings*, 90, 128.

27. Philadelphia *Aurora*, 18 Sept. 1807.

28. James Simpson to Secretary of State, 7 June 1800, *BW* 1: 352–353; Simpson to Secretary of State, 28 Mar. 1803, Washington, D.C., *National Intelligencer*, 27 May 1803; Jefferson, Second Annual Message, 15 Dec. 1802, Richardson, *Messages and Papers of the Presidents*, I, 343.

29. Foss, *Captivity and Sufferings*, 2d ed., 52–53.

30. James Wilson Stevens, *An Historical and Geographical Account of Algiers: Comprehending a Novel and Interesting detail of Events relative to the American Captives* (Philadelphia, 1797), 286–287.

31. Riley, *Narrative*, 91–92.

CHAPTER SIX

The Muslim World and American Benevolence

1. William Bentley, Diary, 1 Jan. 1794, *Diary of William Bentley, D. D.* (Salem, Mass., 1905), 2: 79; Philadelphia meeting reported in Newburyport, Massachusetts, *Impartial Herald*, 4 Apr. 1794; "Benevolence" to [Randolph?], 4 Apr. 1794, State Department, Consular Records, Algiers, Vol. 1, Part 1.

2. George Washington to Mathew Irwin, 20 July 1789, Fitzpatrick, ed., *Writings of Washington*, 30: 357–358.

3. Newburyport, Massachusetts, *Impartial Herald*, 4 Apr. 1794. For other examples of Republican attacks on Britain for supporting Algiers, see Philip S. Foner, ed., *The Democratic-Republican Societies 1790–1800: A Documentary Sourcebook of Constitutions, Declarations, Addresses, Resolutions, and Toasts* (Westport, Conn., 1976), 168–169, 191, 267–268, 283, 347, 372. On the debate over British depradations, see especially Drew R. McCoy, *The Elusive Republic: Political Economy in Jeffersonian America* (New York, 1980), 162–164.

4. See Washington's Sixth Annual Address, 19 Nov. 1794, in Richardson, *Messages and Papers of the Presidents*, I: 163. On the political atmosphere of the 1790s, see especially Thomas P. Slaughter, *The Whiskey Rebellion: Frontier Epilogue to the American Revolution* (New York and Oxford, 1986).

5. Humphreys's Address, Lisbon, 12 July 1794, reprinted in Salem

Gazette, 11 Nov. 1794; Newburyport, Massachusetts, *Morning Star,* 12 Nov. 1794; Boston *Federal Orrery,* 17 Nov. 1794; New London *Connecticut Gazette,* 19 Feb. 1795.

6. Benjamin Lincoln to Secretary of State, Boston, 19 Sept. 1794, State Department, Consular Records, Algiers, Vol. 1, Part 1.

7. Randolph to Humphreys, Philadelphia, 8 Nov. 1794, Frank Landon Humphreys, *The Life and Times of David Humphreys* (2 vols., New York and London, 1917), 2: 227. Robert Montgomery warned Cathcart that Heissel was a British agent. Montgomery to Cathcart, note dated 22 Apr. 1795, on letter 16 Apr. 1795, Cathcart Papers, Box 1, File 2, New York Public Library.

8. Heraclitus, Boston *Federal Orrery,* 13 Nov. 1794.

9. Laurence Sterne, *A Sentimental Journey,* 195–202.

10. Essex, Salem *Gazette,* 25 Nov. 1794.

11. Philadelphia *Gazette of the United States,* 12 Sept. 1794.

12. Washington, Thanksgiving Proclamation, 1 Jan. 1795, Richardson, *Messages and Papers of the Presidents,* 1: 179–180.

13. "Plan of a Continental Contribution for the relief of our American Brethren in Captivity at Algiers," Newburyport *Impartial Herald* , 23 Jan. 1795; Boston *Federal Orrery,* 29 Jan. 1795; *Salem Gazette,* 3 Feb. 1795; New London *Connecticut Gazette,* 19 Feb. 1795.

14. Boston *Federal Orrery,* 26 Jan. 1795, repr. *Salem Gazette,* 27 Jan. 1795. The petition was signed "RICHARD O'BRIEN," though O'Brien was in Algiers, and it was physically impossible for him to have known of Washington's proclamation. Only three weeks had passed since Washington issued it, and it usually took twice that long for news from America just to reach Algiers, and another six weeks for news from Algiers to reach America. The petition's religious rhetoric, its invocations of Jesus, make it completely unlike any other thing O'Brien wrote. The petition's final line, "Thus pray your fellow-citizens, chained to the gallies of the imposter Mahomet," could not have been written by O'Brien, who knew that American captives were not chained to galleys and who was not interested in whether or not Muhammad was an imposter. Instead, this petition was most likely written by a New England clergyman, who used O'Brien's name to give the piece the ring of authenticity, and who used the imagery of galley slaves and imposture to convey a sense of the captives' suffering.

15. William Penrose to a Friend, extract, Boston *Independent Chronicle,* 12 Feb. 1795, reprinted Boston *Mercury,* 13 Feb.; Portsmouth, New Hampshire,

Oracle of the Day, 14 Feb.; Providence, Rhode Island, *Gazette,* 14 Feb.; Newburyport, Massachusetts, *Impartial Herald,* 17 Feb. 1795.

16. Boston *Federal Orrery,* 29 Jan. 1795, repr. Philadelphia *Gazette of the United States,* 10 Feb. 1795.

17. Newburyport *Impartial Herald,* 3 Feb. 1795, repr. *Boston Mercury,* 17 Feb. 1795; Portsmouth *Oracle of the Day,* 11, 14 Feb. 1795.

18. William Bentley, 10 Feb. 1795, *Diary,* 2: 126; New London *Connecticut Gazette,* 26 Feb. 1795.

19. New York *American Minerva,* 27 Feb. 1795; Boston *Mercury,* 10 Mar. 1795; Boston *Columbian Centinel,* 28 Feb. 1795.

20. William Bentley, 19 Feb. 1795, *Diary* 2: 128; Portsmouth, New Hampshire, *Oracle of the Day,* 21 Feb. 1795; Boston *Mercury,* 27 Feb., 13 Mar. 1795; New York *American Minerva,* 28 Feb. 1795.

21. Boston *Mercury,* 27 Feb., 13 Mar. 1795.

22. Boston *Mercury,* 20 Feb. 1795.

23. Abiel Holmes, *A Sermon, on the Freedom and Happiness of America; Preached at Cambridge, February 19, 1795* (Boston, 1795), 19–20; Bishop [James] Madison, *Manifestations of the Beneficence of Divine Providence towards America* (Richmond, Va., 1795), 9.

24. Isaac Story, A. M., *A discourse, delivered February 15, 1795, at the request of the Proprietors' Committee, as preparatory to the Collection on the National Thanksgiving, the Thursday following, for the benefit of our American brethren in captivity at Algiers* (Salem, Mass., 1795), 1, 9, 14. For more on Washington and Moses, see Linda K. Kerber, *Federalists in Dissent: Imagery and Ideology in Jeffersonian America* (Ithaca, N.Y., and London, 1970), 5–6.

25. Story, *A discourse,* 13, 14, 8–9, 20.

26. New London *Connecticut Gazette,* 19 Feb. 1795, repr. Providence, Rhode Island, *Gazette,* 28 Feb. 1795.

27. New London *Connecticut Gazette,* 26 Mar. 1795, repr. from Boston *American Mercury.* "Aletina" defended Seabury by attacking "Connecticut and Rhode Island" for trying to stir up trouble. (New London *Connecticut Gazette,* 16 Apr. 1795, from Newport *Mercury.*)

28. New London *Connecticut Gazette,* 12, 19 Mar. 1795.

29. Philadelphia *Gazette of the United States,* 25 Feb. 1795; Boston *Massachusetts Mercury,* 28 Feb. 1797.

30. Philadelphia *Gazette of the United States,* 10 Mar. and 23 Feb. 1797.

31. Philadelphia *Gazette of the United States,* 14 Feb. 1797.

32. Foss, *Captivity and Sufferings,* 1st ed., 54–55.

Notes

CHAPTER SEVEN
American Consuls in the Muslim World

1. *Claypoole's American Daily Advertiser*, 19 Mar. 1798; Adams to Congress, 23 June 1797, Richardson, *Messages and Papers of the Presidents* I: 247–248. At this time, and until the twentieth century, American consuls were not diplomatic officers; they did not negotiate treaties or oversee political relations between the United States and the country in which they resided. Often they were local traders, whose main job was to help American merchants in distress in the port cities. An individual could be, and often was, consul for several different nations. These consuls had either no stipends or very small ones, but they were expected to make most of their living from their own business interests, augmented by the fees they could charge for their services. By appointing a consul general at Algiers, and consuls to Tunis and Tripoli, who would be responsible for both the commercial concerns of American traders and the political interests of the United States, Adams was anticipating the modern role of consuls, who serve as both diplomats and commercial agents.

2. O'Brien to William L. Smith, Algiers, 13 Sept. 1799, [20–28 Aug. 1799], EA 422, Eaton Papers, HEH.

3. O'Brien to David Humphreys, Algiers, 1 Mar. 1798, *BW* 1: 240; O'Brien to Secretary of State, Philadelphia, 16 Apr. 1797, State Department, Consular Dispatches, Algiers, Vol. 2.

4. O'Brien, Memo on Commerce, 18 May 1797, State Department, Consular Despatches, Algiers, Vol. 2. O'Brien thus anticipated the basic international policies of both the Adams and Jefferson administrations, recommending a navy to fight privateers at sea, as Adams would do against France, and building smaller gunboats for harbor and river defenses and a commercial embargo to coerce Europeans to make peace, as Jefferson would do.

5. O'Brien, Memo on Commerce, 18 May 1797, Consular Dispatches, Algiers, Vol. 2.

6. O'Brien to David Humphreys, 1 Mar. 1798, *BW* 1: 240.

7. Barlow to Monroe, 21 Aug. 1796, quoted in Milton Cantor, "A Connecticut Yankee in a Barbary Court: Joel Barlow's Algerian Letters to his Wife," *William and Mary Quarterly*, 3rd series, 19 (1962), 102–103n. I have drawn this account of the *Eliza* from Barlow, "Declaration on Schooner Eliza," 18 Apr. 1797, EA 29, Eaton Papers, HEH; Wilson,

"American Prisoners in the Barbary Nations," 117–118; and Irwin, *United States and Barbary Powers*, 86.

8. Secretary of State to O'Brien, Philadelphia, 21 Dec. 1798, *BW* 1: 281; Postscript to Joel Barlow, Declaration on Schooner *Eliza*, EA 29, Eaton Papers, HEH; Rand to Barlow, Tunis, 23 June 1796, *BW* 1: 157–158; Barlow to Rand, Algiers, 2 Aug. 1796, *BW* 1: 169; Gorham Parsons and Edward Rand, Petition to Congress for Restoration of Schooner *Eliza*, 9 Dec. 1797, *BW* 1: 225–227.

9. Barlow to Secretary of State, Marseilles, 24 Aug. 1797, *BW* 1: 209. On the *Fortune*, see George Clark, chargé at Algiers, Statement Regarding Ship "Fortune," 19 Jan. 1798, EA 173, Eaton Papers, HEH.

10. O'Brien to Secretary of State, Algiers, 6 Mar. 1798, *BW* 1: 243; O'Brien to Secretary of State, Algiers, 14 Oct. 1798, *BW* 1: 262.

11. O'Brien to Humphreys, Algiers, 27–30 Dec. 1798, *BW* 1: 288–289; O'Brien to Humphreys, Algiers, 21 May 1798, *BW* 1: 250; O'Brien to Humphreys, Algiers, 18 Sept. 1798, *BW* 1: 256; O'Brien to Eaton and Cathcart, Algiers, 20 May 1801, EA 468, Eaton Papers, HEH.

12. O'Brien, Dispatch 1, 23 Jan.–Mar. 1799, *BW* 1: 293–295. Adams's Message to the Senate and House of Representatives, 21 June 1798, Richardson, *Messages and Papers of the Presidents*, 1: 266.

13. Eaton to Secretary of State [Tunis, June–July 1800], EA 201, 107; Eaton Journal, 30 Oct. 1799, EA 199; 258, Eaton Papers, HEH.

14. Eaton Journal, 22 Feb. 1799, EA 199; 37; Eaton to Pickering, Algiers, 10 Feb. 1799, EA 199; 68–69, Eaton Papers, HEH.

15. Eaton Journal, 19 Feb. 16 Feb. 1799, EA 199; 36, 31; Eaton to O'Brien, Tunis, 20 July 1799, EA 199; 196, Eaton Papers, HEH.

16. Cathcart to Eaton, 9 Nov. 1799, EA 70, Eaton Papers, HEH.

17. Eaton to Pickering, Tunis, 8 Aug. 1799, EA 199, 205; WE to O'Brien, Tunis, 20 July 1799, EA 199, 195; Cathcart to Eaton, Tripoli, 9 Nov. 1799, EA 70, Eaton Papers, HEH. Reports of Cathcart's attempt to seduce Elizabeth Robeson appear in Abedin, "In Defense of Freedom," 168, and Louis B. Wright and Julia H. MacLeod, *First Americans in North Africa* (Princeton, N.J., 1945), 30. Cathcart's refusal to make an equal of his servant is omitted from the version of this letter printed in *Tripoli*, 91–98.

18. Eaton Journal, 17 Feb. 1799, EA 199; 33, Eaton Papers, HEH. Though in Eaton's journal this statement refers explicitly to O'Brien's hospitality to Elizabeth Robeson, Cathcart would later recall it as applying to American relations with Tunis.

19. Eaton to O'Brien, 1 May 1799, EA 199, 146, Eaton Papers, HEH.

20. Pickering, Instructions to O'Brien, Eaton, and Cathcart, [18 Dec. 1798], *BW* 1: 268–269.

21. Pickering to Eaton, 20 Dec. 1798, EA 496, Eaton Papers, HEH; Eaton to Pickering, 15 June 1799, Prentiss, 97–98; WE Journal, 15 Mar 1799, EA 199, 91, Eaton Papers, HEH.

22. Prentiss, 75, 78–79; Eaton to Pickering, 14 April 1799, EA 199; p. 122, Eaton Papers, HEH.

23. Prentiss, *Life,* 72–73.

24. Consular Present, Made at Tunis, 26 Mar. 1799, *BW* 1: 314; Eaton to O'Brien, Tunis, 1 May 1799, EA 199; 146, Eaton Papers, HEH; [Eaton?], "Concerning Defences of Algiers and Tunis," [April 1799], *BW* 1: 315–316; O'Brien to Eaton, 2 Dec. 1799, EA 432, Eaton Papers, HEH.

25. Cathcart to Pickering, 14 Apr. 1799, *Tripoli,* 23–24, and 16 Aug. 1799, Cathcart, *Tripoli,* 66–67; Cathcart to O'Brien, 27 Apr. 1799, *Tripoli,* 26–27; Cathcart to O'Brien, *Tripoli,* 13 Apr. 1799, *BW* 1: 322; Geddes denied hearing O'Brien's promise, *BW* 1: 323; Cathcart, *Journal of Negotations,* 13 Apr. 1799, *BW* 1: 306–312; O'Brien's denial of promise, O'Brien to Joseph Ingraham, Algiers, 12 July 1798, *BW* 1: 252. Eaton called McDonogh "a renegade, and of course a rogue." Two years later, Cathcart realized his mistake, saying that McDonogh was "likely to betray the trust reposed in him" and was "dispised by every consul in Tripoli," having by then learned that McDonogh himself had placed the obstacles in Cathcart's path, which Cathcart then paid him to remove. (Eaton to William L. Smith, EA 199; 189; Cathcart to Eaton and O'Brien, 23 Feb. 1801, *Tripoli,* 279; Cathcart to Secretary of State, Leghorn, 4 June 1801, EA 115, Eaton Papers, HEH.)

26. Eaton to O'Brien, Tunis, 2 June 1799, on receiving bill from Cathcart, EA 199, 148–149; Eaton to William L. Smith, Tunis, 18 July 1799, EA 199, 189–190, Eaton Papers, HEH; Eaton to Secretary of State, 23 June 1800, *BW* 1: 358.

27. Cathcart to Eaton, 9 Nov. 1799, EA 70; Eaton to Cathcart, 25 Nov. 1799, Box 1, File 3, Cathcart Papers, New York Public Library; Eaton to Pickering, 8 Aug. 1799, EA 199, Eaton Papers, HEH; 205, Eaton to Cathcart, 10 Oct 1799, EA 66, Eaton to O'Brien, 20 July 1799, EA 199, 195, Eaton Papers, HEH.

28. Cathcart to WE, 27 Aug. 1800, EA 80; O'Brien to WE, Algiers, 13 Dec. 1799, Eaton Papers, HEH, commenting on Cathcart to O'Brien, 20 Aug. and 30 Oct. 1799, in *Tripoli,* 68–71, 83–87.

29. O'Brien to Cathcart, 25 July 1800, EA 201, 167–173; O'Brien to Eaton, 30 July 1800, EA 445; Eaton to Cathcart, 1 Oct. 1800, EA 201, 174–175, Eaton Papers, HEH.

30. Cathcart to Eaton, *Tripoli,* 22 July 1799, EA 62; Cathcart to Eaton, Tripoli, 27 Oct 1799, EA 68, Eaton Papers, HEH; Cathcart to Thomas Appleton, *Tripoli,* 24 Oct 1799, *Tripoli,* 79.

31. Cathcart to Eaton, 5 Nov. 1799, EA 69, Eaton Papers, HEH.

32. Cathcart to Eaton, 6 Feb. 1800, EA 73; Eaton to John Marshall, Tunis, 21 Nov. 1800, EA 201, 223, Eaton Papers, HEH.

33. Eaton to Secretary of State, Tunis, 21 July 1800, *BW* 1: 363–364; Eaton to Secretary of State, 6 Mar. 1801, EA 201, 271–273; Pickering to Eaton, 11 Jan. 1800, *BW* 1: 343–344; Eaton to Cathcart, Tunis, 27 Apr. 1801, EA 201; 301, Eaton Papers, HEH

34. O'Brien to Eaton, 24 Sept. 1799, EA 426; Eaton to John Shaw, Tunis, 14 Dec. 1799, EA 201; 1, Eaton Papers, HEH.

35. The case of Alberganty has been drawn from Samuel Holmes, Protest filed in chancery office, U.S. Consulate, Tunis, 1 June 1800, EA 201, 69–75; Eaton to O'Brien, Tunis, 2 June 1800, EA 201, 78–79; WE to Thomas Appleton, Tunis, 2 June 1800, EA 201, 80; Eaton to Danish consul, 22 June 1800, EA 201, 87; Eaton to Appleton, 27 July 1800, EA 201, 115; Eaton to Appleton, 27 July 1800, EA 201, 116–117; Eaton to Pickering, 1 Aug. 1800, EA 201, 126–127; Eaton to Appleton, 6 Aug. 1800, EA 201, 136; O'Brien to Eaton, Algiers, 14 Aug. 1800, EA 449, Eaton Papers, HEH.

36. Eaton to O'Brien, Tunis, 26 Aug. 1800, EA 201, 140–143; Eaton to William L. Smith, 13 Nov. 1800, Postscript 25 Nov. 1800, EA 201, 205, Eaton Papers, HEH.

37. O'Brien to Eaton, Algiers, 21 Oct. 1800, EA 454, Eaton Papers, HEH.

38. O'Brien to William L. Smith, 28 Aug. [1799], EA 422, Eaton Papers, HEH.

39. Marshall to O'Brien, 29 July 1800, EA 451; O'Brien to Eaton, Algiers, 13 Aug. 1800, EA 448, Eaton Papers, HEH. On Pickering's fall, see Stephen G. Kurtz, *The Presidency of John Adams: The Collapse of Federalism* (Philadelphia, 1957) esp. ch. 17.

40. O'Brien to Eaton, 7 May 1800, EA 441, Eaton Papers, HEH; O'Brien to Cathcart, 19 Oct. 1800, Box 1, File 4, Cathcart Papers, New York Public Library.

41. O'Brien to Secretary of State, 20 Sept. 1800, 22 Oct. 1800, *BW* 1:

371, 389; O'Brien to Cathcart, 21 Oct. 1800, Box 1, File 4, Cathcart Papers, New York Public Library.

42. Eaton William L. Smith, 13 Nov. 1800, postscript 25 Nov. 1800, EA 201, 205, Eaton Papers, HEH; also quoted in Prentiss, *Life,* 190.

43. Eaton to O'Brien, Tunis, 26 Aug. 1800, EA 201, 140–143; Eaton to Cathcart, 29 Dec. 1800, EA 201, 245–247, Eaton Papers, HEH.

44. Wright and MacLeod, *First Americans,* 80–81; O'Brien to Eaton and Cathcart, 20 May 1801, EA 468; Eaton to Cathcart, 17 Feb. 1801, EA 201, 267, Eaton Papers, HEH; Cathcart to Secretary of State, Dispatch 6, 16 May 1801, *BW* 1: 455–460.

45. Cathcart, *Tripoli,* 17; Cathcart to Eaton, 6 Feb. 1800, EA 73; O'Brien to Eaton, Algiers, 17 Feb. 1801, EA 460, Eaton Papers, HEH.

46. O'Brien to Eaton, Algiers, [22 Feb. 1801], EA 463; Eaton to Cathcart, Tunis, 27 Apr. 1801, EA 201, 301; Cathcart to Eaton, 15 Mar. 1801, EA 102; O'Brien to Eaton, 29 Sept. 1800, EA 452; WE to JLC, 25 Feb. 1801, EA 201, 267; Eaton to William L. Smith, 21 May 1801, EA 201, 310, Eaton Papers, HEH. On the election of 1800, see especially Page Smith, *John Adams* (2 vols., New York, 1962), 2: 1046–1048, and Merrill Peterson, *Thomas Jefferson and the New Nation* (New York, 1970), 634–651.

47. Abedin, "In Defense of Freedom," 180–181; O'Brien to Cathcart, Algiers, 13 Apr., 1801, EA 465, Eaton Papers, HEH.

48. Cathcart to W. England, Tripoli, 14 Apr. 1801, Cathcart, *Tripoli,* 313–314.

49. This account of the war's outbreak follows Cathcart to Secretary of State, 16 May 1801, *BW* 1: 455–460. See also Cathcart to Eaton, 13 May 1801, EA 113, Eaton Papers, HEH.

50. O'Brien to Cathcart, [Algiers], 13 May [1801], EA 466, Eaton Papers, HEH.

51. Nicolai C. Nissen to Eaton, *Tripoli,* 28 May 1801, EA 379, Eaton Papers, HEH.

52. Cathcart to Eaton, Lazeretto of Leghorn, 13 June 1801, EA 118; Cathcart to Eaton, Leghorn, 15 June 1801, EA 119, Eaton Papers, HEH. See also a somewhat different version in Box 1, File 4, Cathcart Papers, New York Public Library; Cathcart to Eaton, Leghorn, 19 June 1801, EA 121, Eaton Papers, HEH.

53. Cathcart to Eaton, Leghorn, 5 May 1802, EA 147; W.Y. Purviance for Degen and Purviance to WE, Leghorn, 3 Aug. 1802, EA 196; Cathcart to Eaton, Leghorn, 10 Dec. 1804, EA 156, Eaton Papers, HEH.

54. O'Brien to Eaton, 1 June 1801, 2 Aug. 1801, EA 470, 473, Eaton Papers, HEH.

55. Cathcart, "Passa Tiempos," Plans for Country Seat, Box 4, Cathcart Papers; Cathcart to Charles W. Cathcart, 19 Aug. 1843, Box 3, File 60, Cathcart Papers, New York Public Library. See also Mella Menni to James Madison, 25 Aug. 1806, U.S. Department of State, Notes from Tunisian Legation, 1805–1806; Louis B. Wright and Julia H. MacLeod, "Mellimelli," *Virginia Quarterly Review* (1944); and Walter Prichard, Fred B. Kniffen, and Clair A. Brown eds., "Southern Louisiana and Southern Alabama in 1819: The Journal of James Leander Cathcart," *Louisiana Historical Quarterly* (1945).

CHAPTER EIGHT
Remembering the Tripolitan War

1. Irving's "Jonathan Oldstyle" review, New York *Morning Chronicle,* quoted in William Dunlap, *History of the American Theater* (New York, 1832), 301–302.

2. Joseph Hanson, *The Musselmen Humbled; or a Heroic Poem in Celebration of the Bravery Displayed by the American Tars, in the Contest with Tripoli* (New York, 1806), 7–9, 3.

3. D. Elsworth, "National Felicity," Philadelphia *Aurora,* 15 May 1804.

4. William Ray, "Ode to Liberty," Philadelphia *Aurora,* 15 Oct. 1805; Nelson quoted in Irwin, *United States and the Barbary Powers,* 135.

5. New York *Evening Post,* 19 May 1804; *Post* quoted in Philadelphia *Aurora,* 21 May 1804.

6. New York *Evening Post,* 21 May, 5 June, 28 May 1804; song 15 Mar. 1806.

7. Philadelphia *Aurora,* 6 Jan. 1806.

8. Philadelphia *Aurora,* 10 July, 9 July, 7 July 1804.

9. Philadelphia *Aurora,* 4 July, 7 July 1804.

10. Hanson, *The Musselmen Humbled,* 4–5; Pius VII quoted in Eaton to Colonel Timothy Dwight, Malta, 20 Sept. 1804, printed in New York *Evening Post,* 12 Jan. 1805, also in *BW* 5: 52.

11. Philadelphia *Aurora,* 13 Mar. 1806. Accounts of the *Intrepid* drawn from John Darby, journal, 3 Sept. 1804, *BW* 4: 506; Nathaniel Haraden, sail-

ing master, U.S.S. *Constitution* log, 4 Sept. 1804, *BW* 4: 506–507; Richard O'Brien to John Gavino, Malta, 5 Sept. 1804, *BW* 4: 516–517.

12. New York *Evening Post*, 11 Jan. 1805, reprinted from the Philadelphia *Aurora*.

13. Robert Ker Porter's "Battle of Alexandria," New York *Evening Post*, 22 Aug. 1804; Philadelphia *Aurora*, 21 Dec. 1804; Holland's "Tars in Tripoli," Philadelphia *Aurora*, 27 Mar. 1805; Ray, "The American Captive in Tripoli," *The Portfolio* (Philadelphia), 6 Oct. 1804.

14. Philadelphia *Aurora*, 30 May 1808; "Tars from Tripoli," New York *Evening Post*, 28 Feb. 1806.

15. "An American," New York *Evening Post*, 25 Oct., 21 Nov. 1804, 12 Jan. 1805; see Philadelphia *Aurora*, 4 Oct. 1805, referring to *Political Register,* 2 Aug. 1805; Eaton, Notes on a Speech or Letter, [1804–1809?], EA 261–266, Eaton Papers, HEH.

16. Philadelphia *Aurora*, 9, 10 Jan. 1806. I am indebted to Paul V. Burke, U.S. Marine Corps, for information on the significance of the Mameluke's sword.

17. Philadelphia *Aurora*, 17 Oct. 1805, from Richmond *Enquirer*. On Yusuf Pacha's reign, see Folayan, *Tripoli During the Reign of Yusuf Pasha Qaramanli*.

18. William Bainbridge to George Davis, Tripoli, 22 Nov. 1804, *BW* 5: 155–156.

19. New York *Evening Post*, 24 Mar., 26 Mar 1806.

20. Adams, 1 Apr. 1806, Benton, *Debates in Congress*, 3: 374. Congress voted a stipend of $2400 to Ahmed on the last day of the session, 21 Apr. 1806. George Dyson, naval agent at Syracuse, paid Ahmad Qaramanli $200 each month from July 1805 until Dyson resigned his post in May 1807. The payments were continued by his successor, and in May or June 1807 he gave Ahmad $2400, which Congress appropriated 21 Apr. 1806. (Dyson to Charles W. Goldsborough, 11 Nov. 1807, *BW* 6: 577; Secretary of the Navy to D. Thomas, 16 Nov. 1807, *BW* 6 :579–580.)

21. Eaton quoted in Plumer, *Memorandum*, 480; Plumer, *Memorandum*, 496–497; Jefferson quoted in Plumer, *Memorandum*, 468; Eaton to Preble, 21 Mar. 1806, *BW* 6: 398.

22. Louis B. Wright and Julia H. MacLeod, "William Eaton's Relations with Aaron Burr," *Mississippi Valley Historical Review* 13 (March 1945), 523–536, quote on 526; J. Parton, *The Life and Times of Aaron Burr* (New York, 1860), 491.

23. Robert Treat Paine, "Ode, Written and Sung for General Eaton Fire

Society, January 14, 1808," *Works, in Verse and Prose, of the Late Robert Treat Paine, jun., Esq.* (Boston, 1812), 283–285.

24. Quoted in E. Shippen, "A Forgotten General," *The United Service*, vol. 5, no. 1 (July 1881), 1; Philadelphia *Aurora*, 19 Oct. 1805.

25. James Ellison, *The American Captive, or Siege of Tripoli* (Boston, 1812), 35.

26. Ellison, *American Captive*, 12, 9.

27. Ellison, *American Captive*, 24–25.

28. Ellison, *American Captive*, 20–21.

29. Ellison, *American Captive*, 18–19, 37–38.

30. Ellison, *American Captive*, 51, 34

31. Ode to Thorn, New York *Evening Post*, 15 Mar. 1806.

32. New York *Evening Post*, 9 Jan. 1806; also in the Boston *Independent Chronicle*, 30 Dec. 1805.

CHAPTER NINE
James Riley, the Return of the Captive

1. Secretary of the Navy Robert Smith to James Barron, 15 May 1807, *BW* 6: 523–524; Smith to Barron, 30 Apr. 1807, *BW* 6: 519.

2. See Philadelphia *Aurora*, 7, 11, 13, 18 July 1807.

3. James Riley, *An Authentic Narrative of the Loss of the American Brig Commerce* (Hartford, Conn., 1833), 15–16.

4. Riley, *Narrative* (Hartford, Conn., 1817), 257–258, 259.

5. Archibald Robbins, *A Journal Comprising an Account of the Loss of the Brig Commerce* (Hartford, Conn., 1818); Judah Paddock, *A Narrative of the Shipwreck of the Ship Oswego* (New York, 1818).

6. [Jared Sparks], "Review of Riley's *Narrative*," *North American Review* 5 (1817), 390–391. Riley's *Narrative* was an international best-seller. In 1817 it appeared in Hartford, New York, and London; the following year, it appeared in French and German translations, as well as in an English-language Paris edition and a second New York edition. Riley went to Ohio in 1819 and took his manuscript with him. It appeared in Chillicothe, Ohio, in 1820, and in Lexington, Kentucky, in 1823. Between 1828 and 1851 it was published every other year in Hartford. In 1839 and 1859 it was republished in New York, and in 1876 selections from it were published as *What he Saw and Did in Africa*. A posthumous *Sequel to Riley's Narrative* was published in Columbus, Ohio, in 1851. Gordon H. Evans has published the first twenty-

six chapters of the *Narrative* as *Sufferings in Africa* (New York: Clarkson N. Potter, Inc., 1965).

7. *Sequel to Riley's Narrative*, 387; Henry David Thoreau, *Cape Cod* (2 vols., Boston and New York, 1904, [1864]), II: 102.

8. Riley, *Narrative* (Hartford, Conn., 1833), 260–261.

9. Riley, *Narrative* (Hartford, Conn., 1817), 294, 454.

10. Riley, *Narrative* (Hartford, Conn., 1817), 447, 446.

11. *Sequel to Riley's Narrative*, 384.

12. R. Gerald McMurtry, "The Influence of Riley's Narrative Upon Abraham Lincoln," *Indiana Magazine of History* 30 (June 1934), 134.

Index

Index

Index

Index

Index